D1095248

# A HISTORY OF

By

R. G. G. PRICE

COLLINS, ST JAMES'S PLACE, LONDON

FIRST IMPRESSION AUGUST 1957
SECOND IMPRESSION NOVEMBER 1957

PRINTED IN GREAT BRITAIN BY R. & R. CLARK, LTD., EDINBURGH
FOR WM. COLLINS SONS & CO LTD.

*To Susan*

## ACKNOWLEDGMENTS

I WISH to express my gratitude to : Messrs. Bradbury & Agnew for encouraging me to undertake this book, for giving me access to their records and for allowing me to use pictorial and literary material of which they hold the copyright ; Mr. Alan Agnew, Mr. Peter Agnew and the staff of their firm, especially Mr. W. J. Rutter, Mr. R. E. Williams and Mrs. W. Ashton. Mr. E. V. Knox for information, ideas about the course of *Punch* history and the loan of books ; Mr. Kenneth Bird for much advice on the development of *Punch* Art and for very kindly contributing the *Appendix on Drawing and Reproduction* ; Mr. Malcolm Muggeridge for suggesting that I should undertake the book, for discussing his approach to editing *Punch* and for his insistence that I should write frankly ; Mr. Eric Keown, who had already done a good deal of work on a *History of Punch* before finding it necessary to abandon it, for generously making his notes available to me. His help saved me a great deal of time ; Mr. H. F. Ellis for reading and commenting on my manuscript, as well as for giving me information and ideas ; Dr. P. E. Spielmann for discussing his father's life and work with me ; Mrs. Leonard Messel for reminiscences of her father, Linley Sambourne, for the loan of books and documents and for the opportunity of visiting his house, one of the few remaining examples of untouched Victorian furnishing and decoration ; Mr. Adrian Conan Doyle, Mrs. Stella Mellersh, Canon A. Rhodes, Mrs. Hope Clayton, Mr. Arthur Kidd, Mr. W. Bennett, Mr. Waley Cohen, Mr. R. E. Swartwout, Mr. Douglas Anderson, Mrs. Arthur Helps, Mr. John Lehmann, Mrs. Thackeray Fuller for documents or information ; the late Frederick Linell and the late Anthony Linell.

I have received so much help from members of the *Punch* staff and from past and present contributors that I cannot particularise my gratitude to them.

I cannot express my gratitude to my wife, who has acted as my research assistant, secretary, sub-editor, etc. I could have neither undertaken nor completed the book without her.

I am grateful to the following authors and publishers for permission to quote :

W. H. Allen (*With a Show in the North* by Joseph Hatton).

Art & Technics and June Rose (*John Leech*), Derek Pepys Whiteley (*George du Maurier*), (*Phil May* by James Thorpe), (*Sir John Tenniel* by Frances Sarzano).

Jonathan Cape and J. P. Thorp (*Friends and Adventures*), and Malcolm Elwin (*Thackeray*).

Chapman & Hall and Lionel Stevenson (*The Showman of Vanity Fair*).

Hamish Hamilton and E. B. White (*The Second Tree from the Corner*).

Macmillan (*Autobiography and Reminiscences* by W. P. Frith).

ACKNOWLEDGMENTS

Methuen (*Reading, Writing and Remembering* by E. V. Lucas), (*Owen Seaman : A Selection* by R. S. Clement Brown, Introduction by C. L. Graves), and the late A. A. Milne (*It's Too Late Now*).

John Murray (*The Two Pins Club* by Harry Furniss), (*Sixty Years in the Wilderness, Nearing Jordan* and *Diary of a Journalist* by Sir Henry Lucy).

Oxford University Press and G. M. Young (*Victorian England*) and Gordon N. Ray (*Thackeray : The Uses of Adversity*), (*A Long Retrospect* by Anstey Guthrie).

Sir Isaac Pitman (*Recollections of a Humorist* by Arthur à Beckett), (*A Great Punch Editor : Shirley Brooks* by G. S. Layard).

Sampson Low (*Life and Letters of Charles Keene* by G. S. Layard).

The Dalziel Foundry (*The Brothers Dalziel*).

Sir Alan Herbert (*Anniversary* and *Ballads for Broadbrows*).

Lady Partridge, Derek Pepys Whiteley and *Image* (*Sir Bernard Partridge*).

Also for permission to quote from letters : Lady Partridge (Sir Bernard Partridge) and Mrs. Parsons (Sir Francis Burnand).

I apologise if I have inadvertently overlooked any copyright owner. In a few cases I have been unable to trace anyone to whom I could apply for permission to quote.

# CONTENTS

## APPENDICES

## ILLUSTRATIONS TO TEXT

## ILLUSTRATIONS

## ILLUSTRATIONS

## ILLUSTRATIONS TO APPENDIX IV



## INITIALS AND END-PIECES

*The numbers of " Punch " from which the end-pieces are taken and the artists who designed them are given in Appendix I.*

# PREFACE

THIS IS neither a " House " History sponsored by Messrs. Bradbury & Agnew, the proprietors of *Punch*, nor a work of extensive research subsidised by a University. It is a sketch published by Messrs. Collins in the ordinary course of business. Messrs. Bradbury & Agnew have encouraged me to write the book and very kindly opened their records to me and given me all the help they can, for which I am very grateful to them. They have also read my manuscript in order to draw my attention to possible mistakes ; but they have no responsibility for any facts or opinions in the book. I am an outside contributor to *Punch* and I am not speaking officially in any way.

I have called the book " A History " rather than " The History " because I doubt whether any definitive History could be written, except perhaps in several volumes by a large team of diverse specialists. There is certainly room for a number of Histories and I hope that in time they will get written. One of them should be for the antiquarians, the lovers of detail who write letters of correction to the Sunday papers and would enjoy knowing when some minor artist did his only initial or how Mark Lemon corrected his proofs. There certainly ought to be a History for the professional historians, tracing in detail the effects of political and economic changes on *Punch* and of *Punch* on them. It would go into detail about changes in costume and the political background of the cartoons. The study of the history of British Art suffers from the lack of anything elaborate on the development of Black-and-White in *Punch* and also of *Punch*'s relationship to movements like Pre-Raphaelitism and Vorticism and Social-Realism. There is a need for a critical treatment of *Punch* writing that is not limited to the prosody of Light Verse but includes the relationship of *Punch* prose to the general development of English prose since the paper's foundation. The absence of any large-scale account of the financial and commercial and technological history of *Punch*, of *Punch* as a business, is a gap in economic history that would be worth filling. All these specialist Histories would appeal to publics primarily interested in something other than *Punch*. I am concerned with *Punch* itself, the collection of pictures and letterpress that its readers find when they open an issue. As these contributions are produced by contributors and edited by Editors, I have had to deal with men as well as with articles and poems and cartoons and jokes. I hope I have remembered that *Punch* is not a record of the history of costume or a political force but a Magazine.

The first fifty years were dealt with in munificent detail by H. M. Spielmann in *The History of " Punch "*. He was an Art historian and a bibliographer and Ruskin's favourite conjuror. His main interest was the identification of contributions. For most of the period before indexes begin he is indispensable. He collated the evidence on the origins of *Punch* very effectively and his rare criticism reflects the views of the sensible, cultivated man of his day. Competition with his work would be impossible, but in any case the point of view of to-day is remote from his. A second volume to Spielmann or a new edition of him would be impracticable.

*Punch* has suffered from an obsession with its infancy, encouraged by the excessive use of early material from its pages by illustrators of text-books ; I have slightly weighted my allocation of space in favour of the less familiar modern period. It has also suffered from a tendency to reply to unfair criticism by being over-defensive, by being more concerned to rebut than to affirm. I have the advantage of writing independently and not being tied to a brief. I have admitted charges that seem to me fair and made charges of my own. If I did not think *Punch* was worth writing about I should not waste my time, but, like Mr. G. M. Young in his biography of Lord Baldwin, I have not hesitated to abandon untenable positions the better to make the main position not only defensible but a firm base for counter-attack. It is obvious that to pretend that all the contents of *Punch* have been valuable means that in practice good work will be masked by bad.

Spielmann mentioned everyone who had contributed even a single article or drawing during the half-century with which he dealt. A Roll of Honour of this kind is completely out of the question. I have reduced the names to what I hope is a manageable number ; even so there are probably too many. However, I am very conscious of the loyal servants of the paper, the men whose work attracted readers week after week, year after year, who have been squeezed out. I have sometimes had to select one member of a school because he is representative of all sides of it when he may not be the most prolific or the best. I have had to cut and cut the list of names. This has been particularly distressing in the latest period when I know many of the contributors personally and should have enjoyed discussing all of them at length, instead of having to ignore men who deserve mention and far too often dismiss those I have picked for discussion in so short a space that even very genuine appreciation must sometimes sound patronising or impertinent.

The illustrations are not intended to provide even the most meagre survey of *Punch* art (that is done elsewhere, for example in Mr. R. E. Williams's *A Century of Punch*), but merely to illustrate points made in the text. I have managed to keep a certain amount of factual detail out of the text by collecting it in Appendices.

*December* 1955 R. G. G. P.

During the period between delivery of the manuscript and its publication there have been quite rapid changes in *Punch*, and the final chapter may already seem a little out of date, e.g. in ignoring the brilliance of Alex Atkinson's most recent work, *The New Mayhew*, etc., Ronald Searle's two-page colour series *Heroes of Our Time* and the great increase in coloured covers and special numbers.

" Fougasse " has just produced *The Good-Tempered Pencil*, a survey of contemporary humorous art, mainly from *Punch* and *The New Yorker*. It has appeared too late for me to be able to take advantage of its learning and polemical force and I must simply draw attention to it.

*December* 1956 R. G. G. P.

CHAPTER ONE

# THE VOICE OF THE OPPRESSED

## *The Beginnings, 1841*

THE FIRST number of *Punch* reached the public on Saturday, 17th July, 1841. Archibald Henning's cover shows a group of grotesques in the Cruikshank-" Phiz " tradition watching a Punch and Judy show. Across the page streams the name of the paper in curious wavering black letters with thin white edges. The sub-title, *The London Charivari*, makes the claim that *Punch* is a copy of the famous Parisian journal.

In the foreground a child pick-pocket sneaks into the hip-pocket of a large man in a top-hat and greatcoat, who is watching the show closely. The audience also includes a woman in a bonnet like an oyster-shell, a boy in a Scotch bonnet who has the wide mouth of a ventriloquist's doll, something vacantly horrible in a high wing-collar, and a lank-haired woman with a turned-up nose. Several of the spectators have children sitting on them. This is the early Dickens world of hardships and high-spirits in the streets, nearer to the time of George I than to to-day.

Victoria had been Queen for only four years and London was scarcely aware yet that a new and gentler period was opening. The prevailing mood was fear and bitterness. The high hopes of the Great Reform Bill had been dashed in the decade that followed it. The towns got fuller and dirtier. The poor, by comparison with the effulgence of " The Venetian Oligarchy," seemed to get poorer.

The Whigs, instead of being The People's Friends, turned out to be overweening, aristocratic, indifferent. Just at the time of *Punch*'s birth, Melbourne gave way to Peel's new-look Tories, the Conservatives, who were soon to run into bad trouble with the French and worse with the Irish potato crop. The voice of the streets was harsh and derisive, the tone of Brecht's *The Threepenny Opera* rather than that of its Eighteenth Century predecessor. Whig or Conservative, Peel or Melbourne, Radicals distrusted them all, seeing the political system as a conspiracy to suppress and plunder the nation and the centre of the conspiracy being the Court.

The journalistic world into which *Punch* was born was divided sharply into solid, respectable newspapers or magazines, like the *Morning Post* and the *Edinburgh Review*, and a proliferating underworld of scurrilous, near-pornographic, hysterically abusive papers that fought savagely in Party warfare or private feuds. Opponents were attacked by lies, rhetoric and sneers, and the sneers were as far as the average swashbuckling journalist got towards laughter. Such humour as there was appeared more in the monthlies than the weeklies. When criticism was disinterested it was often pompous. The press as a whole had vigour and much of it was written by clever men, who could not earn a living elsewhere but showed some lingering evidences of education. There was room for a paper that was warm-hearted rather than hot-tempered, happy instead of venomous and clean enough for the Family, a paper that took the Radical line from generosity and not from spite.

The origins of *Punch*, like those of the Cabinet, have attracted a good deal of discussion that is of only antiquarian interest. Detail is misleading. Comic papers were in the air, and some of those published in the previous decade had the word " Punch " somewhere in the title. The staffs of these short-lived periodicals overlapped. Merry fellows met other merry fellows in taverns and talked plans. Sometimes new publications began with a suggestion from a publisher, more often with a group of writers and artists who got together and turned out something that, like amateur dramatics, was half for the fun of it and half with the hope of making a profit.

Scribbled on greasy table-tops in chop-houses, on bar-counters, in college rooms, in the wings of theatres, at smoky sing-songs in dubious cellars, in sponging-houses and Debtors' Prisons, the comic journals showed the embittered raffishness of the milieu from which they came.

There was *Punchinello*, with drawings by Robert Cruikshank. There was *Figaro in London*, which Gilbert Abbott à Beckett started in 1831. He soon lost interest in it, as did his successor Henry Mayhew, although the paper lasted for eight years. The cartoonist was Seymour, the ill-fated begetter of *Pickwick*. In 1832 Douglas Jerrold started *Punch in London*, taking the name from a suggestion made some time before by a printer called Mills. It ran for seventeen weeks, but Jerrold did little work for it after the first two or three numbers. A Whig periodical, *Punch in Cambridge* (1832–5), borrowed items with acknowledgment from the London papers just mentioned. It contained verse signed " Q," later Jerrold's signature in *Punch*.

About 1835 there were discussions in Paris between Douglas Jerrold, W. M. Thackeray and Henry Mayhew about an English version of Philipon's *Charivari*, a periodical built round a large satirical drawing. Discussions followed in London about a *London Charivari* between Jerrold, Thackeray and the Orrin Smith circle of engravers and artists. This had got as far as having some pages set up in proof, when Thackeray scared everybody by suggesting that the partners might be responsible for one another's private debts. (There are occasional references to a periodical of Jerrold's called *The Penny Punch*, but this was probably his *Punch in London*.)

*Punch* was longer-lived than any of its predecessors or rivals and its success meant that there was kudos to be gained from having started it. It is rather a pity that its origins—the least important part of its history—should have aroused passions that persisted into a grotesque feud between the children of the candidates to Founding Parenthood. In Appendix III I have gone into a little more detail about the various claims ; but the more casual the account of this period is, the nearer to what actually happened it is likely to be.

Although something like the eventual *Punch* was in the air, the principal credit for founding the paper must be shared between Ebenezer Landells, an engraver, and Henry Mayhew, a journalist. The group who were interested in the venture published a Prospectus that attracted a good deal of interest, and an Agreement was drawn up. With documents we approach definition. Some of the floating membership of the groups faded out. What finally emerged was a property. One-third was to be owned by the Printer, Joseph Last, one third by the Engraver, Landells, who acted as Art Editor, and the remaining third was divided equally between three Co-Editors—Henry Mayhew, Mark Lemon and Stirling Coyne. Of these only Lemon was still connected with the paper by the time it had solidly established itself.

Mark Lemon's opening article, *The Moral of Punch*, set the tone exceedingly low. It was jocular and had the common sense of a cudgel, but it lacked wit and style and precision in identifying its targets. At least it showed that *Punch* was intended to raise a laugh and that it would be outspoken and irreverent in attacking the usual butts of Radicals. The connection with a Punch and Judy show was worked pretty hard in all the early numbers. Some contributions were supposed to have been written by Punch himself. Articles discussed the effects of electing Punch to Parliament and even tried to assess his political influence. This identification was made between the paper and the puppet deliberately. Apart from cashing in on a lot of goodwill, it was probably a wise move for a new paper trying as fast as possible to be taken for an old one.

The type was small and set closely in two columns. There was a good deal of variation in the length of articles, and the make-up was given variety by sprinkling about the pages short jokes of the kind now collected together at the beginning. Many of these little jokes were puns and the pun remained the commonest kind of *Punch* humour for many years. If some of them were so laboured as to make their readers' response unimaginable, it ought to be remembered that when, as often happens, one term in the comparison was topical, it is impossible for us to judge the impact. There is a further difficulty that sometimes the joke is that they were deliberately bad puns and fathered by *Punch* on one of his first butts, Colonel Sibthorpe. The butt who turned up week after week was often unfairly handled, but did give continuity at a small expenditure of space. By the third or fourth reference, even if only a single line to fill a column, the reader felt a cosy intimacy between the paper and himself. He had become one of the Club.

The illustrations were mainly little black "cuts," connected with the article they illustrated not visually but verbally. For example, after the words "Never mind" came a gap in the text and a little picture of a man on a treadmill. The caption below it was: "Things may take another turn."[1] These infuriating little puns, delightful though some of the cuts now seem as period pieces, were the main humorous use of art for many numbers of *Punch*. The idea of the detached joke-drawing did not evolve completely for a couple of years.

The whole-page satirical drawing, considered so important that its back was left blank, was one of the most important ingredients taken from the French model when *Punch* was started. (Mayhew wanted a large political cartoon, though Last was nervous about it. Landells preferred a lot of little cuts.) In the first number, Henning's *Candidates Under Different Phases—Canvassing, The Hustings,* etc.[2] was wooden and not very competent, but it had vigour.

One of the best political skits was a whole-page *Synopsis of Voting; Arranged According to the Categories of "Cant."*[3] This tabulated in bitter detail the varieties in misuse of the franchise ranging from frank corruption to self-delusion. The mock systematisation and the pin-pointing of the targets—two different types of joke—created a tension between them. This kind of tension is one of the great *Punch* qualities. The standard of writing and pithiness varied very much from item to item. The political material was, on the whole, keener than the social. Though *Punch* attacked separate abuses, it had no programme and no philosophy. One revealing article was simply an attack on politics as a whole: all Members of Parliament were venal, self-seeking and brutish. This, together with the penury of professional humorists, *Punch* took as one of the facts of life.

A conversation between two hackney-coach horses [4] (allegedly contributed by Dog Toby) which had some cheerful street-talk and amiable digs at selfish fares started from a clearly-held point of view : animals should not be overworked. By comparison, a dialogue between Punch and his stage-manager [5] was woolly and heavy-handed. It lambasted Members of Parliament in a boorish, indiscriminate way for corruption, selfishness and negligence. At this date, attacks on groups were normally less pointed and effective than attacks on individuals. Later the position was reversed.

*An Ode Picked up in Killpack's Divan* [6] was full of half-veiled references to a group of Londoners who met there. It had footnotes. It is difficult to judge how effective this was for the contemporary reader. Lamb used to write about real people concealed by initials, and presumably this supplied some kind of gossipy interest. A stronger attraction was the frame-work of a Club or Society that was used so often for comic work. Even serious writing was sometimes felt to need a framework : compare Dickens's trouble with *Master Humphrey's Clock*. The pretence that the written quips sprang from the conviviality of a Merry Crew lasted down to the early days of *The New Yorker*. Perhaps otherwise the reader would have felt slightly repelled by the idea of cold-blooded waggery aimed direct at him by the writer. The last page of the issue, apart from some more topical trivia, contained gossip and dramatic criticism, including the comment,

> " Young Kean's a bad cigar—because
> The more he's puff'd, the worse he draws." [7]

If *Punch*'s earliest preoccupation was The Condition of the People, its most constant preoccupation was the Drama, with which most of the early *Punch* writers were closely connected. Sometimes its politics seemed a little enthusiastic and amateurish. Its dramatic criticism was very professional. W. H. Wills, who wrote most of the notices at first, had an acid pen and a spare, sardonic style. Whatever else has faded, the dramatic criticism is still readable. Its dead-pan descriptions in detail of silly productions and its sensible enthusiasm for rewarding evenings are modern in tone, and one wishes it had had a theatre worthy of it. Mendelssohn said that an illustrated account of the Covent Garden production of " Antigone " kept him laughing for three days.

Of the original proprietors, Last was a man of some importance in the history of printing. His cylinder press was supposed to reproduce wood-cuts better than the old processes. He soon became unhappy about the finances of the venture and pulled out, working later with Ingram of the *Illustrated London News*, and becoming an important figure in magazine production. Landells was more emotionally engaged. He was a brusque, bubbling Northumbrian, a pupil of Bewick and the teacher of many leading draughtsmen, including Birket Foster, who did a few odd jobs in the early volumes of *Punch*. He was fertile in ideas and had a good nose for talent. He was really as much Art Editor as engraver. Regarding the paper as his own enterprise he threw all the finance he could raise into keeping it afloat.

The early numbers were produced against a background of financial strain. Lemon had to write and sell farces to pay some of the bills. The circulation started at about 6,000 and 10,000 was necessary. The price was 3d. (it was not raised to 6d. until 1917 ; it became 9d. in 1956). The trouble was lack of capital and haphazard methods of distribution. What *Punch* liked was the reader who walked to the publishing office and bought the paper there. The first big circulation lift was the first of the annual Almanacks, that for 1842. It had a page for each month, with the calendar surrounded by gay borders, charming headings and a mass of jokes, largely mock-prophecies of the kind that go back to the Sixteenth Century.

Landells had enthusiasm but he lacked financial sense, and he was tactless. In the complicated retreats and delaying actions of the first months, he lost ground steadily. New printers—Bradbury and Evans—gradually took over the paper's debts and acquired the various interests in it. Landells fought under a sense of grievance and, though he went on to considerable success as an engraver, he never realised how far his own casual financing had led to his losing his share in *Punch*. He also bitterly resented not being used as engraver once he had ceased to be a proprietor.

In December, 1842, Bradbury and Evans finally acquired complete control, with the support of Lemon and Douglas Jerrold, the leading contributor. The problem of distribution was attacked systematically: they enlisted the help of W. S. Orr (the London Agent of Chambers's, the Edinburgh publishers), who was the Carnot of *Punch*. The new railways were pushing out into England and *Punch* went with them. Later, the financial interest of Sir Joseph Paxton, though mainly important in connection with Bradbury and Evans's growing newspaper and book publishing, helped to keep *Punch* on the bookstalls. Circulation still depended primarily on contents and revenue primarily on sales; but it was business organisation that made it possible for the potential reader and his potential reading to meet. Booksellers were encouraged by easy terms of "Sale or Return".

The gap between cost of production and revenue and wild fluctuations in circulation did not mean that *Punch* was a failure in repute. It established itself qualitatively, if not quantitatively, very fast. It is important to realise that while part of its strength was in doing new things, particularly the editorial publicity stunts, part of it was doing the same kind of things as other papers and doing them better. The fight for sales was longer and harder than the fight for recognition. As early as the summer of 1842, in an article on popular periodicals, the *Westminster Review* [8] was justifying itself for spending space on discussing literature meant for the masses by pointing out that, in fact, *Punch* was considerably better-written than many papers with much higher pretensions. Its only criticism was that jokes on drunkenness and suicide were in bad taste. The element of surprise in the general welcome to *Punch*'s decent restraint was, according to a later proprietor,[9] partly due to the connection of its earliest printers with scurrilous comic magazines.

Of the three original Editors, Stirling Coyne was the survival of a previous social group. He was a busy dramatist and an organiser of dramatists in defence of their rights ; his plays included *Did you ever Send your Wife to Camberwell ?* He was "An Irishman of portentous appearance with a big head covered with grey hair ; black moustaches of large size over-shadowed his mouth and formed a striking contrast to the grey of his hair. He had little to say and what he did say he said badly."[10] He was not much help but he disliked it when he was edged out of the co-editorship. When Lemon found he had pinched one of his contributions from an Irish paper, he was dropped from the contributors.

Henry Mayhew, the ideas man of the early *Punch* circle, was an attractive, ebullient character, unbusinesslike and unstable. He had run away from Westminster as a boy and had once been a mid-shipman on a tea-clipper. He was full of schemes, but too many of them were dissipated with cigar-smoke. He suggested *Lives of the Engineers* to Samuel Smiles. His later work on *London Labour and the London Poor*, one of the earliest classics of descriptive sociology, showed his powers of observation and classification. In the early 1840's he was chiefly interested in electricity, which he studied dressed in a loosely-made suit of black shiny material. Throughout life his hobby was the artificial production of diamonds. He was full of jokes, full of compassion, full of projects and very bitter when his brain-child was removed from him for what he felt was the trifling reason that it did not pay its way. He stayed on as assistant to the Editor but, before long, he felt increasingly unhappy in the office-work and, as he disagreed strongly with the savage political tone imposed by Douglas Jerrold, who was his father-in-law, he left. Later he tried to start a rival to *Punch* but his quick wits were still ineffectual without system and persistence.

Mark Lemon sharply divided opinion. He was of Jewish extraction and was born behind the present site of Peter Robinson's. His family were in the licensed victualling trade and when he had a failure in the theatre as an adaptor of plays from the French, he fell back on the alcoholic connection. His services to the drama included dissuading Hardy from becoming a dramatist. He was thirty-one when he became Editor of *Punch*.

The other *Punch* men knew him as a busy hack-dramatist and as the landlord of an inn, The Shakespeare's Head, in Wych Street, where young journalists used to read their work to one another. He was at home in the world of the London tavern and the cheap theatre and the cheap press. He was business-like, a good organiser and a born Chairman. One of his friends said : " His likes were stronger than his dislikes, and this balance was of immense benefit to *Punch* in the early days." [11] He was prepared for hard-hitting, but of abuses rather than of persons. He was genial and kindly, and gradually won the affection and respect of his staff. He was born for the job. As he said, and as he was to show, " I was made for *Punch* and *Punch* for me. I should never have succeeded in any other way." [12]

One of his enemies remarked that his race gave him patience, and he would bear a slight or a snub from Thackeray or Leech meekly. Jerrold, Thackeray and Tom Taylor occasionally spoke most contemptuously of him. He knew men's value and tried to get the best out of them. Later in his editorship he became resistant to the idea of new blood, yet his chief lieutenant came over from a rival in which he had been violently attacking *Punch*. His ready laugh and high spirits and talent for fooling, that made Hans Andersen say, " Mr. Lemon is most excellent full of comic," [13] made up for deficiencies of verbal skill, education and gentility. He did not write much, like Ross of *The New Yorker*, whom he resembled in other ways, not least in the courage to feel his way week-by-week towards a dimly-felt idea of the magazine's potentialities. If he had to, he could pile up little *facetiae* efficiently. He had a wonderful output of work and was often editing another paper as well as *Punch*. He made *The Field*, had a good deal to do with the *Illustrated London News* and slashed the circulation of *The Family Herald* by using the Waverley Novels for its serials.

The criticisms of him were based on his ruthlessness and his unctuous manner, with his continual smiling and hand-shaking and hand-washing. It is true that he was evasive and prepared to pull any string to trip an opponent. When he was private secretary to Herbert Ingram, a fiery character who founded the *Illustrated London News* and was at times an ally and at times an enemy of Bradbury and Evans, he learned that Ingram was intending to produce a rival to *Punch* called the *Comic Times*, which Edmund Yates was to edit. According to Yates, Lemon fought hard for *Punch* by the most unscrupulous use of his confidential position. Ingram, who was noticeably dominated by him, even took an accommodation address so that his editor could communicate with him without the correspondence's being seen by his formidable secretary. Lemon finally got Ingram away to Brighton. Yates, who wanted urgent business discussions, went down to Brighton too, sent a message to his proprietor that he was in the town and received an invitation to breakfast.

When he arrived the door was opened by Lemon, beyond whom he could see the meal prepared and Ingram waiting. Lemon smiled expansively, shook hands warmly, and tried to bar his entrance. Yates pushed his way in, shook hands with Ingram and was then caught again by Lemon, who seized his hand and never left off shaking it and gently propelling him until he had shaken him out on to the landing and shut the door. The *Comic Times* was then stopped after sixteen numbers. (*Punch* literature is full of stories about Ingram and denials of stories about Ingram, for instance, that the *Illustrated London News* was founded to puff a longevity pill, or that the Ingram family sat round the table on Saturday nights indulging in a good cry over the week's losses.)

Many years later Lemon's own description of the manœuvres that left him in sole command of a paper thought of, put across and written by other men, was an airy " The Editorship *became* centralised." [14] But would anyone less tough have kept the paper afloat ? Mayhew may have been a gentler man, and was certainly a more presentable man, but Mayhew's projects folded up before opposition. *Punch* lasted.

The new paper had been extensively advertised and it used novel methods of editorial publicity. As a weekly it could scoop the monthlies, in which the wittiest writing was then being published. It was launched in a journalistic world of rapidly appearing and disappearing little magazines. It had one particular attraction. It was free of "grossness, partisanship, profanity, indelicacy and malice." [15] If to us it seems unfair and very partisan indeed, this is owing to a drop in the temperature of public controversy since the growth of the mass circulation press. By contemporary standards *Punch* was not savage. More important was its family appeal. Father could take it home. In words that were later to seem less remuneratively laudatory, the *Somerset County Gazette* said, "It is the first comic we ever saw which was not vulgar. It will provoke many a hearty laugh, but never call a blush to the most delicate cheek." [16] Hitherto, comic journalism had been as closely associated with vulgarity as seaside postcards. *Punch*'s respectability increased its potential public more and more as Regency England became Victorianised, though as late as 1857 Leech, in *The Great Social Evil*,[17] was allowed to make a perfectly frank attack on prostitution. The moral background is vividly summarised in the remark quoted by Mr. G. M. Young in *Victorian England*: "In 1810 only two gentlemen in Staffordshire had family prayers. In 1850 only two did not." [18] If in time this voluntary limitation of the field of humour was cramping, at first the results were wholly good. Writers had to think of other subjects to be funny about and to widen their investigation of the comic possibilities of the world. Standards were applied to a new field and, if they were not strictly literary, application of any standards leads to self-criticism all round.

Lack of sexual jokes did not mean tepidity. Drunks were laughed at. Like stuttering comedians, they were long in arousing sympathy. Families argued virulently over politics, and indignation was felt about a wide range of iniquities. Savage attacks on politicians were quite acceptable to the family trade, and so were attacks on the Consort, the peerage, the episcopate and the services. *Punch*'s appeal at first was to the lower-middle class and it went up in the social scale with it. The Victorian family was rooted and cohesive, with a great deal of energy locked up in its density. It released its tensions in religion, business and madness. There was a good deal of hysteria in the Forties. One vent for hysteria is a Cause, another is humour. In its early days *Punch* provided both.

At every stage of *Punch*'s history there are both star contributors and useful working writers who give the text body and collective flavour. While the stars are generally completely different from one another, the others can be treated only collectively, according to style and theme. Any institution must live by self-effacing loyalty. Many of the devoted journalists who produced column after column, week after week, were nicer men than the stars. But to recall them would be pious rather than enlightening or enlivening. To avoid a parade of now meaningless names it is necessary to speak as though *Punch* were just Jerrold and Thackeray. In fact it was, of course, a gigantic collaboration and the richness and endurance of this collaboration is one of the factors that have lifted *Punch* out of the ruck of commercial journalism into the place where proud volumes stand on accessible shelves, emotions are aroused by the name and histories are written.

Because *Punch* was produced by a small group in constant argument and conviviality, there is a certain unity in the point of view. To begin with, all the contents and not merely the cartoon were discussed by the Staff as a whole, at first amid the uproar of a circle of contributors, friends and strangers, in various taverns, most frequently the Crown Inn, Vinegar Yard. At length it became necessary to have some quiet and order for the business, and the dinners of the *Punch* Staff were separated from the meetings of what was loosely called the "Punch Club," which continued for several years and gradually evolved into the Savage Club. The dinners came to be held at the office a short time after *Punch* had been acquired by Messrs. Bradbury and Evans, and soon became elaborate, with a certain amount of ritual. The date of the first appearance of the present Table is not known, but it appeared quite early and the custom for the Staff to carve their initials on it has been maintained ever since. The arguments over the cartoons were fierce, within the limits of the deep affection that bound the Staff as a whole. Occasionally they went out of town to dine, often to Greenwich for a fish dinner. From time to time luncheons or dinners were given for distinguished visitors like Garibaldi or Mark Twain. The dinner was changed to luncheon in 1925.

The peculiarities of the paper's origin left a valuable legacy. In fact, though not in law, *Punch* remained a partnership between the leading contributors and their printers and publishers. To-day, at the luncheons where the Staff decide the cartoon for the next issue, the Editor takes the chair and senior proprietor acts as his " Vice." Lemon sought and obtained complete freedom, astonishing everybody by the force with which he asserted his rights on the one occasion when they were seriously threatened. This freedom has been defended by his successors with an outspokenness that must be unique in modern journalism. The system works because it is set in a framework of friendship. The original Evans was a close personal friend of the Editor. They respected each other's professional and convivial qualities. The Firm realised the unique capabilities of the members of the Staff: the Staff recognised that when a member of the Firm talked about printing or periodical publishing he was on his own ground. A less expert proprietorship would have tried to interfere more, being less able to recognise expertness in others. The weekly meeting of the *Punch* Table (a curious mixture of " Pop " and a Joint Production Council), with its wit and furious arguments and rather demonstrative friendliness, helped to produce a common tone without producing too narrow an orthodoxy. Evans said, " Sociality is the secret of the success of *Punch*." [19]

Another factor in *Punch*'s success on which Lemon laid great stress was the system of paying contributors a weekly salary and allotting them so many columns to fill. The disadvantage of the system was obviously that it produced hackwork—words for the sake of words—and that it enabled the more industrious to feel they had a *Punch* income at their back and could use their best ideas elsewhere. *Punch*, like *The New Yorker*, was built up on collecting, training and supporting a ring of contributors on whom the paper could rely and who were subject to a certain amount of editorial direction, though very little by the standards of active editing in modern America. When they got past it, they still had to be employed, a pension system being unthinkable at that date. In old age, Percival Leigh, who had once been a very popular contributor, continued to send in work that was set up in proof and paid for. He corrected the proofs and the contributions never appeared. No comment was made on either side. Later, Evans claimed that the generosity of the firm to contributors was one of the advantageous novelties of the early *Punch*. When the paper ran a series of feature articles on Watering Places, one of the proprietors said, " Go to any expense you think necessary and the office will pay—if you want a shilling fly, have a shilling fly." [20]

Almost all written contributions were anonymous, though a series might have some distinguishing signature like Jerrold's " Q," and Thackeray's " Our Fat Contributor " and Shirley Brooks's " *Epicurus Rotundus* " and the authorship might leak out. The artists on the whole signed their work or could do so if they wished. Thackeray and Jerrold were bitter against the system which exalted the paper at the expense of the men who were making it and which obscured the amount of variety to be found in its pages. Some of the outside contributors, especially the amateurs, found anonymity a protection and the revelations of Spielmann's *History* perturbed many elderly gentlemen now shown to be responsible for the follies of their youth. The principle of anonymity was relaxed very gradually and it is only in the last two or three years that every literary contribution has been signed, though the veil was partially lifted in 1902 with the full index giving all contributions and their authors. There may be some reason for *The Times* to give the weight of the paper rather than that of the individual to its news and comments. There can be none for a paper whose contents are as little connected as those of a music-hall bill. Probably, once the fashion had changed and the personal-appearance journalist developed, the main reason for the Firm's continued support of anonymity was, like that of the early cinema proprietors, fear of the creation of a star system with a consequent demand for special rates of payment. In fact, *Punch*'s circulation has always depended partly on a star system, and the advantage of building-up and aggregating good will for a contributor far outweighs any likely rise in his remuneration.

The differentiation between the writer and the artist has fostered the idea that *Punch* is a paper to be glanced through, not read, and has also prevented *Punch* from getting writers who ought to have appeared in its pages. A man trying to make a living by writing wants his name to become known. There have been cases where a man who might have been of value to the paper has left it once he has got his head above water, because if he remains anonymous his career has, as it were, got stuck. Perhaps the most important damage of all that has been caused by this absurd rule is psychological. A humorous journal may be part of literature or part of history but it is also part of the entertainment industry, and in entertainment exhibitionism is a driving force. Anonymity deprives a writer of the satisfaction of having his talents recognised. The contrary point of view was put many years later by Henry Lucy in a letter to Francis Burnand :[21] " There is only one *Punch*, and his contributors should not be more in evidence than the veins and arteries of his impressive body. . . . I remember when I was a boy watching with keen delight a Punch and Judy street exhibition. Suddenly I caught sight of a pair of feet below the framework of the show. Whereupon the spell was broken. Which thing is an allegory. The world oughtn't to see the feet of Mr. Punch's young men."

The first two star circulation builders, Jerrold and Thackeray, soon became identified with the paper although their names did not appear in it. Jerrold's father was a printer specialising in theatrical work and the proprietor of a local theatre at Sheerness. He was a lover of theatrical tradition and always wore Garrick's shoes on the stage. As a baby Douglas Jerrold was carried on the stage by Edmund Kean. He entered the navy as a midshipman, a step up in the social scale. His grandmother was worried about him and wrote to the captain asking to see that the little boy wore his pattens on the wet decks. The captain was Jane Austen's brother and a kindly commander. He let Jerrold keep pigeons and read his own collection of English Classics and books on natural history. Jerrold had an excellent memory and later he constantly drew on the knowledge of Shakespeare and zoology he had acquired at sea.

The end of the French war left him stranded, axed from the navy and with the family business on the rocks. This early experience of a sudden drop in social position occurs frequently in the lives of *Punch* men. Some reacted by attacks on the society which spurned them, some by trying to reconquer what they considered to be their proper place in it. The difference in reaction gives the two elements in early *Punch*, radicalism and gentility, attacks on the privileged and attacks on the climbers. Jerrold fought his way up from Grub Street by hard work. By the time *Punch* began he was well known as a dramatist. Brilliant in comic dialogue, but more commercially successful in stirring naval melodramas like *Black-Eyed Susan*, he had a very ready pen and a vast experience of journalism. His co-operation was regarded as essential to the paper and it was hoped that he would have written the introductory article. He began writing in the second number.

A visitor to his home said he had never seen a handsomer head on an uglier body. George Augustus Sala described him as "the ikon of Montgolfier."[22] He was a tiny, angry man, frequently tossing away the light-coloured lock that fell over his queer blue eyes. His nostrils seemed to work like a stallion's with the least excitement. He was fiery but inefficient in action, torrential and witty in speech. He gave his friends a strong impression of genius, however hectoring they found him. He was a clubbable man and always starting new social activities and, if his wit had been merely acid, it is hard to believe that he would have had so many friends. The generosity that accompanied his radical scurrilities supports his own claim that it was love of the ill-treated, not hatred of the powerful, that drove him. He was often surprised by the harm his tongue did, apparently because he modestly did not think that there was anything memorable in his casual jokes. They were sometimes unfair, like calling Stirling Coyne " filthy lucre," [23] and sometimes silly, but they had the knack of sticking in the mind. Seeing a tall man dancing with a short woman he said, " There's a mile dancing with a milestone " ; [24] he suggested that some men got on in the world on the same principle as a sweep passes uninterrupted through a crowd. His humour was a kind of by-product of his sociability, like Mayhew's.

Jerrold had a clear idea of the kind of satirical paper he wanted and he drove Lemon towards it hard. He was hostile to new talent and at times behaved like a kind of supervising editor ; but Lemon managed to hold him in check and Jerrold probably realised that in a straight fight Lemon's generalship would defeat his wild romantic charges. Written oratory surges too fast through the mind, unless it has plenty of vivid, unexpected comparisons and Jerrold was full of them. There is a Disraelian or Churchillian quality about " The wounds of the dead are the furrows in which living heroes grow their laurels," [25] or " Earth is so kindly in Australia that tickle her with a hoe and she laughs with a harvest." [26] He wrote every kind of article ; in many numbers he had over seven columns. The savage radical diatribes signed " Q " are still vivid with their sweep of passion and their wonderful fertility of illustration. His laugh is searing : the reader is amused in spite of sympathy for even the least deserving victim. James Hannay said he had real satiric genius—spontaneous, picturesque, with the beauty and deadliness of nightshade. Comparing Jerrold, Dickens and Thackeray, David Masson said : " In Jerrold the fiery element of personal feeling is more continually present ; the imagination is not allowed the same passive and prolonged exercise of itself, but is more trammelled by an immediate purpose. His humour, as compared with that of the others, is as Cognac compared to wine; less of it at a time serves." [27] He had a wonderful eye for the betraying detail, as when he picked out two lines from a book of poems by Lord John Manners and made them famous:

> "*Let wealth and commerce, laws and learning die,*
> BUT LEAVE US STILL OUR OLD NOBILITY." [28]

Later his work turned towards fiction or social comedy. His biggest success, *Mrs. Caudle's Curtain Lectures*, in 1845, sent the circulation flying up—it is said that injunctions were taken out to prevent *Punch*'s being sold at street corners to the sound of trumpets—and he was torn between the pleasure of attending dinners as the saviour of *Punch* and dislike of being considered a funny man instead of "A wit with a mission." This series of naggings by a shrew was the first great *Punch* series and still lives. It has Jerrold's gaiety and clarity but it is all rather on one note. One attraction was that the readers would recognise their neighbours in it. It reflected life in a heightened form. The hen-pecked husband is an object of both pity and contempt and it is interesting to see Jerrold siding with the oppressed when the opposition is psychological rather than economic. The Little Man, the hapless victim of fate, whether up against the impersonal, a stronger personality or simply the obduracy of things became a favourite *Punch* subject later on. At times the paper seems to be written in tears of self-pity. Jerrold does not identify completely with the husband and at times he obviously gets some relish from exercising his own powers of invective through Mrs. Caudle. Jerrold lives as a prose writer and ought to be better remembered as a wit.

The other great literary figure who joined *Punch* in the early days was W. M. Thackeray (though Edward Fitzgerald warned him not to as it would harm his position as a writer) some five years before he leaped into stardom with *Vanity Fair*. His first contribution was probably in June, 1842. He was born in India and on his way home as a child was taken by his nurse to see Napoleon on St. Helena. He was brought up in a solid Anglo-Indian family to expect that the Charterhouse and Trinity would be followed by a life about the town. He showed some artistic talent and his youthful drawings were admired by Goethe. Financial troubles early drove him into journalism and commercial art, where he worked for *Fraser's* and some vituperative little papers and made a muddled kind of reputation as literary odd-job man, art critic, light verse writer and illustrator.

It is sometimes forgotten that at first Thackeray was as much a humorous artist as a humorous writer. In *Punch* he not only illustrated his own articles but took his share in providing cuts. Most of his drawings are signed with his device of a pair of spectacles. His first series for *Punch* was *Miss Tickletoby's Lectures on English History*. The Staff disliked them and he sent a hurt letter to say that he had done his best, just as if he had been writing " for any more dignified periodical." [29] He soon joined the Table, where he had to undertake any writing allotted to him, for example, baiting a character invented by Jerrold, Jenkins of the *Morning Post*. For several years after he had first joined the *Punch* Table Thackeray was in an admittedly inferior position to Jerrold, whose contemporary repute was far higher than is now realised. In his biography of Jerrold his grandson claims that in 1851 his popularity, broadly speaking, was greater than that of Dickens. Indeed, the paper had been started partly on the promise of support from this national figure. While Thackeray had done an enormous amount of work, he was not known much outside the world of newspapers, offices and clubs.

Gilbert Abbott à Beckett is one of those ghostly figures that hover round the birth of institutions. He had not only been at Westminster with Henry Mayhew but had run away from Westminster with Mayhew. His wit, versatility and restless flibbertigibbet energy were part of the climate in which Mayhew grew up. While working for the Bar, à Beckett became not only a fluent journalist but a fluent editor. By twenty-four he had started a large number of short-lived journals, among them *The Ghost; The Gallery of Horrors; The Wag; Figaro in London; The Terrific Penny Magazine* and *The Evangelical Penny Magazine*. He was one of the group that produced *Punch* ; his share in this will be considered in slightly more detail in Appendix III. For its first quarter of a century he contributed on the average a hundred columns to every volume, and much of the character of the paper must have come from him. Shy, witty, ardent and clever, he was just the kind of supporting player that the stars of *Punch* needed. It was useful to the paper to have a leading political journalist on its staff—he was a leader writer for *The Times* and for the *Illustrated London News*. It was useful to the paper to have a man who approached the targets attacked with the kind of knowledge that the new reformers were beginning to bring into the Civil Service. As a Poor Law Commissioner, his report on the Andover Workhouse scandals became a classic, and he was made Metropolitan Police Magistrate at an early age on the strength of it, despite some opposition to the appointment of a journalist. He seems to have been a quietly gay, attractive man, slowly gaining in self-confidence and likely, but for his early death from typhus, to have become a considerable public figure. His *Comic Blackstone*,[30] comic histories of Greece and Rome, and various poems and articles about a young barrister called Mr. Briefless had a considerable vogue for many years, but despite both the quantity and the popularity of his contributions to *Punch*, his chief importance was probably in his share in influencing the characteristic *Punch* tone of voice. His son said that, like Thackeray, he hated the humour of the tavern and the pawnshop.

Ever since à Beckett, *Punch* has been closely linked with the law, as since Lemon it has been linked with the stage. Many young barristers have supported themselves while waiting for briefs by journalism, many leading lawyers have spent their off-duty hours in clubs like the Garrick, meeting leading actors, novelists and *Punch* Editors. *Punch* has gained a good deal from its legal connections, not merely in social status, though the importance here should not be overlooked. The dramatic element in advocacy, the power of mastering complicated facts quickly and rearranging them in a manner lucid, attractive and convincing, verbal readiness, variety of experience and political ambition have all made the legal life a good training ground for *Punch* and, rather less often, *Punch* a good training ground for the legal life. Shirley Brooks passed the Law Final but was apparently not admitted. Tom Taylor, Francis Burnand and Owen Seaman were members of the Bar, like R. C. Lehmann, F. Anstey and the second generation of *Punch* à Becketts. Thackeray became a law student but soon found that nature intended him to be an art student. A. P. Herbert followed the law as private secretary to the Attorney-General, reformed it through his *Misleading Cases* in *Punch* and created it as a Member of Parliament, in particular by his Matrimonial Causes Act.

Albert Smith, the last to be mentioned of the earliest *Punch* men, is perhaps more important as a symptom than as a contributor. In the three years his connection with *Punch* lasted his rather slap-dash facetious descriptive articles, his *Physiologies*, were popular and he was useful because as a journalist he was professionally dependable. He produced large amounts of varying material and he produced it on time. He had been a medical student with John Leech, who sponsored and protected him on the *Punch* staff. The trouble with Albert Smith, accounts of whom vary very much, was that he was "low." He was the kind of man whom contributors to an ordinary comic paper might find they had as a colleague, but *Punch* was intended to be several cuts above the ordinary comic paper. The Staff had to put up with Lemon for the sake of his enormous gifts; they did not feel inclined to put up with the vulgarity and bumptiousness of Albert Smith. Jerrold hated him and used him as a butt. When Albert Smith protested and said, "After all, you know, we row in the same boat," Jerrold answered, "True, but not with the same skulls." [31] According to Vizetelly, Rule, the oyster-shop keeper of Maiden Lane, said: "You see, with Charles Dickens, it's all talent and very little tac' but with Albert it's just the opposite—all tac' and very little talent." [32] Albert Smith's Bohemianism had subtle differences from the Bohemianism of other *Punch* men, who felt that knowing him they might end by knowing his friends. Like

Stirling Coyne, he was finally driven out for plagiarism. For years afterwards any suggestion of using members of the Smith circle, like Sala, was met by the objection that *Punch* would become known as Bohemian and blackguardly instead of gentlemanly, and that *Punch* proofs would be flourished in taverns and *Punch* secrets disclosed to fellow boozers.

This policy of deliberate isolation was undoubtedly necessary if *Punch* was to become the first comic paper of standing, but there was a price to be paid in lessened contact with the rawness of life and in the growth of a self-conscious, repudiatory gentility : some of the lesser men tried to make *Punch* artificially exclusive in order to gain lustre from their association with it, instead of conferring lustre on it by their own work. When Albert Smith began to improve his public position by the popularity of his novels in imitation of Dickens and, more important, by the enormous success of his public lectures, " The Ascent of Mont Blanc " and others, he became smoother and some sort of rough-and-ready peace was patched up, though he did not again contribute. But while he was still smarting from his treatment he took a leading part in assisting and organising attacks on *Punch*, and in producing *The Man in the Moon* for Ingram, the twenty-eight issues of which were more concerned with hostility to *Punch* than with effective competition. One of its leading contributors, Shirley Brooks, an unsuccessful *Punch* contributor, later repressed the Bohemian side of him, gave rein to the scholarly and, after becoming *Punch*'s leading contributor, succeeded Mark Lemon in the Chair.

At first Art was regarded as unimportant compared with the text. Artists were hired as cheaply as possible to carry out commissions devised by writers, such as the little punning cuts paid at eighteen shillings per dozen. They were not very distinguished and when artists with outside reputations, like Kenny Meadows, were tried, they were often too fanciful and delicate for the hack-work that was expected. Work was judged by its literary content. When Landells went, there was nobody who was in touch with the artists to develop the pictorial side of the paper with any understanding of its possibilities. Henry Mayhew's dapper little man-about-town brother Horace, known as " Ponny," who wrote anything and everything and did odd jobs in the office, was put in charge of the Art for a time but artists considered they should be in direct contact with the Editor himself. So Lemon devoted a day a week to driving round London and keeping an eye on the artists at work. To some extent Lemon learnt this part of the job as he went along. He became interested in the technical side and later devoted a lot of thought to the use of photography in printing pictures. The artists were not admitted to social intimacy with the writers nor were they given much encouragement or continuity of employment. Lemon's tactlessness in dealing with artists compared with his skill in handling writers is shown by his curt message to one draughtsman, that as Mr. Leech charged so much he would be paid less in future. When artists walked out and joined other periodicals not much attempt was made to stop them. Some were bruisers who wanted to adapt the type of poster work with which they advertised London night life. Some were simply imitators of the great grotesque observers. At times *Punch* seems to be filled with rejected Dickens illustrations. Of these early *Punch* artists, William Newman was the most important and was only gradually eclipsed by Leech, though from the first he was treated as a high-grade artisan and Leech as a social equal of the writers. Henning was rather a blackguard and belonged too much to the atmosphere of the kind of comic journalism from which *Punch* was trying to draw clear. H. G. Hine did a considerable amount of work but dropped out when the position of the paper stabilised and stronger artists came in. Kenny Meadows might, with better editing, have repeated in *Punch* his outside successes and perhaps have developed from there. His work at its best is more delicately fanciful than either Leech's or Doyle's, but he was a victim of the gradually-evolved policy of concentrating all the art work in the hands of the fewest possible artists. Although he took sides in the contemporary battle between realism and fancy, remarking firmly, " Nature puts me out," [33] he once painted a butcher's wife to pay off a bill. She was loaded with jewellery but he left this out, until he was paid in kind for it. He then painted a gorgeous brooch for so many ribs of beef, a length of chain for a number of legs of mutton and the watch on her bosom for countless chops and steaks. He was a convivial but difficult man, and once at a dinner with other *Punch* men there, announced, " Gentlemen, I am *Punch*." [34]

" Phiz "—Halbôt K. Browne, who came of Huguenot stock—drew the second cover and helped with some of the oddments published from the *Punch* office. He did a few minor decorations in the text for a couple of years but left because, according to Spielmann, *Punch* could not support such twin stars as Leech and " Phiz." He came back during the Sixties with initials and little cuts and produced three full pages in the Pocket Book for 1850 (see p. 112 for the Pocket Books) ; but he never really established himself as a *Punch* draughtsman, though the world of Dickens illustration was so close. Because one has grown up with his Dickens illustrations, one is apt to forget that they are very much in the style of a school, not overwhelmingly recognisable as the product of an original talent. One does not feel that using him so little was a serious editorial mistake.

The full-page drawing with no text on the back which was claimed to be a feature linking *Punch* with its Parisian original was discussed over their food and drink by the stars and taken very seriously. At first it was usually headed *Mr. Punch's Pencillings*. It was formal, often allegorical and more effective than the gutter grotesquerie that currently served for political caricature. In the second volume, the *Pencillings* for a time took the form of a series of *Social Miseries* and these were probably the ancestors of the independent joke drawing. A public competition for the decoration of the new Houses of Parliament led *Punch* to submit its own entries, using a technical term for a mural design—" cartoon." The first mock entries appeared in place of the usual *Pencillings* on 15th July, 1843. The name dropped for a time but gradually returned and replaced the *Pencillings*. " Cartoon " has ever since been generally used for pictorial humour, or satire, on political subjects. More recently, the American use of " cartoon " for any humorous drawing has become widespread in England. Among the Staff the cartoon was originally called " The Big Cut."

Some of the atmosphere of the earliest days is recaptured in a letter [35] written in the middle Nineties by an old man who was a lad in the printing office of Bradbury & Evans when *Punch* came there to be printed :

" Its publisher was one Bryant, often spoken of in the earlier numbers as ' Our Bryant.' He was a very bustling man, dressed in a blue tailed coat with brass buttons, and could assist in the unloading of any quantity of pewter and glass. His favourite drink was Cooper, a mixture of stout and porter and he looked sometimes as if the stout had got the mastery of the porter and made him go lopsided. ' Go and see if you can get some copy for *Punch* ' was easier said than done at that time ; you had first to catch your editor and I had some funny adventures in doing that. After a long search on the first occasion I found Messrs. Lemon and Henry Mayhew in the coffee-room at the Edinburgh Castle in the Strand. I was requested to take a seat. I think Mr. Mayhew had an account with the waiter for after a whispered conversation he (the waiter) made some chalk marks on the inside of a cupboard door. There was a par. appeared in *Punch* soon after headed ' How to get beer from chalk.' One very cold night I was sent to Mr. Henry Mayhew's with proofs which I had to take back with me. He was then living in Clement's Inn in the Strand. Mr. Jerrold and several other gentlemen were there, Mr. Mayhew with a very long pipe with a very large bowl, a copper kettle singing merrily on the hob, and they were enjoying themselves immensely. Mr. Jerrold spoke to Mr. Mayhew and shortly afterwards he (Mr. M.) said to me, who was seated on the sofa, 'Will you have a glass with us, Eason?' I thanked him, and he asked me which I would have, gin or rum. I preferred rum and he told me to ' Mix it for yourself, the same as you would if you were at home.' I was enjoying myself I can tell you, and presently Mr. Mayhew asked me if I would have a pipe, but I declined that. . . . Dr. Maginn and Mr. H. P. Grattan were both in the Fleet Prison in Farringdon St. and I used to be sent to each of them. I went one morning to Mr. Grattan and had to wait while he was engaged with Mr. Henry Mayhew in the racquets ground. I got my proofs and hurried off. Once when I was troubled with a raging tooth Mr. Lemon told me to go to Canton's in St. Martin's Lane and tell them I came from Mr. Jerrold and they would draw it for me. He gave me half a crown to pay for it but after Mr. Canton had asked a few questions about Mr. Jerrold and *Punch* he drew the tooth and said they didn't charge *Punch* anything. When I returned Mr. Lemon would not take the half-crown and told me to get some brandy and wash my mouth out. . . . The *Punch* dinners were not at first held in Bouverie Street but Messrs. Bradbury and Evans and the gentlemen used to dine once a week at a hotel in Fleet Street and it was a treat to see them return, Mr. Lemon with his jolly, broad face, usually arm in arm with the austere looking Mr. Bradbury who tried to look as if he had taken nothing but his dinner. Mr. Henry Mayhew generally walked with Mr. Evans, with his red face and spectacles smiling as Mr. Pickwick is described as doing and the other gentlemen bringing up the rear."

FUNNY DOGS WITH COMIC TALES.

CHAPTER TWO

# THE SHIFT FROM RADICALISM

## *Mark Lemon's Editorship to 1857*

PUNCH'S OPPOSITION to the monarchy, its championship of the oppressed and the fame of some of its cartoons, still reproduced in school text-books, have given the impression that in the beginning it was primarily a political paper. It tried to cover everything that was going on and this, of course, included politics, but in many ways its politics were amateurish. Jerrold, the most keenly political mind on the paper, was a scarifier of abuses rather than a political journalist. He never defeated an opponent through knowing his case better than he did himself. The dinner-table discussions over the cartoon, when it had become a formal graphic statement of the considered attitude of the Staff, were of the kind heard between readers of different newspapers in a train. The difference of tone is obvious when *Punch* turned to something it really understood, like the stage, and it is noticeable that the literary parodies were generally more life-like and penetrating than parodies of political speeches.

*Punch*'s radicalism was fragmentary, hopping cheerfully from abuse to abuse. It was warm-hearted and sympathetic to the oppressed. Its most famous blow for the downtrodden, as opposed to blow against the downtreaders, was Thomas Hood's *Song of the Shirt*. Hood sent this rather doubtfully to Lemon, explaining it had been turned down by two other Editors, and asking him to throw it in the waste-paper basket if he did not want it. The Staff unanimously advised Lemon against printing it on the grounds that it was out of tone with the rest of the paper. He overruled them and its appearance in the Christmas Number of 1843 gave a lift to *Punch*'s circulation and repute that are still legendary. It was a feat of editorial courage and flair that, regarded in the context of its own time, is almost unequalled until Ross's decision to devote a whole issue of *The New Yorker* to John Hersey's report on Hiroshima. Hood was much troubled by false claims to have written the poem and *Punch* grudgingly allowed his authorship to become known.

One of the advantages of a satirical magazine is that it can be usefully unfair. It can swing against the winner when the cause has been won, exaggerate to make its points, ignore the disease for the symptom. There are always plenty of people prepared to be fundamental. All too few are prepared to fight for immediate relief. Its radicalism was a robust, furriner-hating, patriotic radicalism. It was, perhaps, too metropolitan to be Cobbett-like; but its attacks on flunkeyism and bad employers, like its equally hot-fisted support of the Volunteers and scorn for papists and Frenchmen, looked back to the roast beef and broken heads of an ideal past before enclosures and the Georges. Attacks on the papacy, partly caused by the papal record as temporal sovereigns, gained fierceness when Newman went over to Rome. Attacks on Puseyites were uninhibitedly Protestant. Religion was not yet divorced from questions of national security. Richard Doyle later resigned over this anti-Catholic policy but Thackeray joined in with a whoop. It was attacks on Napoleon III, whom he saw as a defender of property against anarchy rather than as a plebiscitary dictator likely to indulge in military adventure, that repelled him.

*Punch*'s attacks on continental despotisms got it at various times banned in France and Austria. Jerrold liked to represent foreign tyrants as blenching before the onslaughts of the terrible hunchback, and timorously keeping his unsettling pages from their subjects' eyes. When he was refused admission to Austria he remarked: "That shows your weakness, not my strength." [1] At times news-vendors might have copied the French example and claimed that that week the Editor was *diablement enragé*. After *Punch* had ceased to constitute any serious threat to the stability of thrones, its enormous prestige as a concentration of British attitudes made casual jokes or tactless slights seem to the more thin-skinned nations the best possible evidence of British views. On the whole, its representative character has been over-rated abroad and its literary and pictorial quality under-rated. Perhaps the extremes of foreign reaction have been the ceremonious burning of a complete set of Nineteenth Century *Punches* by the German Army in the last war and Mr. E. B. White's recent remark: "*Punch* is as British as vegetable marrow . . . The *Punch* Editors not only write the jokes but they help make the laws of England." [2]

*Punch* also continually attacked royal neglect of the arts and learning. It thought the monarchy Hanoverian rather than true British, as Sir Max Beerbohm did forty years later, and it emphasised the contrast between civilised rulers like Elizabeth I and Charles I, interested and appreciative, and the Philistine court of Victoria. The Prince Consort's support for the South Kensington scheme was not recognised at the time as being so far-sighted and intelligent as it turned out to be. His own taste was remote from that of the comparatively advanced circles in which the *Punch* men still moved. After the Prince Consort's death, the intellectual and artistic standards of the Court were even lower. The decline in the culture of the Court was certainly not offset by any development in the culture of the Government. Peel gave Tennyson a Civil List pension at thirty-seven; Salisbury made Alfred Austin Laureate.

*Punch* grew less political after its early years and by the end of 1845 it was only occasionally that articles of any length dealt with politics. Jerrold had revolutionary opinions but they did not go as far as revolution. He had, after all, been as bold a midshipmite as ever Tom-thumbed defiance at the gods. The veiled, unwillingly respectful antagonism of Thackeray and Jerrold revealed a difference in policy that was resolved in Thackeray's favour, especially when with the *Snobs of England* in 1846, he began to draw ahead of Jerrold. Between losing his upper-middle-class background and regaining it, Thackeray had been a pretty tough kind of journalist. He may have felt a difference between himself and men like Maginn and Lemon, but he was still generally classified with them. Mr. Malcolm Elwin points out that the *New Monthly*, reviewing the collected volume of *Punch* travel articles, *Cornhill to Cairo*, treated Thackeray as the traditional cockney, impudently inquiring, knowing, confident, democratically materialist. *Punch* had inherited the reputation of the Leigh Hunt circle. But as soon as possible Thackeray steered for gentleness, fun, kindly sentimental humour, and the political and social attitudes of the West End clubman. Jerrold thought the paper should have a purpose, that there was a duty laid on it to fight on the right side. In a letter to Dickens in 1846,[3] Jerrold said, "*Punch*, I believe, holds its course. . . . Nevertheless, I do not very cordially agree with its new spirit. I am convinced that the world will get tired (at least I hope so) of this eternal guffaw at all things. After all, life has something serious in it. It cannot be all a comic history of humanity. . . . Unless *Punch* gets a little back to his occasional gravities, he'll be sure to suffer." In fact, Jerrold was prepared to provide more fanciful fun and Thackeray to take a stronger political line than the sharp distinction may suggest—Thackeray once said, "I have always told you I can hit harder than any man alive, and I never do," [4]—but it was a very real distinction, and the decision that England should not have a strongly satirical paper, and should therefore be the less European, was taken when Thackeray and Leech began to lead *Punch* upwards in the social scale.

## II

Increasingly, the *Punch* man who was known to be in the middle of things became Thackeray. Tall—Carlyle called him a half-monstrous Cornish giant [5]—distinguished in appearance, despite his broken nose, he was kindly but remote and rather condescending. He was so anxious to sing sentimentally for " the dear boys," he even wrote a moving song for them, " The Mahogany Tree," typically ignoring the fact that the *Punch* Table is an unimpressive deal. He entertained them lavishly, told them improper stories, raised funds for their widows, smoothed over their quarrels ever so expertly ; but it cannot have pleased the dear boys when at a dinner of admirers in Edinburgh organised by Dr. John Brown, Thackeray was presented with a silver statue of *Punch*. When in an article in the *Quarterly Review* in 1854 he suggested that a number without a drawing by his close friend Leech could have nothing to appeal to the reader, they revolted and he had to apologise abjectly, explaining that in trying to do honour to a man he admired he had quite inadvertently seemed to express views about his other colleagues which were the very opposite of those which he held.

Thackeray resigned twice from the salaried staff. While writing *Vanity Fair*, and still more when writing *Pendennis*, he was finding the *Punch* work a drag and lecturing was much more remunerative. About July, 1850, he resigned : " There appears in next *Punch* an article, so wicked, I think, by poor Jerrold that upon my word I don't think I ought to pull any longer in the same boat with such a savage little Robespierre." [6] The proprietors withdrew the offending article and declined to accept the resignation. For another eighteen months he continued to work intermittently, finding it increasingly irksome as he was in the full tide of novel-writing, and also worried by *Punch*'s abuse of the Prince Consort, the Crystal Palace and Louis Napoleon. In December, 1851, coming from Edinburgh, he bought a *Punch* containing the cartoon of a Beggar on Horseback, in which the Emperor was depicted galloping to Hell, with a sword reeking with blood.[7] He promptly resigned from the Staff. After this he contributed only a few occasional articles but continued to attend the dinners from time to time. Though Thackeray himself attributed his resignation to points of principle, Mark Lemon later said the real trouble was a question of salary. In a later letter to the proprietors, however, Thackeray said that as an outside contributor he was paid at a lower rate and as he had lost money by having his last two novels published by Bradbury & Evans because of his old friendship with them, he did not feel inclined to continue writing for *Punch*. There were several rumours about the reasons for the resignation and he was annoyed that there had been no contradiction from the firm of the story that it was due to *Punch* resentment at his *Quarterly* article. Whatever the reasons for the parting, it is quite clear that personal and political difficulties had made his position impossible. "I often think about old *Punch* and having left him : but I am sure it is best for my reputation and the comfort of some of that crew that I should be out of it. I fancied myself too big to pull in the boat ; and it wasn't in the nature of things that Lemon and Jerrold should like me." [8]

*Punch* was essentially a gay little paper. Even when it was dealing with serious topics it managed to remain light-hearted and conveyed the impression of a bustling, amusing world with *Punch* right in the middle of it enjoying the absurdities of its butts. One of its butts was Alfred Bunn, amateur poet and manager at Drury Lane. (Vizetelly says he sold his wife to a Colonel Berkeley.) Goaded beyond endurance, he hit back with a pamphlet, *A Word with Punch*, which closely imitated *Punch* in appearance. Bunn was assisted, to what extent is not known, by George Augustus Sala, and probably by Albert Smith. Landells did the engraving. Its attacks were whole-hearted, those on Jerrold being noticeably more good-humoured than those on à Beckett. There were amusing quotations of bad verse by Mark Lemon, who was jeered at for being a publican, for being conceited, for being a plagiarist and for wanting to be Lord Mayor. After this *Punch* laid off Bunn, whose riposte had been the most effective in the history of the paper.

It lived its life in public more by a kind of instinctive feeling for the limelight than by any systematic campaign to get publicity. Much of its fame was caused by its opponents. Comic papers lived in a perpetual slanging match. Because *Punch* was successful, and also for personal reasons now lost without record, the attacks of rivals were venomous and continuous. *Punch* hit back hard and followed its own jokes into the columns of its contemporaries. Few of the early rivals, some of which had opposition to *Punch* as their *raison d'être*, survived. Showing the editorial works to the readers and enlisting them in its quarrels was not only good publicity; it bound readers to the paper in comradeship. Perhaps Jerrold's personification of the paper as "Mr. Punch" helped to focus their loyalty. It remained for the *Sunday Dispatch* to investigate the possibilities of a readers' tie, but that was just the kind of stunt that *Punch* liked. For a time it printed on the first page extracts from the sillier contributions submitted to it with its own comments.

The social life of *Punch* men brought them into contact with many of the leading artists, writers and actors, and especially with the Dickens circle. Bradbury & Evans, who were leading publishers of fiction as well as of newspapers and periodicals, published several of Dickens's novels and he edited the *Daily News* and *Household Words* for them. He dined at the *Punch* Table but never contributed, though a rejected contribution exists in manuscript. When Dickens parted from his wife, he published a justificatory statement in *Household Words* and because it did not appear in *Punch* also, despite the fact that it could have had no conceivable place in a comic periodical, he not only broke with Bradbury & Evans but for some years severed all social relations with Lemon and his other *Punch* friends. The breach was widened by his famous quarrel with Thackeray over the expulsion of Edmund Yates from the Garrick, which occurred about the same time. Dickens unsuccessfully tried to break off the engagement of his son Charles to Evans's daughter, Bessie.

*Punch* men, having so many connections with the drama, were active in amateur dramatics. Their theatrical usefulness helped their social life. The Dickens circle had always been getting up performances. When a member of the Staff fell into debt or died and left his widow hard up, funds were raised enjoyably by public performances. Of these, one of the most elaborate was after the death of C. H. Bennett in 1867. It began with *Cox and Box*, a lyrical version of Maddison Morton's farce *Box and Cox* by Burnand, with original music by Sullivan. Then came an Address by Shirley Brooks, followed by Tom Taylor's drama *A Wolf in Sheep's Clothing*. In this Tenniel was the success of the evening as Colonel Churchill and the part of Keziah Mapletoft was taken by Miss Ellen Terry. The evening ended with a Bouffonnerie Musicale by Offenbach, and a farce by John Oxenford. One of the *Punch* enterprises was co-operatively writing a pantomime for the management of Covent Garden. When the completed book was to be read to the company, the *Punch* men sat on a row of chairs on the stage, and Mark Lemon rose and read to the horror-struck acrobats, clog-dancers, mimes and buffoons, *King John; or Harlequin and Magna Charta.*

*Punch* was a London paper and many of its writers were never happy for long out of London. It tried to bring an air of the capital to outlying pockets of education or sophistication all over the country. It was read in rectories and country-houses and the red-brick homes of Midland solicitors and amid the chill discomforts of Scottish high-life. The assumption was that what went on in London was what mattered. In its early days *The New Yorker* gave the same feeling of being in the centre of a place where an infinite number of exciting and amusing things were happening. In *Punch* of the Forties there was always something going on. The paper took a considerable interest in London local government and published a musical setting of the Queen's speech.[9] It kept an eye on new building and agitated for the removal of abuses like the filth and confusion of Covent Garden and Smithfield Markets. It ran a series of *London Interiors* and devoted a whole issue to the *Lions of London*,[10] a number of pieces about places and institutions. This London interest remained a central theme in *Punch* for many years. In the middle Fifties the dirty Thames and in the middle Sixties the congestion of City traffic were hammered at over and over again. Other targets, still under fire to-day, were Mock Auctions and Jewish Abattoirs.

One or two of the little jesting paragraphs of these years have become historical and have played a part in building up the legend of the *Punch* back-numbers. On 18th May, 1844, under the heading *Foreign Affairs*, was the suggestion that Caesar's *Veni, vidi, vici*, was beaten for brevity by Sir Charles Napier's dispatch to Lord Ellenborough on the capture of Scinde—*Peccavi*. There is some mystery about this, as on 22nd March, 1856, appears the following :

TRUMPING THE ELEPHANT

" *Peccavi*—I've Scinde," wrote Lord Ellen, so proud.
More briefly Dalhousie wrote—" *Vovi*—I've Oude."

—which gives the impression that the author did not know the earlier *Punch* dispatch to Napier. It was often quoted as genuine.

*Punch*'s adaptation of a popular advertisement,

WORTHY OF ATTENTION

ADVICE TO PERSONS ABOUT TO MARRY,—Don't,

is so familiar to us now, perhaps the most famous joke ever made, that it needs an effort to realise how neat, ingenious and profound it must have seemed at the time. It appeared on the January page of the 1845 Almanack. Innumerable people claimed to have sent it in : Spielmann says mysteriously, and without giving any details, that chance had placed in his possession the authoritative information that it was Henry Mayhew. Mark Lemon told Henry Silver that it had been sent in anonymously but Lemon is not quite a reliable authority as he always tended to play down Mayhew's importance in the early history of the paper.

When Bulwer Lytton attacked Tennyson for taking a Civil pension and Tennyson scribbled off an angry reply, Forster sent it to *Punch*. *The New Timon and the Poets,*[11] signed Alcibiades, is much too long to quote in full, but its odd, jerky, conversational verse, looking forward to early Eliot, is an illustration of the range of treatment as well as of subject that *Punch* was prepared to admit.

> " So died the Old : here comes the New.
> Regard him : a familiar face :
> I *thought* we knew him : What, it's you,
> The padded man—that wears the stays—
> Who kill'd the girls and thrill'd the boys,
> With dandy pathos when you wrote,
> A Lion, you, that made a noise,
> And shook a mane en papillotes."

Very popular were Albert Smith's various *Physiologies*, groups of social observations in which he surveyed medical students, evening parties, London idlers, etc. A number on English watering-places was rather repetitively facetious but quite a lot of its humour came from picking out the odd, amusing point from the history of places it covered.[12] Several of the descriptions of architectural and topographical oddity echoed Dickens. The use of comparisons, either to make reality vivid and thus show its inherent humour or to add a joke to it, stretches from *Pickwick* to Wodehouse, though in the early Twentieth Century it became for a time fresher and more vivacious in the United States than England. *Punch*'s descriptive writing in the early Forties was tighter and more exuberantly metaphorical than it became later. The model school textbook was another hardwearing form. Many of the devices of the far more inventive *1066 and All That* were used, e.g. the mock examination paper, the mock archaic poem, the anachronistic confusion of names, like Godwin and William Godwin. The humour of exaggeration, often a pretended American news item, was a runner-up to the pun, though far below it in frequency. The auction catalogue with pledges by politicians and the Political Euclid are early humorous forms still met with, like the discussions of *The Times* " agony " column—a kind of ancestor of the extracts or " pars " that have been for a long time as popular with readers as with sub-editors filling up a short column.

In the first number of 1843, *The Story of a Feather*, Jerrold's most popular work after the *Caudle Lectures*, began. The record of the wanderings of an inanimate object was one more attempt to give unity to a series of detached scenes, like the devices of an imaginary journal or a club, or a notebook. These episodes had a good deal of heavy-handed satire of court flunkeyism. The parasitic trades like plume-making showed snobbery operating right down the social scale. Scenes of poverty were contrasted with the luxury of the rich. (It is interesting that in these the style became far more Dickensian.) *Punch*, without any particular intention of widening its scope until it became a general magazine, was prepared to admit tears as well as laughter. A scene like the death-bed of the poor seamstress's mother was printed, simply because life was like that. Compassion was Jerrold's starting-point. He attacked Peel because in Peel's England poverty-stricken death-beds were common. He did not, like some later journalists, begin from hatred of a Minister and cynically drag in the pathetic to reinforce his attack. The effect of these series in consolidating readership was shown by the use of characters from them in cartoons nearly as often as Dickens or Shakespeare characters.

In the pages there was an incessant use of proper names. Politicians, shops, actors and businesses were continually mentioned by name. Even in an item dealing with invented characters the background would be described by reference to existing people and addresses. The decline of the proper name in *Punch* is due partly to the crippling effects of a law of libel whose encroachments have never been seriously opposed by the press, partly to pressure from the advertising departments not to attack advertisers and not to puff non-advertisers. When it became obligatory to say that a character in a story got off the bus outside Harridges, retreat from reality was complete. The retreat began early.

Thackeray's series on *Snobs* [13] had much less detailed and accurate knowledge than Albert Smith had shown in his descriptions of Society. However, the funny names and moralising and double-bluff support for the snobs were carried on the gentle music of Thackeray's style, a style surprisingly tough and vigorous. He needed space and the Snob papers were merely sketches for the novels. They included some of the more irritating faults of the novels without having either their sweep or their depth ; yet they would suddenly fire into readability. Thackeray's best *Punch* work was burlesque, descriptive writing and verse. His articles attributed to " Our Fat Contributor " were light and a good contrast to the low comedy of the rest of the paper. They filled much the same place as E. V. Lucas's articles in the Twenties and early Thirties. The burlesques of novelists appealed on two grounds, that they were dreadful likenesses of the originals and that they were funny. The fun varied in subtlety, but even when it was rough and ready there was something refreshing in finding Thackeray prepared to be rough and ready at all. They were effective enough to make G. P. R. James and Charles Lever emend their styles.

Forster was furious with them and Dickens patched up a reconciliation, though saying, " They do no honour to literature or literary men and should be left to the very inferior and miserable." [14] The Staff vetoed a parody of Dickens, to whom Malcolm Elwin suggests Thackeray had transferred the jealousy he no longer felt for Jerrold when, in the late Forties, Jerrold's reputation began to slip after a couple of bad failures. When in the early Fifties Jerrold made a success of editing *Lloyd's Newspaper*, Thackeray remarked, " I am quite pleased with myself at finding myself pleased at a man getting on in the world." [15]

*Punch* was vigorously anti-French, though it charmingly guyed the defence movement that followed the French scares of the early Forties in Leech's *The Brook-Green Militia-Man*, a domestic little character with his toy-soldier's uniform and his wife-bestowed comforts. *Punch*'s attitude to France became complicated with the Revolution of 1848. It was torn between its robustly insular contempt for foreigners and its feeling that foreigners who stood up to tyrants in the way that *Punch* did should be encouraged. The final fizzle of Chartism gave an opportunity of making fun of the faked signatures on the Petition and for a general gaiety of relief; but in the early part of the year there was clearly some uncertainty. Leech's Special Constable says, "Now mind, you know, if I kill you it's nothing; but if you kill me, by jingo, it's murder." [16] *Punch* showed some fear of the effect on liberties of an amateur force with legal immunity, though Lemon and Leech were themselves Special Constables. Of the continental revolutions, the French was the most exciting, partly from proximity, partly because it was like a piece of recent folk-lore come to life. *Punch* was always popping over to Paris to see what was going on and on the whole it approved. At least Louis Philippe, one of the *Punch* butts, was out. You did not have to be a dangerous Radical to approve the fall of a monarch who was still remembered from the war scares of seven years before.

*Punch* was for the oppressed against the privileged provided the oppressed were obviously, even vividly, oppressed. Its Radicalism was the old anti-aristocratic Radicalism—the kind of Radicalism that survived in Wells. Ducal landlords, princes, bishops, Court flunkeys were the targets that roused it, the dying but still powerful class that survived the Reform Bill so well. *Punch* was born when Melbourne was going out and Peel was coming in, and Cabinets represented a greater acreage of land than ever before. Its attacks on Melbourne and the Whigs were as bitter as its attacks on Peel and the Conservatives. It had the advantage of growing up in a period of small majorities. Between the Great Reform Bill in 1832 and Disraeli's extension of the franchise to the urban artisan in 1867, political parties were fluid. Speeches and pledges could affect votes in the House and there were outstanding individuals in politics whose party allegiance was loose. Gladstone was offered office by

*Vol. IX, 1845. P. 183* *John Leech*

THE MOMENTOUS QUESTION.

*"Tell me, oh tell me, dearest Albert, have* you *any Railway Shares?"*

both Conservatives and Whigs in the same week. *Punch* regarded Ministers as royal servants, and it criticised Peel for taking office in the same tone in which it would have attacked the acceptance of a Court post by a minor politician hitherto on the Opposition side. Though *Punch* was never Republican in the sense of wanting a complete abolition of the monarchy, it disliked both the corruption of the Georgian monarchy and the expensive insipidity of the new model.

By the end of the Forties *Punch* was still outspoken by modern standards, but it was becoming increasingly outspoken against change. The Forties were Radical but the Fifties were Whig. *Punch*'s hero was Palmerston and its butts, like Louis Napoleon and the Pope and Disraeli, were attacked as men likely to threaten the *status quo*. It must be remembered that the early Twentieth Century alignment of Conservatives on the Right and Liberals on the Left does not apply to the mid-Nineteenth Century, when the Whigs were well to the right of the new-look Conservatives, so that the shift in *Punch*'s attitude is greater than it appears. It was still capable of generous enthusiasms, still opposed to survivals of the bad old days, but it was no longer tugging at Parliament to go faster. The changes in *Punch* between its foundation and the end of the Fifties were due partly to the attainment of some financial security, partly to the amelioration of English life—the Hungry Forties ended in the fizzling out of Chartism and that godsend for *Punch*, The Railway Bubble, was followed by the comparative prosperity of the Fifties —and partly to the growing cohesion of the *Punch* staff.

## III

Apart from Lemon, Thackeray and Jerrold there was one early recruit who must be mentioned. Tom Taylor arrived as early as 1844 but he did not get the Editorship until thirty years later. He was a Northerner whose father was described as 'a respected and attractive brewer'.[17] At Cambridge he was one of the Tennyson set. He won a Trinity Fellowship, went to the Bar, wrote leaders and was very popular in Society for his high spirits and knack of getting people together and organising them into enjoyment. Nevertheless he inherited a solemn strain from his Northern father and German mother. For two years he was Professor of English Language and Literature at London University. He was an important Civil Servant and ended as Secretary of the Local Government Board. He was also art critic of *The Times* and one of the butts of *The Gentle Art of Making Enemies*. He was nearer to what one thinks of as a great Victorian than most of the *Punch* men. As the record of his charitable enterprises and public functions extends, one feels he is turning into marble before one's eyes. He was a strenuous character, versatile, learned, scholarly and full of knowledge of what was going on in politics and literature and art. He was also a busy dramatist. His plays included *The Ticket of Leave Man*, *To Oblige Benson* and *Our American Cousin*, in which Sothern, who had quarrelled with the Management, tried to wreck the show by gagging and pinching scenes, though his part as Lord Dundreary was only a small one ; instead he turned the play into a smash hit. It was the straight version that Lincoln was watching when he was assassinated. Gruffly kind, incredibly energetic—he liked to get in four hours' work before breakfast—able and aggressive, he brought *Punch* some learning and a much more intellectual grasp of politics than Jerrold. He used to say, " We must not attack the man but put down the system." [18] If his work became increasingly heavy and dull, he linked the *Punch* mind to the serious review mind and gave its humour an academic foundation on which other men could have built. He was an odd fish. Once Birket Foster did some drawings for the Dalziels, the famous engravers and entrepreneurs of art books. They invited Tennyson to write verses to go with them, but he turned the commission down. When Taylor was asked, he suggested he should get *Once a Week* terms, £100 for thirty poems. He wanted his wife to be included in the commission : " I may say that she is homely born and bred, and that her verses would be above the mark of my own, as far as I can judge." If the Dalziels refused his terms, he suggested they might apply to William Barnes.[18a]

It was Leech who made the public look first at the pictures. He had been at the Charterhouse with Thackeray. The shift from " The Charterhouse " to " Charterhouse " had not yet taken place and on *Punch* they rather clung together in the presence of the sureness of Henry Mayhew and Gilbert à Beckett who had been at Westminster. At the Charterhouse, life for the boys was tough, but not as hard as Leech later found it, and a sharp drop in his father's income, owing to an unsuccessful scheme for *table d'hôte* dinners, forced him to leave Barts, where he had been studying medicine like a gentleman. He was apprenticed to a physician whose main interests were pigeons and strong-arm gymnastics.

His early drawings were mainly street scenes, things that had caught his eye in the tangy, slummy world in which he now moved. He learned the job of pictorial journalism under the pressure of trying to regain his former standard of life. After a slow start on *Punch*, where by late delivery of his first commission he made Lemon miss the publication date, he turned the *Pencillings* into something far more varied and adroit. His rebus, a leech wriggling in a bottle, began to be looked for by readers. From the *Social Miseries* he went on to develop the illustrated joke, though always with some sharpness of social observation. He never really liked political work and gradually yielded it to Tenniel in the later Fifties. A hostile painter said he left off where difficulties began, but Miss June Rose more kindly says, " He is content to leave unsaid what he cannot say well."[18b] Frith claimed that nobody had been so successful in conveying action of wind on objects.

When we think of the early *Punches* we think inevitably of a generalised Leech world. Drunken cabbies sit on cobbles, leaning back bemused and bucolic against conduits. Boys, terribly thin, but jerked into vivacity by the edgy derision of the slums, jeer and play japes. Fat parties, with truculent timidity, undertake complicated journeys by boat and train, their voluminous baggage often including pets and barrels of oysters. Weary men about town of extreme youth quiz the belles at assemblies, pityingly discuss their parents with schoolfellows, and are precocious with churchwardens and brandy-and-water. Sharp-tongued mammas war with sharp-tongued daughters on seaside promenades, where winds disclose ankles to military men, real and imitation. It is a world of cabs and bathing machines, chop-houses and seaside lodgings. The terseness

*Almanack, 1854* *John Leech*

PATERFAMILIAS MAKES HIMSELF INDEPENDENT OF HOTELS.

of his captions pleased the Victorians and also his gradual extension of comic art to include the kind of milieu to which his public belonged. Ruskin called Leech's *Punch* work " the finest definition and natural history of the classes of our society, the tenderest flattery of its pretty and well-bred ways with which the modesty of subservient genius ever amused or immortalised careless masters." [19]

Leech distorted reality to get a humorous effect, though in part it was a traditional distortion going back behind the caricaturists of the Napoleonic war. Both Dickens and Thackeray praised Leech not for accuracy but for beauty and elegance, ignoring the burlesqueing and distortion that to modern eyes seem fundamental in him. Part of what seems to us distortion may have been a realistic representation of stunted, warped, blotched bodies and may also have had an element of distorting hatred. As soon as he began to make his way, he became not only very, very gentlemanly in behaviour and opinion, but virulently opposed to the working class. Thackeray's was a blander disdain, often merely a hedonistic evasion. Leech was less brutal than his predecessors but he was a long way from sharing Jerrold's attitude to the poor and perhaps even more than Thackeray steered *Punch* towards the rapidly rising sections of the middle class.

Tall and distinguished, to his friends Leech was gentle, kindly and rather melancholy, though Lemon said he had always been a spoilt child. He was no actor but he rather lackadaisically joined in his colleagues' simple sports. When he played Slender in the *Merry Wives of Windsor* he was heard to say, " Oh sweet Ann Page " with a note of impatience. There was an odd tendency for the leading *Punch* artists to be reserved, sad men, whose only contribution to conviviality was to sing a song by Barry Cornwall called " King Death." Trelawny told Millais that Shelley and Leech were the two men he had loved best. In his early days he liked to entertain the *Punch* men to simple little meals, shyly served by his simple little wife, whom he had seen and loved at sight in the street and was his model for beautiful women ever after. As he went up in the world, she turned into rather a silly woman, and he spent a good deal of time hunting with his fashionable friends. Leech's social observation was far less penetrating and subtle than Thackeray's. He devoted more of his attention to field sports and a good deal of it to the cockney sportsman, the vulgar bounder who does not know the proper usages. Leech as a landscape and sporting artist, above all Leech as a drawer of horses, both in *Punch* and in the great Surtees illustrations, has been remembered better than the London and seaside Leech, but his range, and the sharpness of his political and social humour in the early days, are as much one of the glories of *Punch* as the anatomical accuracy of his hunters. Much of the pleasure that a reader was intended to gain from the social cuts was recognition, not surprise. He was expected to think, "Yes, that's it," not, "I never thought of that," still less, "How on earth did he think of that?" In Leech, the identification of the incident depicted with common experience was foolproof because it was his own notorious clumsiness on horseback that he guyed in Briggs.

*Vol. XVIII, 1850. P. 170* *John Leech*

*Farming Uncle:* "*You don't see such muck as this in London, Ben?*"
*Cockney Nephew:* "*Oh, don't we, though. You should see Eaton Square!*"

He attacked his own failures in others. Later *Punch* humorists tended to claim for themselves more failures than they were entitled to. *Punch* in the early days was extravert and unlikely to admit weaknesses. This made it sometimes dishonest and often unfair but it gave a masculinity to its fun. Jerrold in real life was quite useless with his hands but he used his tongue and pen to supply the lack of one dexterity by another, rather than to excuse maladroitness by humorously exaggerating it.

Amusing and vigorous as Leech's hunting scenes are, there is a loss of power from his early urban work. Or it may be that whereas *Punch* art as a whole greatly improved, Leech repeated past adequacies, though the drawing of his landscape backgrounds continued to develop. He himself said frankly he could not draw as well as Tenniel. But the promise Flaxman had seen in the boy suggests that the painful gap between him and Charles Keene in the early Sixties was due to some failure to develop, and this may have been caused partly by the diversion of energy from being an artist to being a gentleman—a diversion that worried his colleagues. There have been many good artists who were excited by social advance without its doing them any harm. His early death, partly from a nervous disorder that made him violently susceptible to the noise of street bands and organs, was a blow to *Punch*, but not such a blow as had been feared.

For a time, the *Punch* artist second in public favour was Richard Doyle, son of the leading political caricaturist, HB. He has remained a name because after trying several covers *Punch* used his and with minor modifications it is the Doyle cover that is familiar to-day. The procession at the base was adapted from Titian's *Bacchus and Ariadne*. The mask represents Brougham. He first attracted attention with a series of comic borders, *Punch's Triumphal Procession* (one of which enclosed Hood's *Song of the Shirt*), in the number for 16th December, 1843. He did a good deal of odd-job work like initials and borders and, for a time, about one cartoon to Leech's three. Some of his series were very popular, the illustrations to *Manners and Customs of Ye Englyshe* [20] in particular : the Pre-Raphaelites bought the issues to study the grouping. His real strength was in fantastic illustration and much of his *Punch* work seems heavy and uninspired. His imitations of early English drawings, in what he called the etched outline manner, are repetitive and in his anachronisms the drawing adds little to the caption. His view of the past lacked a dimension, like that of his nephew Conan Doyle in *The White Company*. Holman Hunt said Doyle had a delightfully amusing laugh, which always seemed to be indulged in apologetically, with the face bent into the cravat and the double chin pressed forward. He was an admirer of Scott and shared his interest in demonology. Victorian interest in fairies, down to Gilbert or even to Barrie, needs explanation. Doyle touched some nerve that we cannot guess at. Some of his best work was inspired by the California gold rush of 1849, which seems to have been sufficiently outside his usual range to stimulate a dying originality.

Doyle never quite fitted in with the rowdy, boozing *Punch*. He was a little prim and a little socially superior. Also, he was a strong Catholic and increasingly unhappy at the dinners when attacks were made on the Pope, whose revival of the Catholic hierarchy in England in 1850 led to a no-popery outburst, cheered on by Lord John Russell. Doyle finally resigned over an anti-papal cartoon.

*Vol. IX, 1845.* P. *212* *Richard Doyle*

The discussion with Jerrold and Thackeray, who tried to stop the resignation, is revealing. They said the Catholic writers on *The Times* did not resign, though its anti-papal language was often violent. Doyle replied, " *The Times* is a monarchy, whereas *Punch* is a Republic." [21] Lockhart had a rumour—it came from John Murray—that Doyle had been threatened with excommunication by Wiseman if he did not resign.

Jerrold, Thackeray, Taylor, Leech and Doyle were the big names of the Forties. The Fifties brought only three new contributors of major importance. Shirley Brooks was perhaps the best all-round writer that *Punch* ever had. He was the son of quite an important architect and a descendant of that Earl Ferrers who drove to execution behind six cream-coloured ponies in good spirits. His biographer is reticent or evasive about his early life and education until he came to Oswestry to be articled to a solicitor uncle. There seems to have been a financial struggle and he finally fought his way up through journalism and not through the law. He married one of the sisters Walkinshaw, known from the difference in their complexions as Night and Morning : Mrs. Brooks was Night.

Brooks was a trained journalist, broken in to filling column after column with readable, accurate material against a deadline. He was astonishingly able to apply the same skill to verse. He once wrote six songs in a day at three guineas each. He became a leading Parliamentary writer and as a special correspondent investigated agricultural labour in Southern Russia for the *Morning Chronicle* in a series of articles parallel to Henry Mayhew's *London Labour and the London Poor*. He attacked *Punch* in hostile comic papers, being a close friend of some of *Punch*'s persistent opponents, and for almost the only time in its history *Punch* bought over opposition, though it is fair to add that Brooks had wanted to join *Punch* from the start. Lemon, although increasingly unwilling to admit new blood as he grew older and very happy now among the band of brothers that he liked to treat as sons, seized on Brooks and in a short time was relying on him more and more until he was his destined successor, though Percival Leigh was the official deputy.

Brooks wrote every kind of article and poem. His *Essence of Parliament*, which began in 1855, was the first thing of its kind and has remained one of the best. It was not only attractive to the country reader who felt it kept him in touch with the political realities behind the sober reports in his newspaper, it linked *Punch* with a political world which was just beginning to learn the advantages of personal publicity : *Punch* men would be met at political dinners. It is true that by becoming to some extent the house journal of the political world, *Punch* lost some of its sting. It ceased to be extreme, but by modern standards its descriptions of members and their speeches and its sharp record of the odd incident were outspokenly unkind. Yet there were only the acids of personal distaste, not those of a Cause, behind its slighting words. Brooks did an enormous amount of outside journalism and wrote several novels, but it was in *Punch* that his powers had their chance. If early *Punch* was Lemon and Jerrold, *Punch* later became Lemon and Brooks.

He was always that little bit quicker in suggesting a cartoon. He had always seen the news item that was wanted, often in the most obscure provincial paper. He was an out-and-out Tory in politics and said he assumed that every *Punch* reader would have read *The Times* and that the paper was not produced for cottagers.

Nobody knew how Brooks got through his work. He did not, like Thackeray, digest his ideas before he wrote but sat down and scratched away until it came. Taylor's output was a result of long hours and grim determination. Brooks always seemed to have just stopped lounging over a novel or magazine, just stepped in from a club or reception. He went everywhere and, happy as he was at home in his study, he managed to combine domestic reading with incessant visiting. He made excellent speeches at the banquets of rich City Companies. He was accused of social climbing, blackguardedly pastimes, snobbery—but his upbringing had been pious and he retained a shamefaced piety behind his man-of-the-worldliness. Like Lemon and Jerrold, he was a Freemason. Jerrold's son described him as a literary man of the old French type. There was a serene contentment in him. He had a fantastic verbal memory and a very good memory for people. Somebody described him as "A clear skinned, rosy-cheeked, fresh-looking gentleman-farmer sort of man, with thick fair hair, bright blue eyes, very clear, and a ready smile with a slight curl of the upper lip which gave a look of cynicism when he joked or laughed." [22] His heartiness had been polished and he had the air of a fashionable physician. He prepared his conversation before dinner parties, though there was no need to. His wit needed a setting; he was not quotable in isolation like Jerrold or Wilde. He cultivated letter-writing and his diaries and letters, scattered by events only darkly hinted by his biographer, might be worth collecting and publishing. High living undermined his health and he died young. As Burnand said, "That generation were boozers." [23] But Brooks was altogether a lighter-minded boozer than men of the generation of Mayhew and Coyne. Brooks combined some of the learning of Taylor, the sheer writing ability of Jerrold, the gaiety and ideas of Mayhew and the politic toughness of Lemon. One curious foretaste of later standards of professionalism was that Brooks always took his coat off to work. The most presentable of his children, Reginald, did some work for *Punch* and joined the Table for a year or two under Burnand. He did not fit in. At one time he was editor of the *Sketch* but he found his niche as "Peter Blobbs" of *The Pink 'Un*. He died young through dissipation.

Doyle's resignation left *Punch* in urgent need of a decorative artist. Jerrold saw John Tenniel's *Aesop* illustrations and suggested him to Lemon. Mr. E. V. Knox thinks Tenniel the greatest single acquisition *Punch* ever made. Lemon considered comic genius less important than grace and professionalism, as Leech was still going strong. Tenniel did not distort, but he was in his early days a master of the smooth grotesque. His illustrations for *Alice* owed something to Carroll, who supervised them closely, though he was sufficiently co-operative to offer the Baronet and the Butterfly when Tenniel objected to the Walrus and the Carpenter. Jerrold had prevented Lemon from using John Gilbert with the dictum " We don't want Rubens on *Punch*." [24] The appointment of Tenniel was a victory for High Art : his colleagues regarded him as a leading exponent of black-and-white. As a young man, Tenniel's inclination had been for the grand style and the mediaeval revival. He thought of himself as doing murals of men in armour. Like some of his fellow-students he first came to black and white as a means of supporting himself until he had achieved his ambitions. The interest in wood-engraving awakened by Bewick, and the work of Germans like Menzel and Rethel were very slowly exciting the young who were going to be responsible for the sudden blazing out of English book illustration in the late Fifties and Sixties. Tenniel drew with a 6-H pencil on the wood block and did not, like some of his contemporaries, experiment in going to meet the engraver more than half-way. Considering the difficulties of working against time for the cartoon, Swain engraved Tenniel fairly and adequately ; inevitably his grey lines came out black and hard. In time, Tenniel naturally began to some extent to draw for Swain. His book illustration was generally more fluent.

*22nd August, 1857* REVENGE FOR THE INDIAN MUTINY *John Tenniel*

THE BRITISH LION'S VENGENCE ON THE BENGAL TIGER.

Tenniel was like several of the artists—a shy man worried about his health. Twenty years before his death he told a London hostess that he was breaking up. Blind in one eye, like George du Maurier, he had a good visual memory and hardly ever worked from photographs or models. Unfortunately, having once looked at something he saw no need to look at it again, and the appearances he drew in *Punch* became increasingly divorced from reality. It was difficult to persuade him that a politician had aged or that one had even grown a beard. In her essay on him, Miss Frances Sarzano comments that he had an agreeable eye for pattern but " draws the features of things without their personality. He remembers how a wall is built but not the stoniness of stone."[25] Like F. C. Burnand and Tom Taylor and R. C. Lehmann and George du Maurier, he came from mixed English and continental stock. His wife was a foreigner and after her death he was cared for by her presumably equally-foreign sisters. This increased his remoteness from his colleagues and from the people he interpreted.

The reproduction of Tenniel's work in school histories has made us see Victorian England through his eyes, but he made it colder, more formal, more classical than it really was. When he gradually took the cartoons over from Leech it was obviously a suitable arrangement for both sides but it made cartoons less funny and also removed Tenniel's humorous fancy from the other pages.

In considering Tenniel's cartoons it is important to remember the brilliance of the early ones, not to allow the competent dullness of his later years to overlay the memory of them and not to confuse the exaggeration of some of Tenniel's weaknesses by his successor, Bernard Partridge, with his own best work. Compare *The British Lion's Vengence on the Bengal Tiger,*[26] suggested by Shirley Brooks, with the even more famous *Dropping the Pilot,*[27] in which Gilbert Arthur à Beckett's idea was everything, though the public probably assumed that Tenniel thought of it himself, rather as the public assume that every word spoken by Groucho Marx or Sid Field was their own. In the earlier cartoon the design has a tremendous melo-

DROPPING THE PILOT.

dramatic verve. The tiger is really tigerish and the whole composition has the force of intense conviction, like some of the biblical subjects of the generation after Blake.

It was Tenniel, and the *Punch* table working through him, that changed *Punch* from one of the ruck of comic papers to a National Institution. Tenniel's style suited the change and the change sobered his style. It also cramped it. A cartoonist heading for a knighthood and a public dinner presided over by Balfour could hardly cock snooks. Tenniel himself scarcely ever suggested a cartoon idea or requested any but visual alterations. He was a Conservative at a time when most of the staff were Liberals and he kept quiet. The commission given him was generally no longer to strike a blow for a Cause or right a burning injustice. It was to undertake a descriptive job in which no convictions mattered but those of professional draughtsmanship. His membership of the staff was cherished by them for not any fancy or wit or flow of ideas but for a certain silvern sweetness. His colleagues disputed whether he more resembled Don Quixote or Colonel Newcome. He was a very nice man and in the early days he found something in the *Punch* companionship that comes out in his picture of his colleague Ponny Mayhew as Carroll's White Knight.

The other great acquisition of the Fifties was Charles Keene. He came of solid professional stock and though he spent his early years in London the family moved back to Ipswich and he always considered himself a Suffolk man and hated to be thought of as a cockney. In *Punch* he began by redrawing jokes for a friend and only gradually consented to allow his name to appear. In time, he did almost all the odd jobs, including fourteen cartoons, but what he liked doing and what he did incomparably best was illustrating jokes. Some of the jokes he heard, some were invented by himself—many were sent to him : *Bang went saxpence* [28] came from Birket Foster. A remarkable friend, Joseph Crawhall, kept albums of jokes with his own rough illustrations and Keene drew heavily on these in later years. Keene's case is curious. He was looked upon at first as another Leech, as an amusing sketcher of popular life. Though his facility at getting a likeness might have made him a good political cartoonist, he was out of sympathy with making fun of individuals. His targets were generally classes whose idiosyncracies were revealed in typical members. As Leech gradually specialised in sporting subjects Keene succeeded him as chronicler of the life of

*9th December, 1871* *Charles Keene*

"PATENT SAFETY!"

*Portly Female:* "*Be careful, Cabman; I'm so Afraid of his Tumbling Down. It's very Slippery on that Asphalte.*"
*Cabby:* "*All Right, Mum! You 'Set' well back, Mum, and I'm Blessed if he could go Down if he Tried!*"

the streets, gradually extending his range to include the Volunteers and the Highlands. It was not until the death of Leech that he became one of the stars, after he had been contributing for thirteen years. In time his drunks and abusive cabbies and bottle-nosed parsons and ghillies were looked upon as low and he seemed to be a slightly regrettable survival into the world of du Maurier's soirées of the old *Punch* of sanded floors and churchwarden pipes. He came to be regarded a little as Defore was regarded by the Swift circle, though *Punch* resented the refusal of the Royal Academy to honour him in recognition of English black and white.

Meanwhile among the more advanced artists his reputation was slowly growing. In Germany and France and among the Whistler group in England he was becoming recognised as the greatest English artist since Hogarth. As Sickert said, he saw things that nobody had seen before—like reflected lights in shadows. He may have had more influence on the Impressionists than Constable. Like many *Punch* men his training had included a period with a wood engraver and he took his share in the great period of illustration in the Sixties. He illustrated *The Cloister and the Hearth*, *Evan Harrington* and a book on gout. He drew reality, and because reality is sometimes funny, his pictures were funny, though they were often quite straight illustrations for a joke, and it was by the joke he was judged. He was not a caricaturist like Leech and it is difficult to see any tradition of English art into which he fits. He was as near to a pure genius as it is possible for a draughtsman to be.

He experimented ceaselessly, mixing inks of varying shades of brown, trying different kinds of pens, even dipping splintered penholders in the ink. He liked old paper coloured by age. He completely disregarded the engraver, who could not reproduce many of his effects at all. Existing Keene sketches are normally, of course, notes for the drawing worked up afterwards, as, until the development of photographic processes, the original had to be cut with the block. It was only in the Pocket Books that Keene's etching on copper could be used by *Punch*. (He was oddly worried by his growing reputation in Paris as an etcher, partly because he felt he had produced too few etchings.) In a letter [29] he said, " I maintain that Bewick was a greater artist than wood-engraver, and that he worked in and was hampered by an ungrateful material, that he could have done more with copper. . . . We have not beaten the old masters of wood-engraving in my opinion, but have tried to do too much with it and failed." As a young man he had been influenced by the Pre-Raphaelites, but perhaps the strongest influence on him was Menzel, for whom he reserved his greatest admiration. In later years he much admired Whistler. Perhaps naturally, Ruskin omitted him in discussing *Punch* artists in *The Art of England*.

*3rd December, 1881* *Charles Keene*

"NEM. CON.!"

*Chatty Passenger (on G.W. Railway): "How plainly you can see the Lights of Hanwell from the Railway!"*
*Silent Man (in a corner): "Not half so plain as the Lights of the Train look from Hanwell!"*
*(All change at the next Station*

He had been a fellow student with Tenniel, from whose shadow he emerged slowly, and shared with him an old-world outlook and a kindly, taciturn manner, though Tenniel became far more of a public figure and went about more. Keene's whole odd personality has been described so often that it has come to seem synthetic—a bundle of quotable traits. We keep hearing of his love of old books and music, of the junk in his various cobwebby studios approached by rickety staircases down ramshackle alleys, the meals cooked over the spring of a gibus, of the pork gravy mixed with marmalade and brown sugar, the golf score kept on an oyster shell, the foul dottles smoked in stumpy seventeenth-century clay pipes, the love for East Anglia and friendship with Fitzgerald, the whimsical gentleness suddenly interrupted by imperious irritability, the horror of any critical discussion of art. To deter himself from using the Underground, which he considered unwholesome, he always travelled first-class on it. When staying at Cromer he used to paint pieces of bread to represent plum cake, place them on low walls and watch the effect on passing children.

Yet each facet of his rugged and archaic personality can be related to his work. Like Hopkins in poetry or Acton in history, he looked both backwards and forwards ; because he belonged to an earlier age, he also belonged to a later one. He was only intermittently a recluse and behaved more like one than he really was. He sang and played old music and fished and even danced. But compared with the *Punch* standards of sociability, which in the mid-Victorian period were frenetic, he seemed retiring. His chief contribution to male conviviality was anecdote, in which his own enjoyment of the humour, pointed by a curious slow wink in which the lower lid rose, was infectious, and though as he aged the stories became increasingly complicated the effect became increasingly ludicrous. In later life he had only one story, an unintelligible account of a recipe that ended with the words, delivered with enormous emphasis, " That *was* a Bakewell Tart." One night he startled and delighted his audience by breaking new ground. " The other day," he began, " I was walking down Kennington Road." Here there was a pause and he added, " When I say the other day, I mean forty years ago." [30] It was on his advice that Lily Langtry went on the stage.

## IV

As we dip into the *Punch* of the Fifties, we notice a greater evenness of standard. If there was nothing quite as good as the early political articles there was nothing quite as bad as the early pictorial puns. *Punch* was still youthful enough to be able to get excited, for example, over the Great Exhibition, held in the building that Jerrold in *Punch* christened "The Crystal Palace." It also got curiously upset over the British Museum catalogue, fretting that it was an impossible job, a neglected job, a fantastic job and probably simply a job. In 1851 a paragraph headed *Latest Literary News* said, "It is rumoured that the official catalogue of the Great Exhibition is to be trusted to the rapid pen of the same writer who has dashed off the catalogue for the British Museum." After suggesting that the museum catalogue has been held up so that both can be issued together it reported that in this "The pleasing effect of the alphabetical arrangement creates a sort of familiarity with letters which is no less instructive than agreeable." [31]

In 1853, Jerrold's last serial began. He was doing less and less work and the proprietors continued his salary rather doubtfully, though till his death in 1857 he was still a full member of the staff. In this year there also began an intermittent pictorial series called *Servantgalisms*. These were mainly jokes about the demands of servants, their supposed apeing of their masters and similar subjects that modern taste finds unpleasant. However, the disturbance of the due order of Society has been a traditional subject for humour for so long that it is unfair to tax any particular periodical or artist with indulging in it. *Punch* also campaigned against the crinoline. This fashion has gained a kind of folk repute. It did not last very long, and it was not as silly as the bustle, but it is still the only fashion to have become a legend between the male wig and the short skirt. Most of the *Punch* artists disliked it and Keene had for it almost the same intensity of hatred as Leech had for barrel organs.

The Volunteers began to provide some affectionate fun about this time, though none of the innumerable drawings about drills and tents and the conversion of civil to military attitudes have the poignant charm of *The Brook-Green Militia-Man.*[32] Both the attempt to control cab fares and the pollution of the Thames aroused *Punch* the Londoner. With the Crimean war, mismanagement was displayed on a larger scale and though *Punch* followed the Palmerstonian line as usual it showed more interest in defects of commissariat than in the question of the Straits. Leech's famous cartoon on the Czar's death, '*General Février' Turned Traitor*[33] marked the final emergence of *Punch* on Olympus. It was a good cartoon, neat in idea and dramatic in execution, but there had been sharper jests and finer drawings. What is important to the history of *Punch* is that here was a comment that was Olympian without being pompous. It was not for anything or against anything. It simply summed up memorably and ingeniously what people had not realised they were feeling. It included a double point by the way. The treachery was both in killing the Czar and in allowing the Russians to be defeated in the snow, for the dead Czar's hand held a notice of the Russian defeat at Eupatoria. In the later Fifties, articles of more than half a column in length became exceptional. *Punch* was a collection of quips with sometimes a single serial, the most solid item usually being the Parliamentary report, which criticised peers and members as outspokenly as Mr. Kenneth Tynan criticising actors. In one number a single contributor had fifteen separate items.

Typical of the tone was a sharp attack on the delay in completion of the Wellington memorial, by Shirley Brooks.[34] A jeering account of the prematurely released design by a sculptor described as Baron Marrowfatti included this : " Well, before the sham doors is to be a figure of victory—outside mind—though the Duke instead of keeping victory away from him was usually very much at home with her. This, however, is of less consequence as the Duke himself is to be outside his own mausoleum, indeed to be perched on top of it. For this there are two good artistic reasons. Were the Duke inside we could not see him and secondly he cannot be put inside because the mausoleum doors are sham ones. The effect would seem to be that of a lady weeping against the front door of a house while the party she is bewailing has got out on the roof."

By now it was noticeable how much better the political satire was than the social satire. There was a lack of articles springing from the fancy rather than the week's news. Jerrold's political leaders, by discussing political subjects in imaginative language, rich in comparisons and the unexpected, had to some extent kept a footing for invention in *Punch*. After him there was a period of fumbling, before, with a revival of literary burlesque and the invention of the article of personal experience, Burnand showed the way. Nearly everything still worth reading in the issues of this period was by Brooks.

In its first sixteen years, *Punch* attained and consolidated a position that was glorious but dangerous. It was well ahead of any rival in political and social influence. The danger was that it might lose its urchin light-heartedness and test a joke by whether it was the kind of joke that a National Institution ought to make. It was on the verge of moving from the outside of the centres of power and prestige into the same building as the ministers and bishops and peers and swells and it was going to become difficult to attack with the old recklessness men its staff knew at their clubs. As the tone of debate between the two main Parties lost any background threat of violence, politics became less suited to satirical baiting and personal attacks. *Punch*'s strength at the beginning had been that it was attacking from a point well to the left of the main parliamentary groups and the main periodicals. Unless it was to become merely eccentric, supporting some perennial minority, it had to move into the two-party system. On the whole political satire is funniest when there are a number of small parliamentary groups. (John Scanlon shows how much a satirist can gain from belonging to a group that is never likely to have to exchange the negations of opposition for the affirmations of power.)

CHAPTER THREE

# TOWARDS RESPECTABILITY

## *Mark Lemon and Shirley Brooks, 1857–1874*

IN THE Sixties, *Punch* was not so much neutral between the Parties as ambidexterously hostile. Political opinion among the staff was divided. Strict political orthodoxy came in only with the decline of *Punch*'s political power. Criticism of the Liberal Party was rather less penetrating than criticism of the Conservative Party. The entry into the firm of the Agnew family towards the end of this period encouraged a more whole-heartedly Liberal attitude that eventually became Liberal-Unionism.

The death of the Prince Consort stopped attacks on the Crown and it took time for the effects of the prolonged widowhood to rouse comment. In ecclesiastical affairs *Punch* was Erastian, not because it particularly liked the State but because it mistrusted the Church. It disliked privileged power. For example, it supported Garibaldi more because he was defying the Vatican than from any particular sympathy with the mob. At home, however low its opinion of Cabinets, at least they were to some extent responsible to an electorate. *Punch* had a low opinion of the Episcopate except for Temple and Tait. It disliked Romanism and has always hated fanaticism, attacking from time to time the Salvation Army, Moody and Sankey, and Billy Graham. Its heroes were Charles Kingsley, Frederick Denison Maurice and Dean Stanley, though its religion, never exactly mystical, stayed short of Christian Socialism. It was, in the Sixties, Broad Church and socially-conscious. It adopted by imperceptible gradations "Public School Religion," the virtues and vices of which, and its slow decline, can be traced in *Punch* for the next fifty or sixty years. It was worried that Shaftesbury, so enlightened on industrial questions, could support the narrowest Sabbatarianism. *Punch*'s attitude to small questions, like whether the British Museum should be open on Sunday, and to large questions, like whether Foreign Missions should be supported at the expense of the home field, was roughly that of Dickens.

It also took the Dickens line on America. America repudiated debts, was vulgar, boastful and provincial. You expected other foreigners like the French or the Pope to be disreputable, sometimes menacing, sometimes contemptible ; but for an ex-British colony to behave like that threw blame on Britain's rôle as governess. Imperial policy was only beginning to affect ordinary thinking after its long dormancy and there was certainly no idea of re-conquest. With the Fenian movement Irish violence imported bitterness into Anglo-American relations, where before there had only been bad manners. On the whole *Punch* supported the South in the Civil War, the side generally taken by upper class England. The North represented a bullying, vulgarly commercial civilisation that seemed to be coercing an agricultural, more gentlemanly civilisation. A small nation was being bullied into accepting a centralised government dominated by thrusting business men of the type that ran the English Poor Law and seemed favourable to Fenianism. The North's treatment of the South was equated with Russia's treatment of Poland. *Punch* was obsessed by the North's interference with what she considered our maritime rights in the *Trent* and *Alabama* cases. The support of Lancashire and the English working class for the anti-slavery side, even at the cost of the loss of Southern cotton and the consequent unemployment in the textile trades, redounded to Lincoln's discredit ; he was accused of using emancipation as a card to be played only when it was to his advantage. Taylor's generous lines on Lincoln's assassination were only partly a withdrawal.[1]

On the whole the *Punch* staff, now ageing, were content to let the reforms of their hot youth remain as the high-water mark. Political excitement over Parliamentary Reform found *Punch* a little on the defensive. It ought not, it felt, to oppose any extension of the franchise, and yet it was beginning to defend the last revolution against the future as well as against the past. Leech, who was hysterically opposed to the poor—an attitude now rarely expressed except by the poor themselves—argued furiously that the proposed new voters would be incapable of properly using their vote. *Punch* committed itself to some cautious but not completely hostile views on the franchise and hurried on to other questions as soon as possible, but there was an uncertainty that Jerrold would have scorned. Disraeli's extension of the franchise to the artisan class of the towns resulted in larger majorities and probably more real difference between the Parties. It also resulted in *Punch*'s finding it more difficult to keep a lively distance between them. In the end it was probably Ireland more than any social question that swung it to the right.

II

Lemon, who died in 1870, had won his way through the social barriers. His daughter married the first of the legal dynasty of Romers. As things became easier, he became smoother, went out into better Society, relaxed his wariness. Able men made him their constant companion. Dickens liked to take him with him on his night-walks, and he joined enthusiastically in the amateur dramatics of the Dickens circle.

In later life, when he was an established public figure, he toured in his own adaptation of *Falstaff*. This was expurgated, and slanted in favour of Falstaff. Opinions differ on whether he played it very slightly padded, or with no padding at all. His admiring companion, Mr. Joseph Hatton, whose various pro-Lemon accounts of early *Punch* days are at least evidence of some strongly-marked good qualities in Lemon—Hatton was no fool—remarked : " In the early days of the entertainment when the actor was not thoroughly master of the dialogue, his acting lacked finish," but went on to describe a reasonably triumphant tour.[2] *Punch* was no longer jeered at for its pot-house origins and *Punch* men could be found in those country houses which admitted leading actors and painters. With the deaths of Thackeray in 1863 and Leech in 1864, Lemon was surrounded by his own appointees. He was smoothed by success and no longer needed the iron hand under the velvet glove; and the velvet itself seemed of better quality. Cumulatively, the changes in the staff had strengthened it. Men tried to get on to the paper and the test of acceptance was not readiness but indispensability. Lemon took on fewer and fewer men but those he did accept were outstanding.

*Punch*'s rivals continued to rise and fall rapidly, unsteadily and sneeringly. The most successful was *Fun*, which lasted thirty years. It was frankly based on *Punch* and had a good staff, several of whom it lost to *Punch*, but it never became more than a collection of contributions of varying merit. Both commercially and politically *Punch* was the stronger and *Fun* could not compete, though its editors included Tom Hood and its staff H. J. Byron and Ambrose Bierce. The Dalziel Brothers bought it when its previous owner retired to devote himself entirely to the development of Spratt's Dog Biscuits. A couple of years later the Dalziels bought *Judy* and ran two comic papers, *Fun* Liberal and *Judy* Conservative. (Charles Ross, *Judy*'s editor, created Ally Sloper, and when Dalziel started *Ally Sloper's Half-Holiday* for him, *Punch*'s closest rivals gave up the fight and aligned themselves with the gay vulgarities of the popular press.)

In 1865, the older generation of Bradbury and Evans handed over to their sons, and the firm of Agnew, the art dealers, was brought in as partners. The younger Bradbury married an Agnew daughter. In 1872, the younger Evans left the firm, nobody seems to know why, and it became Bradbury, Agnew & Co.

During the last years of Lemon the clinging to old friends and old ways became stronger. Brooks was quite capable of writing the entire paper himself and did not, as a young second-in-command should have done, act as a talent-spotter. Sometimes some friend of a friend introduced the work of a young artist or writer to Lemon. Lemon then gave an order for initials or decorative work and having encouraged the man—sometimes to the point of getting him to leave another newspaper—when pressed with submissions became hostile. His biggest failure was with W. S. Gilbert. He turned down *The Yarn of the Nancy Bell* as too cannibalistic for his readers' tastes—in itself an odd sign of the softening effect of a quarter of a century's success on *Punch*. After a few drawings and articles had been taken, Gilbert submitted fifteen poems with his own illustrations, but Lemon said he would publish nothing of his unless he gave up all connection with *Fun*. Gilbert reasonably asked to be put on the permanent staff and Lemon sharply refused. Gilbert remained outside, and there was always a slight edge on his relations with *Punch* men. Burnand resented that after *Cox and Box* Gilbert replaced him as Sullivan's librettist. Many years later, they met at dinner. Rather fatuously Burnand remarked, "All the good things are sent to *Punch*." Gilbert snapped, "Then why don't you put them in your paper?" [3]

By the end of the Sixties, Lemon was doing a good deal outside *Punch*. His son Harry acted as his secretary and at the end as sub-editor, very much over-shadowed by his father, who gave him plenty of mechanical work to do but no real advancement. When he was away Leigh deputised for him, but Shirley Brooks acted both at the Table and in the office as the leading member of the staff and almost co-editor, though in the last resort Lemon would smack him down in public. He was a man who liked his ease but never at the expense of his authority. On the whole they seemed to have got on pretty well. Both were kindly men. Both were devoted to *Punch*. Each was able to appreciate the other's qualities. Lemon said, "Shirley's is the most graceful pen in London." [4] At this time Lemon was usually half-way through a novel, with several plays on hand; he became increasingly involved in wild-cat financial schemes and a Fund was raised for his family. Throughout his career his firm defence of the independence of the paper was varied with rather soapy letters to the firm asking for financial assistance—usually in the form of backing bills.

I feel, among other inadequacies for the post of *Punch*'s historian, no greater weakness than my inability to understand the Victorian Law of Debt. The archives of the firm are filled with letters on everyday business, ending casually with a request that the week's proofs should be sent to some sponging house. Salaries were usually drawn, or at least mortgaged, in advance. The early *Punch* world was one of flight from creditors and this background got into the columns. Article after article, picture after picture assumed that the normal condition of man was to be on the run. Friends put their names to paper for other friends. Gentlemen lived at Boulogne, or in some sanctuary like the precincts of Windsor castle. One always looked both ways on leaving lodgings for fear of duns. At his death, Lemon seems to have been as involved as when he first took on the editorship. The boom in industry had made the amateur financier feel that for really big profits and quick returns you had to find a small investor and stake him, and this Lemon was always doing. He was particularly interested in sanitary inventions. Unbusinesslike in everything but getting words into print at the right time, he got deeper and deeper. The fecklessness of the journalist—dear Richard Steele, dear Richard Savage—was partly an excuse, partly an apeing of aristocratic disdain. The age of the artist as amoral for the benefit of the moral was on its way.

In tracing the history of any institution, length of tenure and patterns of promotion are of great importance. The fact that once Lemon had seized power—" He seized the place, perhaps the place was his " [5]—he remained in daily contact with the paper for almost thirty years, combined with the fact that he was capable of developing with the paper, made his Editorship one of the greatest advantages any paper ever began with. A fidgety beginning is quite common, with several rapid changes of policy, each intended to get better results next week. It is a rare and invaluable advantage to begin with continuity. The early death of Shirley Brooks after only four years in the Chair was a serious blow. But the paper was strong enough to stand it. If Lemon had died after four years *Punch* might never have outdistanced the field.

### III

One of the successes of the Sixties was Shirley Brooks's *The Naggletons.*[6] These used the dramatic form, later picked up for other purposes by Anstey Guthrie, and consisted of a number of varied squabbles between husband and wife. Mr. Naggleton was a Caudle who bit back. In the course of the series he became rather more often the aggressor. The background was realistic, apart from an unbelievably silly ending. The dialogue's cut and thrust was brisk and compressed. The attitude of the series was cynical, bitterly amused and admirably hard. Here was the eye that Jerrold turned on politics turned on to the family.

Another successful series of Brooks's was *Mr. Punch's Table Talk.*[7] The separate oddments were supposed to be addressed to a dining circle of *Punch* men. Some weeks there were up to forty items—puns, bits of curious lore, public complaints, statements of taste and prejudice or anything else one might find in a Notebook. The tone is probably much the tone of Brooks's dinner conversations, thrusting and impatient.

> " Godiva is amends for Eve."
>
> "Let us all go into decent half-mourning for brave Tom Sayers. Say one black eye."
>
> "A street block fifty yards a-head of your Hansom, is aggravating enough. But I appeal to the consciences of all of you who ride in such a vehicle whether there is not more aggravation in the obstinate fact that the block must be over before you can get to the point at which it is occurring, and so you will not be able to abuse anybody."

"Anchovy on curried toast is very much to the purpose."

"When a wise man uses the weak argument because the strong one would be unacceptable to the many, and he is abused for shallowness by the few, they do not thereby prove themselves to resemble him."

"When good photographers die, they go to Brighton."

"In one of their abominable parodies of the psalms Brady and Tate set forth that as for the wicked man,

'The ravens shall pick out his eyes
And eagles eat *the same.*'

The courtesy of the ravens, in extracting the food, and leaving it for the superior birds, is above praise."

"I perceive an advertisement for the place of a groom. The advertiser is a young married man 'who has lived with a deceased incumbent seven years in Warwickshire.' A Ghoul-Groom."

"You are aware that the Beaver is not a beast, or at least that the Catholic Church permits its being devoured during fasts. Hence, I suspect, came the old vow, 'If I don't do it, I'll eat my Hat.'"

"I like the enthusiastic old Herald who pitied Adam because he had no opportunity of studying genealogy."

"The love of evil is the root of all money."

"What could be more polite than the remark of the knights when they were about to slay Thomas à Beckett. '*Impossibile enim est ut ulterius vivas*'?"

The only important acquisition among the writers in the Sixties was Francis Burnand, who was working for *Fun* when they refused his burlesque of the sensational serials in the *London Journal*, *Mokeanna*.[8] He took it to Lemon, who had already been watching his work with interest. *Punch* published it with the original artists burlesqueing their own work and, as *Punch* was printed by the same firm that printed the *London Journal*, it was easy to burlesque make-up. The imitations were sufficiently close for Bradbury to run up from the seaside in a panic when he saw the issue. Thackeray said he wished he had written *Mokeanna* himself.

Burnand was half-foreign, Savoy-Swiss and possibly Jewish. He was an Etonian, a Catholic, founder of the Cambridge A.D.C., a Barrister and a busy writer of burlesques for the theatre. He was a cheerful, rather bumptious young man who wrote puns with great versatility. In some ways he was a throwback to the facetious, convivial, dress-rehearsal scribblers of the old days. He could tackle anything and did all the ordinary journalistic jobs on the paper; but where he excelled was in fooling, and at a time when *Punch* was becoming more sober it was a good thing that youthful high spirits should be heard in it once again. Mr. E. V. Knox makes a more serious claim for Burnand, that he was the real originator of the humorous article of personal experience and misadventure. This, with parody, has been the dominating form down to very recently and its invention, or even its first important development, is something that should claim at least a footnote in histories of literature.

Burnand was here, there and everywhere in the Sixties and Seventies. Shirley Brooks was witty, light-hearted, happy, but he was very rarely amusingly absurd. Nobody else really tried to be funny at all. In his burlesques, his spoof journalism and his serials, Burnand did sometimes overstrain a joke. He sometimes rattled away too vigorously for his material, but he is often very amusing and it is easy to see that before generations of humorists had copied him he must have been very amusing indeed. *Happy Thoughts*, which began in 1866,[9] was his best-known serial, though not his only work worth re-reading. It had a narrator who was the centre of a number of physical and social predicaments. He stayed at country houses, got mixed up in country pursuits and punctuated his accounts of his trials with mental notes headed "Happy

Thought." The comedy of the relation of intention and performance, or good resolution and inept practice, was developed skilfully. Above all there were plenty of good jokes. No scene went on too long. The other characters were real enough to carry their part in the design though not so individual that they converted a series of linked sketches into a serialised novel, and there was a freshness about the discovery of this new world of humour that is still very attractive. *Happy Thoughts*, which was much admired by Dickens, was funny in several different ways. Despite all the bad puns and churned-out plays and determined jocularity, Burnand did what Thackeray never succeeded in doing, except perhaps when burlesqueing other men. He wrote a humorous classic in the pages of *Punch* that lives on outside them.

## IV

The Sixties were one of the great periods of English book illustration. The rise in the standard of the decorative and illustrative work in *Punch*, which is very marked compared with the slap-dash draughtsmanship of the early hacks, is linked with a marked decline in the humour of the drawings. After Leech, none of the major artists showed any element of caricature or distortion or clowning. The joke was printed underneath and the drawing illustrated it. Although Keene sometimes drew a man whose amusing characteristics looked funny on paper, it was many years before humour was again an integral part of the art work.

In the Sixties du Maurier was the most important new artist. He stamped his strong, graphic personality so firmly on *Punch*, he went on so long and so regularly, his series and characters became so famous that when one mentions his name one calls up a composite image. As Dana Gibson later made the Gibson Girl, du Maurier created the tall woman of the period. (He is said to have added inches to British womanhood—vertically.) Mrs. Ponsonby de Tomkyns, the social climber, Sir Gorgius Midas, the *nouveau riche* vulgarian, Maudle and Postlethwaite, the Aesthetes, the children with their funny sayings to nannies in cosy nurseries or beside frozen Hampstead ponds, the soirées and feathery décors and diptychal compositions are remembered as characteristic du Maurier, but they are not the whole of du Maurier.

*1st March, 1884* *George du Maurier*

"OLD FRIENDS"—HOW TO SNUB THEM.

*Mrs. MacSmythe (who has got into a New Set) : " Oh-er-how d'ye do ? So sorry I couldn't come to You and the Girls last night. Had to go to Mrs. Masham's ! "*
*Mrs. Fitzjones (her oldest Friend) : " Indeed ! I hope it was a pleasant Party ! "*
*Mrs. MacSmythe : " Oh : very much so ! Everybody one* knows *was there, you know ! "*

The du Mauriers were French, descendants of Jean Bart. They had once had a family glass-blowing business, as this was the only trade allowed to the *noblesse*. On his mother's side George was descended from Mary Anne Clarke. Brought up mainly abroad, he was bilingual. He came to England to study chemistry and his father started him off as an analytical chemist, but annoyed him by refusing to let him have a piano in his laboratory. He went abroad again and was a gay art student in Paris with the Whistler group and in later life he retained amid the increasing grandeurs of his home a taste for simple high spirits, for singing snatches of French songs, for light, gay chaff and for emotionally-expressed tenderness. In the accounts of *Punch* men that have come down to us—a very partial body of evidence—there is no one whose attractions seem less attractive than du Maurier's. His " dear boy-ishness," remarks like, " While you clever old cockalorums are talking about politics, I'll take a nap," [10] and his pose of boredom strike chill upon a mid-Twentieth Century mind. Those tremendous house parties, the parade of smart-art Society, the insistence of Father and his favourite companions, his children, that everything should be " amusing," remind one of accounts of " The Souls." As against this, must be put the effect he had on the men who actually knew him. Opinions differed about the ebullient Burnand. I have found nothing but affection for du Maurier. He was the companion men chose. He was uncensorious and thought the only sin was cruelty. His family loved him, despite occasional fits of petulance of the kind much exaggerated in his son Gerald. He had lost the sight of one eye when an art student, and to worries over money and social success were added worries over blindness. His appointment to the *Punch* staff on Leech's death in 1864 was followed by a period of relaxation, of the mannered inertia that was his weakness. Lemon came down on him heavily and told him that unless he worked he would be sacked. In his relationship with this new and difficult member of a generation he found puzzling, Lemon showed his flair for getting the best out of men, the eye for the possibilities, the avuncular encouragement, the toughness when needed.

du Maurier became *Punch*'s most popular contributor. Unfortunately his range narrowed as he began repeating successes. The absence of an art editor made this possible. To appreciate what that range was at its fullest it is important to examine his *Nightmare* drawings. In them fear came out of the illustrations to Victorian children's books and into *Punch*. There is a common frontier between humour and horror, as there is between humour and sentiment. His picture of the boy who saw a cockhorse,[11] or his odd series about the little man who married a giantess,[12] showed a coarsely horrible imagination that later receded and was hidden behind a façade of fashionable boredom.

du Maurier has been compared to Thackeray, the elegant, gentle satirist and flatterer. He himself violently swung away from the Leech tradition, though a picture like his mistress explaining that a damp bedroom was good enough for a servant was in sharpness of idea and style of drawing very near to Leech. Though he claimed to have learned his art from the work of Keene, he swung away also from Keene's preoccupation with low life. Lemon, who liked to have a few outstanding men all contrasted and balanced, urged him to use his decorative sense to be delightfully amusing rather than funny, to " be the tenor, while Keene, with his magnificent, highly trained bass, sang the comic songs." [13] In a letter to Henry Lucy,[14] du Maurier referred to " the inevitable comparison with Leech, whose aims and methods were the antipodes of mine. . . . I can only wish to point out the distinction between the artist who tries to depict people as they really are, and the artist who has the enviable gift of so exquisitely distorting them that the sacrifice of truth is more than compensated by the side-splitting laughter the performance creates. . . . Nobody feels more than I do (who know him thoroughly by heart) that Leech stands alone, unapproached hitherto and probably unapproachable. (I have generally stuck to the ' classes ' because C. K. seems to have monopolised the ' masses '.—Division of labour.) "

Keene came to seem increasingly old-fashioned in comparison with the smart young Hampstead society artist, despite the attempts by a small clique of highbrows to draw attention to his genius as a draughtsman. As he went out less and less he did not always realise that his jokes were not very new, and since the public judged, as they still do, by what was done and not by how it was done, his popularity dwindled at a time when his art had slowly ripened. Some of Keene's ghillies and volunteers and cabbies are still funny and all of them have the same kind of stale beery flavour

**A LITTLE CHRISTMAS DREAM.**

*Mr. L. Figuier, in the Thesis which precedes his interesting Work on the World before the Flood, condemns the Practice of awakening the Youthful Mind to Admiration by means of Fables and Fairy Tales, and recommends, in lieu thereof, the Study of the Natural History of the World in which we live. Fired by this Advice, we have tried the Experience on our Eldest, an imaginative Boy of Six. We have cut off his " Cinderella " and his " Puss in Boots," and introduced him to some of the more peaceful Fauna of the Preadamite World, as they appear Restored in Mr. Figuier's Book.*

*The poor Boy has not had a decent Night's Rest ever since !*

that made George Robey evocative even to those whom he did not amuse :

> Irascible old gentleman : " Waiter ! this plate is quite cold."
> Waiter : "Yes sir, but the chop is hot, sir, which I think you'll find it'll warm up the plate nicely, sir." [15]

Some of this atmosphere spilled over on to the models. Frith tells a story [16] of a drunken model saying to a Magistrate : " You call yourself a Beak ? Why, you ain't up to the situation ; and I'll tell you what, I'm an artist's model, and I sits for them as draws for *Punch* ; and I'll have you took and put in *Punch*, you see just if I don't." The Magistrate changed the sentence from three weeks to six.

Keene took great trouble with his captions, especially when they were in dialect, for which he had a scholarly ear, and was worried when editors mangled them. The length and obviousness of *Punch* captions at this period have been exaggerated though they certainly bear more weight than the drawings, and they tell the reader things that might have been conveyed to him more simply by gesture. Sometimes they simply describe a situation and the drawing shows one stage in its development, or even the characters after the situation has occurred, but the florescence of the " collapse of stout party " type of caption comes later.

Taste has shifted towards Keene and away from du Maurier who, except for period charm, is now as much under-rated as he was once over-rated. Any comic artist who turns out such a mass of work as du Maurier will repeat himself, but his jokes, taking his work as a whole, were very varied and until towards the end of his life the illustrations of those jokes were varied too. He had a knack of drawing as well as he could and then, if some essential item that he could not manage were required to fit the caption, covering inability to do more than indicate it with a charming scrawl that is a kind of pictorial shrug.

He did a good deal of writing in prose and verse for *Punch*, enough for it to be suggested that he ought to get a writer's salary, and his very carefully composed captions were themselves one form of writing. When he expressed surprise at the success of his amateur novels, a colleague pointed out that he had been learning to write for years. The dialogue in the novels is said to reproduce exactly the tone of the conversation. His wonderful *Legend of Camelot*

*6th March, 1875* *George du Maurier*

A WHISPERED APPEAL.

"*Mamma! Mamma!* Don't *Scold him any more! It makes the Room so Dark!*"

should be better known. It was published in five issues beginning on 3rd March, 1866, and republished in book form. It is a burlesque of the Pre-Raphaelites. The five parts are brilliantly sustained both in verse and drawing. They are still funny and as near the original as C. S. Calverley or Max Beerbohm or Richard Mallett.

Of the artists of the Sixties it is necessary to mention C. H. Bennett because of his contemporary reputation. He seemed a big man to big men and their view must be recorded. He was long remembered for his personal charm and fantastic imagination, but the fun has evaporated from his general decorative work and his illustrations to *Punch's Essence of Parliament*. Like Doyle, he festooned his pages with outline grotesques. He put large naturalistic heads

*13th January, 1872* *Linley Sambourne*

on small naturalistic bodies, and at least he showed *Punch* artists, at a time when the pictures were improving in drawing and deteriorating in humour, how wide the pictorial possibilities for *Punch* still were. Linley Sambourne arrived in 1867, but his work belongs properly to a later date, though in the early Seventies he was getting enough of the initials and headings for his draughtsmanship to make some of the regular contributors look dowdy. His most imaginative early work was his fantasies on fashions.

## V

*Punch*'s humour has generally come from three main sources. First comes a jealously guarded quirk in a semi-hermit, a private joke matured in isolation and often developed over the years as an escape from life. Then there is the journalist's humour, the sharp eye for what is going on and the rapid extraction of the odd and silly from the press. Here the humorist is perhaps an editor or anthologist rather than a creator. Lastly there is humour that springs from the meeting of private amusement and public fact in a social setting. The funny man at the party is sometimes not so funny in print, and sometimes even a danger to the paper, but there is obviously a type of humour which ripens at its best in a convivial atmosphere.

The Dinners of the Staff were only the centre of *Punch* conviviality. *Punch* men visited one another, they went for holidays together. They dined out of town in small parties. They punted up the Thames. They ran over to Paris or Boulogne. They met at their clubs—the Garrick, the Savage, the Reform and the Athenæum in particular—as well as in all the small private clubs and night-clubs, often scandalous, of Thackeray's day. The dangers of this kind of inbreeding were serious and in time any addition to the staff seemed unnatural. New appointments were made only to fill vacancies caused by death. The advantage was that from the cut and thrust of minds within the framework of strong feelings of friendship, humour might be born and standards maintained. The strongest single incentive was the opinion of fellow craftsmen. The readers were remote and so was the sack.

This golden age of *Punch*, one of its golden ages, is reflected in the Diary of the Dinners kept by a quiet, shy, observant member of the Staff, Henry Silver, who did much of the straight journalism in the paper. He left the manuscript to the proprietors on his death. He was Jerrold's successor on the Table and resigned when Brooks succeeded Lemon as Editor although he continued to contribute frequently. He was a priggish young man and boasts a little of his own inarticulateness and of how Lemon confided in him, finding him quiet and reliable. He died many years later, very rich, law and business having proved more remunerative than journalism. The large sums left by a few *Punch* men like Silver, Keene and Lucy worried the others, who imagined that the public would think they were all highly paid.

At the Dinners arguments were hot, though not as hot as in the early days. Suggestions for the cartoon were thrown out all round the table and then the Editor made the decision in accordance with general opinion. There was chaff and gossip, literary and political. Thackeray was grand, Leech die-hard, Taylor kindly, fussy and overbearing, Leigh knowledgeable but old and indifferent, Lemon gay and talkative, du Maurier, when he appeared, charming and detached, Tenniel and Keene silent and well liked, and Shirley Brooks so dashing in his intellectual and convivial gifts that he caused the slightest of strained feelings. There is a good deal of convivial impropriety, necessarily not reproduced here. The most famous English Limerick, *There was a young lady of Gloucester* . . . appears in 1868. Apart from the intrinsic interest of the conversation, Silver's Diary shows the soil in which the mid-Victorian *Punch* grew and it is worth raiding at some length.

1859 . . . Discussion on the Policy of *Punch*—take the right side and not the bright side. . . . John Leech against Jerrold's radicalism and low breeding—clearly he inclines to the Clubbish view of things. Query if not a worshipper of No. 1.

. . . Says Thackeray, a man who produces cannot hope to read much.

. . . Leech thinks the petty British shopkeeper the meanest creature in creation. Advantage of high birth is that a man has no need to cringe—can look men in the face, and has no fawning. Therefore pleasanter. Ponny (*Horace Mayhew*) walks into Aristocracy. Says Reform is wanted. Percival Leigh says doubtful—no need to excite the country—wait till they ask for it. Shirley Brooks says, But Government ought to legislate in advance, and not wait till Acts are clamoured for. . . . Brooks fills his pockets for his " brats," explaining that the Proprietors have to pay for the dessert whether eaten or not.

. . . Tom Taylor comes merely " to hear what you fellows say about the Reform Bill." Thinks people look to *Punch* and that *Punch* should take a decided course. Leigh and Lemon think we should stand by and see how the stream runs first. . . . Splendid mill between Ponny Mayhew and Pater Evans and Leech. Ponny lets fly by saying *Punch* is standing still—used to take the lead but now fears to do so. " Avançons ! " Evans returns, that times are altered, my dear Ponny ; and *Punch* alters with the times. Strong language has done its work and there's now no need of it. Nobody talks now about the trampled working man and the dignity of labour. Poor not crushed now as they were 15 years ago. Says Leech, I'm a man of extremely simple tastes—Give me my claret and my hunter and I ask not for more.

1860 . . . Leech when in quod used to get Leigh to sell lithographic caricatures for him. Used to kiss female prisoners through the bars.

. . . Funny to see others as anxious as oneself for the insertion of their articles.

. . . Charles Keene wants to have rifle regiments sing part songs to march to.

. . . *Mill on the Floss* dreary and immoral. Evans bid for it—Brooks says he's well out of it.

. . . Leigh explains to nephew, asking why the Band of Hope marched with trumpets and trombones blaring, that Teetotallers are persons who act when they are sober just as other people do when they are drunk.

. . . Lemon says *Punch* keeps up by its keeping to the gentlemanly view of things and its being known that Bohemians don't write for it.

. . . Talk of " my dear Forster "—says Leech, " don't see why we should hate him so : he's not been so *very* successful."

1861 . . . Lemon tells of Thackeray's intrusion at dinner given to Dickens, when Forster says, " Here are our two greatest writers—one extracts good from evil and the other finds evil in everything that is good."

. . . Tom Taylor says Rubens's landscapes and animals his best work. Brooks says no painter has produced a luscious woman, one carnally desirable. Keene says Titian has, and Leech, Lely. Brooks says a man needn't paint to criticise painting. Leech, Keene and Tenniel differ from him. Say Ruskin can draw well. Taylor would write a criticism on Chaldee if he were asked. Brooks ranks a caricaturist like HB or Hogarth or Leech above all painters—stamps the image of his times ineffaceably.

. . . Thackeray savage at Edwin James's reception into American Bar, " And I have only a twopenny ha'penny thunderbolt to hurl at him." . . . Thackeray calls Tennyson the greatest man of the age—" has thrown the quoit furthest." Brooks says *Vanity Fair* ranks higher than anything of Tennyson's. " Would you change your reputation for his ? " " Yes." " I don't believe you." Thackeray, Brooks and Leigh all praise Scott, Brooks and Leigh the most—stirs the blood—but, says Thackeray, I don't want to have my blood stirred. Says Brooks, Bulwer might much improve Scott's language. Curious felicity of words, says Thackeray. (Thackeray often talks just as he writes, and I fancy so did Douglas Jerrold.) . . . Bradbury when savage at Chambers's close competition used to cut down all Scotch thistles with walking stick.

. . . War talk predominates. Leigh throwing cold water on the fire of indignation. Thinks people too prone to fight. . . . Thackeray says, British ships are British soil—and if we submit the Yankees will get the notion that British Bottoms are made to be kicked. . . . Has 5000 dear relations (invested) in the States : " but yet I, Makepeace, declare for War . . ." N.B. Fighting cut always sends the sale up—this week 2000 above average.

. . . Taylor reads poem by a young imitator of Young Bulwer, Swinburne. First line proves it wouldn't do for *Punch* or *Cornhill*, 'I'm not quite right in my innards, Bill.'

1862 . . . Horace Mayhew queries if a deadlock be opened by a skeleton key. . . . Brooks speaks of how rosewatery the critics are and how little the public cares for the puffs they emit. *Punch* has been too mealy-mouthed by half. Well, Lemon be thanked for it. As we walk home discuss this with Lemon, who says, "I don't agree with Shirley that *Punch* should be all pitch in and no praise." . . . Taylor thinks du Maurier "not much use to us—drawings too liney"—whatever that may mean. Lemon asks me to do a bit about the Miners, who are aggrieved by Leech's sketches and are good customers of *Punch*. But Leech's cuts are at Staffordshire, not Newcastle.

. . . Lemon says he didn't use my last dram. letters: the public would think me finding fault without assigning reasons. It's hard to be savage with such a corrector of the press, cutting out whatever's cutting. Said Horace the other day, "Your letters are too favourable. What the public wants are criticisms, not advertisements."

. . . Thackeray thinks Freetrade is the right policy in literature and art—man takes his work where he's best paid for it. . . . Lemon thinks a Mag. should have a regular salaried staff of writers, and room for occasional outsiders. This would secure an evenness of quality. Don't want a genius at £3000 a year—A good sensible ready-handed man at £500 better. The genius don't read other articles than his own, or if he finds a good one is apt to be jealous . . . Lemon tells of his daughter saying "Let me go into the drawingroom" to her sister. "I've as much parlour blood in me as you." . . . Leech disapproves of Frith's *Derby Day*. Not a bit like life! Swell in black cloth trowsers! Says a man should like horses to paint them.

July 23. *Coming of Age Dinner to Mr. Punch*. Turtle soup, Salmon, Cutlet, Cold Beef, Pineapple fritters, cheese, Strawberries and cream, cherries, pineapple, Punch, champagne, sherry, and claret. " Man wants but little here below," but likes that little good . . . Evans proposes health to Mark Lemon. *Punch* met with obloquy in its start, as its printer and engraver were those of *The Town* and other ribald comic papers. No light honour to a man to have kept such a team together as the *Punch* lot—to have so kindly borne and foreborne, and reconciled and bound together men of such diversity of talent and of tastes.

. . . Lemon's system is to let each man write what he likes, subject to his supervision. " All cleverer fellows than I am," says he—but is not his judicious editing a talent they can't show an equal to ?

. . . When the Papal Aggression came, Lemon foresaw he'd lose Doyle, and thought the circulation would fall, but it didn't, and he thinks their firm tone then showed the public *Punch* was in earnest and was something more than a buffoon. His plan as editor had always been to avoid dictation—reserving merely the power of correction—thereby has the benefit of a variety of minds, unfettered by his own.

. . . Lemon advises Keene to take a weekly salary—tells how Jerrold received £300 and 30/- a week for *Caudle*. Is sure the system has been the making of *Punch*—keeps men from jealousy . . . Thackeray tells how Forster was annoyed by his hit at him in *Esmond* as " Mr. Addison's man," Charles Dickens being Mr. A . . . Lemon thinks that the *Punch* light style of writing has had great influence on *The Times* and other leader-writers.

1863 Big Cut. Lemon and Brooks agree that Lincoln's proclamation as to slaves being free should be noticed. Abraham Lincoln made a law and a proclamation—Slave reading proclamation and saying, " Yes, massa, but you beat him first." Southerner with pistols cocked, " Wal, why don't yer go ? " Joe Youngs, a rabid Northerner, says that *Punch* has surprised and offended the Americans more than anything else. *Punch* always as yet in favour of justice and now to pat rebels on the back.

*March* 11, *Prince of Wales, his Wedding*. . . . Taylor tells how the old dowagers emerged from their queer coverings like fairies out of witches. . . . Noticed the gleam of sunshine on the royal pew as the Queen entered—the one black spot. Something selfish in such sorrow, surely. Rumour says she wished the chapel hung with black and that the Prince said, " Then I'd better bring my Bride in a hearse." . . . The Beauty of Alexandra is not merely in her features—looks good and amiable and wishing to please, and as if she had brains and used them. . . .

. . . Thackeray talks of Frank Stone's history forming the *Shabby Genteel Story*. Now his son Marcus it is said has behaved ill to mother.

. . . Mayhew offered £50 by Duberg of the *Haymarket* to say a word for him in *Punch*.

. . . Pater feelingly proposes Mark's health and success to his novel (*Wait for the End*), his maiden effort in a new path of penmanship. Mark replies with tears in his voice—and hopes his friends will pardon him for any discredit the work may bring—it was written to relieve him from a temporary distress and not for any selfish feeling of ambition.

1864 . . . Mark begs for earlier copy—and Evans says the circulation now renders it necessary that the number should go to the press Saturday night. Then we must try and reduce the circulation, says Leech. . . . We all agree that Leech is out of health and should take rest—but Mark thinks he wouldn't give up his dinner engagements. To get into Society has been the aim of his life, and now he seems to have lost all taste for enjoyment. Mark and Leigh both say it annoys him to think *Punch* could go on without him—even for a month. He has always been a spoilt child, says Mark, lets petty worries master him, and it is sad to think that his great gifts have not made him a more happy man.

. . . Brooks says the first number of *Our Mutual Friend* is a very weak one. Dickens can't draw a gentleman or a dinner-party—Thackeray could.

. . . Brooks says he takes for granted every reader of *Punch* has read *The Times*. Objects to making quotations from newspapers. Lemon and Leigh say *Punch* should hit low as well as high. . . .

*John Leech obit October 29th; aetat 46. Special meeting at the Bedford to consider what is to be done. . . .* Lemon thinks that *Punch* dinners have not been looked on as part of the week's work so much as they ought to be—begs for better attendance and for more business talk at them. Thinks everyone should come with suggestions, both for cuts and articles. . . . What artist shall be asked to join us ? Keene and Tenniel both say du Maurier and Silver speaks for him as anxious to join us.

. . . Mark says the circulation of *Punch* now is as large as ever—but not larger than it was at the close of the *Caudle* papers—these and *Jeames' Diary* and the *Snobs* increased the sale—great cuts seldom do, except the *Bengal Tiger*, for instance . . . du Maurier tells of Whistler and Rossetti's rage for old china—and how R. once left his guests at dinner and rushed off to buy a piece for fear W. should forestall him.

1865 . . . Talk of criticism. Lemon says it should be " I think " and not " we think " or still less " It is." Criticism is a matter of opinion. du Maurier and Keene object to Tom Taylor's *ex cathedra dicta* in *The Times*. du M. says Leighton and Rossetti are the best critics he knows.

. . . Big Cut. Slavery abolished by order of N.Y. Senate. Shirley thinks it an event for History. Lemon thinks it humbug. " A thought strikes me—let us again emancipate the slaves," says Tenniel. . . . Paxton commends *Punch* of late, advises us to write over readers' heads a bit—circulation keeps up, so let us keep up the tone.

. . . du Maurier and Brooks agree that a man may be justified in suicide. Shirley says, " God is too hospitable to turn away an uninvited guest."

. . . Bradbury and Evans getting old, have put their sons in their stead and taken the Agnews into partnership.

1866 . . . du M. tells of little boy of some artist saying to Miss Ionides, ' If you are a Greek girl, why are you not naked ? '

. . . Tom Taylor tells of small boy being told that God is everywhere and saying, " Then how can he move about ? "

. . . Shirley wishes Tenniel to modernise the John Bull he draws—and whom Arbuthnot invented.

. . . Albert Smith was a stingy beggar. Had a lithographed circular refusing charity.

1868 . . . Pater says Ponny and Mark remember the early struggles of *Punch*—how we met at the Edinburgh Castle once and debated whether to go on ! We paid literature more liberally than had been done—were laughed at by our fellow publishers, but set the fashion of liberality to authors.

1870 . . . Tom Taylor says Trollope's man's wages depend on his making his master get out of bed.

## VI

*Punch*'s Editors have been able and varied and on the whole each new reign has meant attention to some part of the work hitherto neglected. The least of the changes was the change from Lemon to his right-hand man. The qualities that have already been described made Brooks nearly as good an Editor as contributor. He united awareness of what was going on with a sense of continuity and tradition. He was subtle and skilful. He made no big changes, but then it is probable that he had been responsible for a good many of the improvements during the previous ten years. The paper was still scrappy, but the profusion of short paragraphs did at least mean that if the proper length of a joke was two and a half lines it got two and a half lines and not a whole column complete with introduction about the man who told it to the narrator. What have come to be considered normal length *Punch* articles were limited to one or two per issue, often forming part of a series. The importance of a series in building and retaining a public is obvious ; its importance to the anonymous contributor was equally great.

Obituary poems, whether for *Punch* men like Lemon and "Pater" Evans or for public figures like Palmerston or Dickens, marked the victory of the official over the impish in *Punch*. They were graceful exercises, as the Cartoon was becoming, and, though occasionally, like the poem of recantation on Lincoln's death, they made a statement, more often they merely versified sentiments. One of the best of these funereal items was a joint poem on Samuel Wilberforce and Lord Westbury, comparing the general view of them in life with a kinder estimate produced by their death.[17] No modern obituary poem would mention so frankly the exact criticisms made of a bishop and a judge.

By the middle Seventies the sea-sick joke and the drunk joke had been joined in a repellent trio by the old maid joke. This of course goes back into the mists. It seems to have got renewed sourness and popularity in the mid-Victorian period. The kind of joke that makes Gilbert's modern audience writhe was to be found also in *Punch*. One certainly gets the feeling that the urban family was both tighter and crueller than the country family, though the spinster-aunt joke is used in the Dingley Dell scenes in *Pickwick*. Perhaps in villages spinsters helped on the farm and had more occupation than among the genteel *déracinées* of the town. Cruelty seems oddly at variance with the humanity that was always evident in *Punch*. If crossing-sweepers and mudlarks were sympathised with, why were the sea-sick or the unwanted jeered at? Perhaps these were minor sufferers in a world of cholera and rat-ridden hovels and birchings at schools. Sympathies develop unevenly and, while to-day we compassionately press finger-tips to the foreheads of sufferers from hang-overs, we annihilate whole cities. The Victorians might have laughed at drunks, but at least they believed that the end of the world should be left to God.

*Punch*'s attitude to women, apart from an occasional foray against their economic exploitation, was not as misogynist as that of much traditional humour, but was strongly anti-feminist. The dear creatures must be fled when nagging and petted when feather-headed. The Dickens range of female character, from Mrs. Gamp to Dora Copperfield, may be found in *Punch*, but nothing corresponding to Meredith's women in fiction or the great ladies of Victorian Oxford and Cambridge in life. Some of du Maurier's women were witty though not intellectual. Woman's place was the home, or, if she were surplus, someone else's home, and she was entitled, whether a seamstress or a governess, not to be starved or bullied. The slightest evidence of feminine migration within the economic or the intellectual worlds roused the bachelor clubman in *Punch*. From the jokes of 1853 against conductresses in omnibuses to the assumptions of First War joke-drawings that the appearance of a waitress where only waiters had been known was an evidence of the instability of things so frightening that it had to be met by laughter, *Punch*, considering its large female readership, was strangely blind and petty in its references to a change which, in a few decades, began an independent history for half the human race. Its attitude to the Suffragette Movement was uneasy on the question of justice, though firmly against the violence. *Punch* always regarded women as a kind of domesticated Irish, anyway.

The Franco-Prussian war naturally enough caused some comment but it was rather pompous in tone. Napoleon III was still suspect but the King of Prussia was not much liked either. Britannia was going to keep out of it unless Prussia invaded Belgium ; meanwhile she would tell France that though it was her own fault sympathy could not be withheld. Papal infallibility and the end of the temporal power suited *Punch* better as a subject. Until the Catholic Burnand became Editor the Papacy was fair game. The proportion of comment to satire in cartoons was shooting up but ecclesiastical cartoons still retained for a time the edge that had once been the cartoon's sole justification. From this time on cartoons were better drawn but on the whole much duller than in the early days.

*Punch* wished Gladstone were a bit livelier but respected him. Once it suddenly and incomprehensibly asked, " Why is Mr. Gladstone like a Welsh apposition pronoun ? " The answer came pat, " because when he is marked by emphasis he retains his radical and strong form." [18] Disraeli was distrusted though he courted and flattered *Punch* ; but the staff were slowing down in their reactions to contemporary change and they still saw him as a political adventurer and traitor to the Radicals, who had coldly transferred his allegiance to the place where it could do him most good. It became a little politer but not much less suspicious. Politicians on both sides said they were afraid of *Punch*'s influence. The paper was treated with reverence and sometimes almost as if it were minor royalty. Since the great debate in the Conservative party over whether to accept the end of Protection, *Punch* paid comparatively little attention to economic questions except in-so-far as employment was occasionally linked with The Condition of the People. Imperial themes were rare in the middle Sixties and early Seventies and perhaps the end of one period of colonial history was marked by the obituary poem to Livingstone in 1874.

The issue for the week of Shirley Brooks's death, 28th February, 1874, showed comparatively little change in form or arrangement from fifteen years earlier. It contained forty items. There was a fall in vivacity and lightness since Jerrold's death. *Punch* was relying too much on a few stars—Brooks, Burnand, du Maurier, Sambourne, Keene and Tenniel, and only two of these were writers. In Brooks's own words, " Our horses make excellent running but they don't take fences." [19]

CHAPTER FOUR

# FOR SCHOLARS AND GENTLEMEN

## *Tom Taylor's Editorship, 1874–1880*

THE EDITORSHIP of Tom Taylor has been so constantly criticised that it is surprising to look at the paper he produced and see how much of it lives. He had four big men as his artists and he gave them freedom, though he was more autocratic than Brooks over the cartoon. Taylor had served *Punch* for thirty years and finished a distinguished career in the Civil Service before he became Editor at the age of fifty-seven. He was a public figure quite apart from his *Punch* work and he did not want it forgotten. His social ebullience dimmed with the years and his scholarship turned to pedantry. As an Editor he was vacillating and fidgety. He was kind to his Staff though brusquely impatient. The older men, who had known him for years and appreciated his good heart and friendly fun, supported him. He was a generous host, a warm-hearted friend and an unfailingly cheerful Uncle to innumerable Victorian families. His house, Lavender Sweep at Clapham Common, was a frequent meeting place of the leading Victorian Academicians, *littérateurs*, musicians and upper-middlebrows of high birth.

Undoubtedly *Punch* became too heavy, too much a weekly journal of opinion under him. But the heaviness of *Punch* had always been there, in Taylor's own contributions, in the work of Percival Leigh, in the weak puns of " Ponny " Mayhew, though it had been restricted ; there had generally been enough gaiety to make the prosiness seem a concession to old readers and old writers. Now the loss of Shirley Brooks was combined with a drift away of occasional contributors and Taylor's new blood was, except for Milliken, unimportant. He discouraged sporting contributors, including the very popular Georgina Bowers, who told Spielmann that she had specialised in " hunting and flirting scenes." Taylor at least established a tradition that *Punch* was related to the academic world and, while this meant some narrowness and some rather obstrusive classical references, it also meant that its aims were high, and that it aimed at quality of product as well as quantity of sales. The fact that it is the only non-technical magazine whose bound volumes are still saleable suggests that the solidity Taylor fought for long before his appointment to the Chair had been achieved.

An ancillary factor in building up *Punch* was the attention attracted by *Punch* publications additional to the weekly issue. The Almanack was an annual feature, varying slightly in title (at Christmas 1890, for example, it was called *Punch Among the Planets*). In time the chronological side of the Almanack faded away, and it became a Special Number making some attempt to depart from the weekly formula, and at times specialising in longer illustrated stories. Later it was joined by a Summer Number. These special issues generally had a bigger sale over a rather longer period than the weekly issues, and were of considerable importance in extending knowledge of *Punch*'s leading contributors.

As well as the Almanack, *Punch* produced an annual Pocket Book, but while the calendar side of the Almanack lacked utility and eventually became purely vestigial, the Diary and compendium of useful information included in the Pocket Book never faded away sufficiently for the remainder of the little volume to settle down to an independent life as an annual. Contributors tried to put their very best work into it and no expense was spared in the production. The value of the Pocket Books to the paper was more as a shop window for *Punch* talent than as a source of income. Leech's elaborate coloured frontispieces and Keene's and Sambourne's work in later days have given them a value in the sale-room that mere rarity would not have done. Information about them is sparse even by *Punch* standards, and one can sympathise with Spielmann's blandly referring to the Pocket Books without explaining what they were. There is even some doubt about how many go to the complete set : it seems to run from 1843 to 1881.

On special occasions *Punch* produced separate numbers or supplements, for example to mark stages in the paper's history, to celebrate Coronations and Exhibitions and to mourn the deaths of sovereigns. Occasionally the Obituary page or article would be supplemented by quite elaborate selections from the dead contributor's work. One such enterprise, which does not quite fit into any of the above classes, was that devoted to the Centenary of the Railways in 1925.

The line between the book publishing enterprises of Bradbury and Evans and those of *Punch* is faint. Thackeray's novels, for example, were sometimes under one imprint and sometimes under the other. Down to quite late one or other did a good deal of reprinting of contributions in volume-form and also produced collections of cartoons relating to particular periods or statesmen.

Internally the Taylor régime is without much interest. Recluses and eccentrics continued, only slightly more so : there was not much young blood. Burnand continued to keep up a flow of spirits that slightly irritated the primmer and more subtle of his colleagues but he carried the paper on its literary side. Much of his fooling was poor stuff ; too often he relied on chuckles and nudges in print to convey the impression that tremendous fun was being had by all and that *Punch* men were monstrously funny fellows ; he worked the pun to death ; but he did insist on writing humorous articles, never allowing it to be completely forgotten that *Punch* was a humorous paper.

## II

Taylor's editorship coincided with Disraeli's last and most important Ministry. Cross was carrying out a number of useful domestic reforms, the *sanitas* side of Disraeli's *imperium et sanitas*. The news that struck the public imagination, when it was not of murders or divorces, both ignored by *Punch*, came from far away, from the North-West frontier of India, from the unsettled tribal lands north of Cape Colony, from the Canadian prairies with their threat to British agriculture. It was in this decade that Britain lost its absolute lead over the rest of the world in steel. The Irish question was at its height and while *Punch* delighted in the vigour of Parliamentary life under the stimulus of the Irish members it was unhappily conscious of the evictions and boycotting and murder and starvation in Ireland itself. While judging any attempt by the Irish to revolt into independence to be simply and flatly disloyal, it remained as guiltily conscious of the weaknesses of the British handling of Ireland as it had been back in 1844, when Leech's cartoon showed Victoria sitting under a map of Ireland and saying to the Czar, sitting under a map of Poland, " Brother, Brother. We are both in the wrong." [1]

In the cartoons Tenniel was always supported by his professionalism but he obviously felt more at home and more inspired by the sharper criticisms of twenty years before. He would draw nobly and ceremoniously for a plain statement but there was not much to interest him in it. (Sambourne probably suffered less than Tenniel from waste of powers because he had begun as a much more purely decorative designer, though this is not to say that his charming and ingenious fashion drawings do not show comic invention.) There was a good deal of foreign politics—Saki's Balkans were beginning to dominate diplomacy—with a certain amount of anti-Turkish criticism. Colonial wars appeared and disappeared in the news and

*Punch* opinion was obviously divided between the old radical mistrust of imperial adventure and the new schoolboy gusto at extension of the flag and the removal of tyrannical coloured rulers by landing parties. France's attempt to recover after the defeat of 1871 was treated with a cold superiority.

*Punch*'s rudeness to America began to give way to a warier hostility. The " rebellious colonies " had made good and might in time threaten English commercial power. There was some recognition of the vitality of American journalism and show business and a good deal about the charming vivacity, outspokenness and unexpected *chic* of the American girl in English Society. Her freedom from the conventions that were strangling English social life was perhaps reprehensible, but how delightful. Taylor had a considerable American connection as a dramatist, though he may not have gained much financially from it considering the amount of piracy there was. This may have moderated *Punch*'s tone—the tone that tended to crop up from time to time later on, until the Slump showed that the colossus was humanly fallible.

## III

A typical issue of Taylor's *Punch* seems at first sight to consist mainly of du Maurier, not always very good du Maurier, and *Punch*'s *Essence of Parliament*. The Editor wrote this himself and he saw no reason to stint his readers. It is obvious he would have been happier with a straight report or a political leader. Succeeding Shirley Brooks, he floundered and desperately tried to brighten his columns with forced puns and heavily facetious whimsies. To some extent the *Essence* was carried by Linley Sambourne's increasingly elaborate initials inspired by C. H. Bennett, which took up most of the page and gradually changed to a second cartoon. For some reason these designs were full of barometers and thermometers.

Sambourne had now begun to emerge as a major figure after years of rather dull drudgery. He was a descendant of an old family that included Sheridan's beautiful Miss Linley of Bath. His daughter, Miss Maud Sambourne, was one of *Punch*'s few feminine contributors ; his grandson is Oliver Messel. He had been trained as an engineering draughtsman but disliked office work. A friend showed one of his sketches to Lemon, who immediately asked him to take on some odd jobs. Nothing in his early work justified Lemon's faith ; but Lemon's flair was right. His small social cuts steadily improved in humour and invention, and soon his illustrations for the *Essence* were showing a fresh and decisive talent. Influenced by both Keene and Leech and later by Tenniel he never showed much resemblance to the men on whom he came to model himself.

Although to-day perhaps few critics would put Sambourne over Keene as a draughtsman, foreign opinion in the late-Nineteenth Century often bracketed them together or put Sambourne first. Their aims and results were so different that the comparison seems inept. His strength was in the classical, the formal, the decorative and the contrived grotesque. Purely as a cartoonist, despite his knowledge and sense of composition, he must take second place to Tenniel. When a junior cartoon was started for him, he inevitably adopted Tenniel's aims and succeeded him as chief cartoonist on his retirement as a matter of course. His formal decorative work, as in the Index heading that was used until 1949 and in the Pocket Books, had tremendous verve and variety ; it is a great pity that *Punch* never turned his gift for illustration to full account. The illustrations to *Our Holiday in the Scottish Highlands* of 1875 or the Venetian illustrations to *Childe Harold* of 1878 show another side of his talent that *Punch* might have used.

Where Tenniel relied on eye and memory, Sambourne worked from an extraordinary collection of props and 10,000 photographs. He built his pictures up in sections. His Britannia incorporated the selected charms of four models. He carefully drew his figures in the nude and then patiently added the uniform or dress on the top.

# THE RELIEF OF LADYSMITH

*7th March, 1900* *Linley Sambourne*

**AT LAST!**

*Sir George White : " I hoped to have met you before, Sir Redvers."*
*Sir Redvers Buller, V.C. : " Couldn't help it, General. Had so many Engagements ! "*

He shared du Maurier's preference for tall women. Unlike Tenniel he liked working with process. The change from the old method of reproducing the art work by cutting into wood, which depended so much on the engraver's skill, to photographic methods is discussed in more detail by Mr. Kenneth Bird in Appendix IV. It was not simply conservatism that made Tenniel prefer the methods in which he had been trained and in which he became so great a master. Wood blocks continued to be used for his cartoons long after they had been dropped in favour of process for the rest of the paper. He said, " Even the perfect facsimile would be too weak and pale and utterly lacking in the *striking* effect which I take to be—has ever been—a most important feature in the opening pages of Punch." [2] The cartoon rush always worried Sambourne and his conscientiousness about details worried him still further. This tightness showed increasingly in his work.

It is interesting to trace the rising social importance of *Punch* from Leech's little dinners for his colleagues right up to the formal dinner parties of Sambourne's prime. He entertained the statesmen he caricatured and was on terms of close acquaintance with all the leading painters. He was a happy, kindly man, very energetic and always rushing off to shoot or hunt or yacht. " Sammy " was loved by his colleagues, who were amused by his naïvety and respectful of his goodness. Nobody knew whether his mistakes were intentional, mistakes like " There was such a silence afterwards that you could have picked up a pin in it," " You're digging nails in your coffin with every stroke of your tongue," or " I don't care for Lady Macbeth in the street walking scene." [3] He certainly enjoyed the amusement they produced. The deliberate butt has been rare among *Punch* men except on paper. It is of some interest that when much later the Liberal party split Sambourne became a Liberal-Unionist and eventually rather more conservative than Conservatives. Politics, that flavoured all the columns in the radical days, were now kept on the whole for special occasions and by the mid-Seventies there was rarely more than a passing dig at a politician's foibles outside the cartoon and the *Essence of Parliament*. It is perhaps a pity that Sambourne's considerable political knowledge was not further tapped.

In his Slade Lectures, *The Art of England*, Ruskin devoted some idiosyncratic attention to some of the *Punch* artists. He referred to Leech's tenderness and rather surprisingly, while praising du Maurier for never degenerating into caricature, praised him for a closeness of delineation the like of which had not been seen since Holbein. To some extent, here as elsewhere, Ruskin's aesthetic theories and his politics were at odds. He pointed out that *Punch* resisted attacks on property and held up as a model for children the British hunting squire, the British colonel and the British sailor. Leech made not a single endeavour to represent the beauty of the poor. The middle class were usually represented reclining on a sofa, surrounded by charming children, with whom they were usually too idle to play. The charm of the children depended to a great extent on their back hair and the fitting of their boots. As they grew up their girlish beauty was more and more fixed in an expression of more or less self-satisfied pride and practised apathy. There was no example in *Punch* of a girl in society whose face expressed humility or enthusiasm, except in mistaken directions and foolish degrees. Ruskin complained that *Punch* always showed John Bull as a farmer, never as a manufacturer or shopkeeper. Its foreigners were extremely delightful but represented of the Continent little more than Boulogne. Ruskin ignored Keene, but asked what a genius such as that of Tenniel would have done had the best been asked of it. Tenniel had much of the largeness and mystery of symbolic imagination which belonged to the great leaders of classic art : in the shadowy masses and sweeping lines of his great compositions there were tendencies which might have won his adoption into the school of Tintoret : and his scorn of whatever seemed dishonest or contemptible in religion would have translated itself into awe in the presence of its vital power.

The innumerable artists who came and went included Randolph Caldecott. He did not do very much and his most characteristic work is, of course, outside *Punch* ; but it is worth remembering, amid all the talk in *Punch* reminiscences of closed and open boroughs, that in turning over past volumes one is always liable to come upon the work of men primarily associated with other periodicals, and these visits from other sections of the art world were not only agreeable for the readers but stimulating and fertilising to the regular contributors. These "guest artists" have included Sir John Gilbert, Millais, Arthur Rackham, Heath Robinson and Feliks Topolski.

Keene's nephew and protégé, A. Chantrey Corbould, was a contributor of hunting and country scenes, apparently more popular with the readers than with the Editors. Both he and Keene took his non-appointment to the staff as personally insulting, but he was essentially a supporting player with a very narrow range. People who were fond of horses liked to see horses well drawn, but he showed insufficient versatility for editorial work, and since the early days artists appointed to the Table had been expected to have strongly individual genius. The lack of this requirement in making literary appointments may account for the divergence in the repute of the writing and the pictures towards the end of the century.

## IV

Taylor's one find was E. J. Milliken, for many years the main editorial writer. He suggested most of the cartoons and wrote verses to face them. He took on any job that needed doing. His verses about 'Arry the cockney bounder were very popular.[4]

The basic prose style of *Punch* has, of course, varied with literary fashion. Jerrold and Thackeray had strongly marked styles and are usually identifiable. In the early issues the tone of the shorter pieces was gay and charming and clear, and must reflect the tone of the conversation among the Staff. They were written by different men. The waggishness which threatened to clog the paper came in a little later. Taylor liked a solid Germanic type of humour and, though he would not have admitted it, feared the frivolous and the imaginative. One important theme in the history of *Punch* is the relation between the style of the descriptive or feature columns and the style of the purely humorous columns. Later it is possible to compare Burnand and Seaman when they are writing dramatic criticisms and when they are aiming at raising a laugh. On the whole, divorce between straightforward clean English in the descriptive columns and the more florid, consciously-quizzical style of the comic items has been unhealthy. *Punch* has been strongest when the humour has been in the attitude and the whole range of the language has been used to express it so that whether a man is writing about a play or his visit to the sea-side, about the Chancellor's introducing a budget or the extravagance of some popular dietician, he uses words in the same way. If he has a very curt style and the language is strained to produce an effect and does so successfully, then he is still inside the best *Punch* tradition. Nearly always the weakest periods and weakest contributions have been when the writer shows he has sat down to be funny against the grain and has made up for lack of subject matter or lack of a humorous approach by verbal clichés.

Burnand did not invent the pun nor did he end it. From the beginning *Punch* had printed puns, often political and usually appalling, some of them by Thomas Hood. The trouble with Burnand was that he produced too many puns. They are quite mechanical. As soon as he met a combination of sounds he automatically coupled it with a similar combination of sounds. Burnand's puns rarely had a point. He made the readers pun-shy. Reaction from his methods was never complete ; but unfortunately he made word-play editorially suspect at a time when the language was taking on a new flexibility and richness from its contact with the American language and with Anglo-Irish. Of recent years, the only artist in puns has been Richard Mallett, who has generally used them poetically to create mad beauties of his own. An example of the kind of jest which Taylor enjoyed was a paragraph in which the words " glad " and " stone " were translated into Greek, then the Greek letters were transliterated into English and the anagram produced, " Oh Midlothian Sue." [5]

CHAPTER FIVE

# KINDLY GAIETY

## *F. C. Burnand's Editorship, 1880–1906*

WHEN BURNAND took over on Taylor's death in 1880 he had a stiff task ahead of him. *Punch* had already lived much longer than the average humorous paper and there was no reason to assume that longevity would be in itself an attraction to the public. He had to reverse a slow downward trend and to kill the idea that *Punch* had lived its day and was dying. The birth of new periodicals was news ; the continued existence of a periodical had to be made into news. It was one of the great achievements of *Punch* editing to train the public to think of *Punch* as having a corporate and continuous character, like *The Times* or the *Encyclopædia Britannica*. The first fifty years were celebrated by *An Evening With Punch*, a solid brochure mingling selections from back numbers, snippets from the history of the paper and gossip about contributors. This advertised a reprint by *The Times* Publishing Company of the collected issues, two years to a volume with notes and introductions. These, together with Spielmann's *History*, helped to compel the public to realise that *Punch* existed in its past and its future. Each number began to gain weight from the half-acknowledged realisation that it was a back number to come. There was, of course, a danger in all this, but it did not develop into a serious threat until much later.

The distance *Punch* had come in its domestic life may be seen in the contrast between the old days of a joint of mutton and a bowl of punch at a tavern and the menu of the Staff's Jubilee Dinner at Greenwich. As one of his staff said, " for William Bradbury nothing was too good for his boys, whether in the way of meat or drink, and, regardless of cost, they had both in abundance ". [1]

| | |
|---|---|
| E. I. Madeira | Potages à la tortue claire et tortue liée gras verts au jus |
| Ponche à la Romaine | Aileron de tortue étuvée aux fines herbes |
| | ——— |
| Amontillado | Carrelets souchés ; Saumon de Severne souché ; white-bait |
| | Rissoles de Homard. Christines à la Mantua |
| Rüdesheimerberg | Boudins de Merlans à la Danoise |
| Pontet Canet | Anguilles étuvées à la Bordelaise |
| | Truite grillée, sauce à la Tartare |
| | Omelette de crabe au cordon bleu |
| | Filet de sole à la crème au Parmesa |
| | Côtelettes de saumon à l'Ecossaise à l'Orientale |
| Sorbet à la | Whitebait à la Diable |
| Française | Kari de Crevettes au riz |
| | Soufflé d'Ecrevisses glacé |
| | Filet de Volaille à l'écarlate |
| Irroy Carte d'Or, | Epaule d'agneau grillée et Haricots Verts |
| vint. 1878, | ——— |
| and | Canetons rôtis et petits pois verts |
| Moët dry | ——— |
| Imperial | Asperges en branches glacées |
| Champagnes | ——— |
| | Cailles rôties et salade à la Française |
| | ——— |
| | Bacon and beans |
| | ——— |
| | Jambon grillé à la Diable et salade de tomates |
| | ——— |
| | Crème d'abricots. Dames d'honneur |
| | Meringues à la crème ; éclairs aux chocolats |
| | Mille fruits glacés |
| | ——— |
| Liqueurs | Pailles de fromage |
| | ——— |

| | |
|---|---|
| 1865 | Glaces |
| Brown Sherry, | Crème d'ananas. Eau de Cerises |
| Ch. Larose, | Crème aux fraises. Eau de Citron |
| 1870. | |
| Port 1863 | ——— |
| | Fait boire |
| | Dessert |
| Punch Bowl | Ananas, melons, pêches, nectarines, fraises, raisins, conserves[1a] |

Burnand was a vigorous, confident man. He had been on the staff long enough to remember the editing of Lemon and Brooks. He allowed it to be known that he welcomed newcomers and invited promising young men to let him see their work. He did not force his own opinions on the paper, though in deciding the cartoon he summed up opinion quickly and saw that a firm decision was reached without more debate than was convivially enjoyable. He was a Catholic and banned anti-Catholic jokes, which were anyway getting rare ten years after the loss of the temporal power. He was hampered in his opposition to the drunk joke by Keene and to the anti-Semitic joke by du Maurier. This progressive elimination of minority targets, which perhaps began when Shirley Brooks stopped the anti-Welsh joke and du Maurier ended the tradition of the gesticulating, ludicrous Frenchman, resulted in leaving the area of life that could be dealt with considerably smaller than the area that could not. Burnand believed in fun and in kindly humour. As it is difficult to be kind where you feel deeply, and as most people feel deeply about most of the things that matter, *Punch* began to lose its contact with life as a whole, to write more about leisure and less about work, more about the few and less about the many, more about behaviour and less about action.

On the other hand, width of treatment expanded. Variety was transferred from " what " to " how." (*Punch* Editors have swung alternately from placing subject matter first to placing treatment first. Seaman, for example, was a " how," Malcolm Muggeridge is a " what.") Burnand liked burlesque and was far too fond of the pun, but his own sense of humour was more delicate than the forms in which he expressed it. As E. V. Lucas said, he did not realise how good some of his material was. He liked his contributors to exude a hearty cheerfulness and wanted readers assured that in *Punch*'s pages there would be endless family fun. At first this was a necessary change after the heaviness of the Taylor régime. Later the lack of fineness of point, the substitution of the jovial for the humorous, the lack of subtlety, tension and irony became tedious. However, new brooms are entitled to be judged as such. When he took over he saved *Punch* by converting it slowly into a different paper. On the evidence of his first ten years as Editor he is a much bigger man than on the evidence of his last ten. In the late Eighties Bryce remarked, " I used formerly to look through the pictures in *Punch* and lay the number down ; now I read it through." [2]

The brash young Etonian dramatist and journalist quietened down once he was in authority. He remained kindly and genial, but he was not so noisy and he went out of his way to conciliate. He liked responsibility. He was not a scholarly or artistic or even a very clever man, but brisk and competent. Some of his literary inventions—the article of personal experience has already been mentioned—seem in retrospect to have been bigger departures than they seemed to be at the time.

Gradually Burnand's interest in innovation waned. As with other Editors, the early years were a time of reform and hard feelings, the later of warm fellowship and resistance to change and refusal to reconsider the nature and purposes of the periodical. No reform is ever enough and soon Burnand's were taken for granted and something more was required. His increasingly hand-to-mouth editing and disinclination for the daily grind caused friction with the proprietors, who in 1891 offered the Editorship to Henry Lucy. Lucy refused it on the grounds that he could not go behind the back of a man who had advanced him, and difficulties were patched up. The declining repute of *Punch* caused public concern. The *Nottingham Express* devoted an article to the decadence of the paper : " During the last few years the journal has entirely lost touch with Society. None of the new social absurdities have been caught or castigated. . . . The new forms of snobbishness have been overlooked ; the ' bounder ' has never been interpreted : nor has fresh merit in art, literature, or the drama lately been welcomed. There is no use blinking the fact that *Punch* has become anaemic and feeble for want of new blood, and its influence in consequence is steadily decreasing. It made the fatal mistake of never welcoming outside contribution and thus became the organ of a clique. It is thus that mediocrity is attained." [3] However, it says something for *Punch*'s status that a variation in quality should attract serious newspaper comment. *Punch* has fairly often been praised or blamed in print, not only at a change of Editorship. Did any newspaper ever discuss fluctuations in the standing of *The Field* or *Little Folks* or *The Journal of Hellenic Studies* ?

By 1906 something had to be done. Burnand was forced into retirement and showed considerably more activity over the loss of his Editorship than he had over its exercise. His farewell note in *Punch* sounded cordial enough, but in other intemperate newspaper articles he published his side of the case and stumped the country with lectures entitled *Nearly Fifty Years of Punch*. He was given a substantial pension by the firm but with some ingenuity added a Civil List pension to it. Except for his appearance at the Table when Mark Twain was entertained the year after he retired, Burnand had no more to do with *Punch*.

The active proprietors were no longer jobbing printers, slightly surprised to find themselves owning a leading periodical, but members of an extensive family, prosperous, solid and engaged in activities ranging from expert fine art dealing to membership of the Liberal Party in the House of Commons. The links between the Bradbury-Agnew family and the world of country gentlemen who were M.F.H.s at home and Members of Parliament in London helped to give *Punch* more access to the world of power than it had had fifty years before, but also helped to diminish its urchin irresponsibility.

Gradually the general publishing business, which in mid-

Victorian times had been very important, was allowed to lapse. The proprietors, after one quarrel towards the end of Lemon's time, in which he threatened that he and the Staff would secede, made no sustained attempt to reduce the unusual amount of editorial independence, until their intervention became drastically necessary under Burnand. With the development in the Twentieth Century of *Punch* as an advertising medium, the need for a stronger commercial direction became felt, and there were sometimes tugs between the attraction of the life of a country gentleman and the need for initiating, or at least approving, commercial development. The growing professionalism of the *Punch* organisation was mitigated by close personal relations, sometimes dating back to schooldays, between leading members of the proprietary families and of the Staff. The courtesies and benevolences of the old family firm have survived in *Punch* to an extent unusual in the world of periodical publication. The agreement of both proprietors and Staff that *Punch* was a National Institution, whatever its legal status, produced a curious relationship of proprietor and Editor, more like that of Godolphin and Marlborough than that of Lord Beaverbrook and Arthur Christiansen. Sir William Agnew, for example, became a baronet and a very influential Member of Parliament, but the Staff thought of him first as a dining companion and " an admirable mixer of salads ".[4]

In later years, while Burnand concentrated on writing his reminiscences and enjoying life in Ramsgate, the actual running of the paper was left more and more to his deputy, Arthur William à Beckett. He was a busy journalist who expected that Lemon would put him on the paper as a son of Gilbert à Beckett and never really recovered from his cold-shouldering. He finally won his way on under Taylor. He was very prolific and spent his youth on the usual Bar, Newspaper, Theatre round of the better Victorian journalists. He knew everybody and was popular. His varied journalistic experience included editing the *Sunday Times*. He was a Catholic, like his close friend Burnand, and once tried to sell Cardinal Manning a racing paper which he had run into difficulties.

When Manning refused to buy it he passionately asked whether they could appeal to the Pope. Cheerful, negligent and very self-assured, he was filled with a family piety that allied easily with his natural self-importance. He regarded *Punch*, as one of his colleagues said, as an à Beckett family property. He was ready to take on any job and gradually Burnand let the reins drop into his willing hands. He never took a holiday but slaved in the office and presided at the Table in Burnand's absence. He liked the same kind of writing as Burnand and assumed he would succeed him.

Arthur à Beckett's two autobiographical volumes, *The à Becketts of Punch* and *Confessions of a Humorist*, are really dreadful. Written after his ejection from the Assistant Editorship in Seaman's favour, smarting with fury, full of pompous references to his resignation and the alleged need for new blood and to his fresh enterprises, they show clearly enough why a radical change was needed. He boasted, though not in print, that he allowed only one per cent. of the post from outside contributors to reach Burnand, and in the drop in the quality and vivacity of the paper before Seaman initiated yet another revival can be seen the effects of the sieve. This might perhaps account for Burnand's laments about the exceeding smallness of the supply of new blood, which he claimed to be constantly seeking.

On the evidence of his autobiographies, à Beckett was a silly old man, whatever he may have been in his youth, and no paper has been so threatened by silly old men as *Punch*. Bufferdom has to accept changes in science and warfare and technology. It digs its toes in when its entertainment is concerned and in entertainment it includes all the arts. *Punch* published Thackeray and Keene, for example, both infinitely greater men than the majority of its readers, but to the buffer they were merely comedians hired by him. All papers attract correspondence from lunatics : the *Punch* letter-box has a strong attraction for the gaga as well. Buffers expect all humour, all drawing, all writing, to be much the same as when their taste was formed in childhood. Buffers write in to the paper complaining of the absence of contributors long since dead or discarded and attacking contributors who try to do anything new.

When they praise they use language that itself debilitates any urge towards change, as, for example, in these laudatory remarks of Lady Edmond Fitzmaurice, " What responsible people you are to be sure, who keep alive for us, like a little wax taper burning before the altar of our ideal, this good old wise Punch." [5] While they remained a minority of readers they could be replied to politely or ignored and the policy of the paper could develop organically. The trouble began when they got right into the office. Percival Leigh became a buffer young, but his contributions were dropped. Taylor had a bit of the buffer in him but he was a man of sufficiently varied public life to prevent his sinking altogether into the elderly clubman. The buffers really got into the works with à Beckett, and even he had been quite light and entertaining in youth.

## II

Though *Punch* became kinder to the monarchy with the death of the Prince Consort, it did not become mealy-mouthed. It is interesting to notice that right to the end of the Nineteenth Century, *Punch* was more outspoken than in the Twentieth Century, or at least the first half of it. In September, 1881, a bitter little mock diary of a royal Princess, perhaps by R. C. Lehmann, hit straight-forwardly at the material selfishness of the Queen and the tedium of her Court. The tone can be judged from these extracts :

> 19th Osborne.—Dear A——, came with the children and pressed for me to be allowed to join them on the yacht, and see the regatta, and have a real sail, and spend a quite too lovely day ! No use ; so she went back, and I took a walk as usual with Mamma, had luncheon as usual with Mamma, and dined as usual with Mamma. Everything *very much* as usual. Stay, though ; I am forgetting. I must add a two hours' steam up and down on the *Alberta*, a mile and a half away from everything, which the

*Court Journal* will no doubt describe as "witnessing the regatta" with Mamma.

20th to 27th.—The usual Osborne routine. Of course, I am perfectly happy doing nothing else but walking, taking luncheon, driving and dining continually with Mamma; though I should like to be able to get away a *little* now and then. In one of our drives round the island, we passed several groups of happy girls enjoying themselves, in the society of their relatives and friends, in various healthful and innocent ways (with the permission of *their Mammas*).

28th to 29th.—Off again to Balmoral, without waiting for the State ball on the 30th. Journey full of novelty.

In politics, the Eighties began with *Punch*'s rejoicing over the Conservative defeat; but it became increasingly difficult for a Liberal to find anything to rejoice over. There is always a difficulty when a Party supported by a paper is on the defensive. Gladstone's preoccupation with Ireland could not provide Liberals with a complete policy. He became almost a one-man-Party towards the end. *Punch*'s decreasing political interest was partly owing to lack of any clear-cut line to follow on major issues. The proprietors set a Liberal tone and this was the traditional allegiance. The Conservative opposition to the Franchise Bill helped to keep *Punch* Liberal. Tenniel thought it his duty to suppress his own Conservative inclinations in carrying out commissions for the cartoon. Keene's Conservatism was crusty and either accepted as one of his character-props or ignored as a defect of age. A colleague said that for him life would have been endurable but for its new moons. The new generation was less politically-minded than its forerunners and more liable to prejudice. One feels that arguments were less heated and evasions more common. From now on *Punch*'s policy was that described by C. L. Graves in a phrase borrowed from Bagehot, "animated moderation." The most famous cartoon of the period—*Dropping the Pilot* [6]—was comment, and rather polite comment, on the internal affairs of another country, not a blow in any Cause. It put into a phrase what people were thinking, but its fame was partly due to lack of competition.

Burnand was a man of the clubs and increasingly a man of the home. Most of his club life was a matter of good food, rich cigars and kindly chaff. Slightly more energetic, but *only* slightly more, was the famous Sunday morning riding club, The Two Pins Club, called after Turpin and Gilpin, and consisting of leading *Punch* men and leading lawyers—Burnand, Sambourne, Willie Matthews, Frank Lockwood, Tenniel and Charles Russell. Burnand had none of Brooks's knowledge of what was going on and nothing like his wit or intellectual interests. When he became Editor, the first French revolution was within living memory and he left the editorship after Einstein had published his Special Theory of Relativity. *Punch* ignored ferment and was unaware of the overlapping of old and new. Its coverage of the arts lacked sharpness. Art was treated primarily as a commodity ; in the Seventies and Eighties nearly every number had a joke about a painter or his patrons. There was a stereotype of a modern artist or poet and that remained as fixed as Keene's drunken cabbies or Tenniel's national bestiary. *Punch* attacked the Aesthetic Movement without much clear idea of how the Aesthetic Movement was developing, and with the *Yellow Book* it was even more at sea. In the Sixties, *Punch* had recognised Meredith and Whistler well ahead of the general public, but now more and more it reacted to vitality with philistine guffaws. There was far too much about Wilde's poses, far too little precise satire of the Movement he publicised. Generally speaking, *Punch* under Burnand, as under Seaman, was interested in art only for its eccentricities. The new was sneered at, but the old was not intelligently praised. For years at a time the subject was virtually ignored.

The Nineties, of course, are not important solely in the history of the arts and entertainment. It was also the great decade of imperialism, which *Punch* saw from the point of view of the explorer and administrator. It was unsympathetic alike to South African millionaires, Kipling, missionaries and anti-colonial agitation. The impact of European civilisation on backward peoples often provided amusing incongruities and it was held against *Punch* overseas that it was conscious of the incongruities only on one side. (Perhaps it is fair to remark that there is a limit to the amount of school-mastering a humorous periodical can be expected to take on.) Ominously, America was beginning to attract not merely horny-handed immigrants but established businesses and, above all, inventions.

The Nineties were also a period of rising self-consciousness in the working class. The unions edged forward doubtfully into parliamentary politics. The attack on poverty, of which less had been heard in the comic press since the Forties, was in the Nineties not an appeal to a change of heart in the rich or an attack on the muddle of the vestries. It was a matter of Trade Boards, of housing schemes, of gas-and-water municipal-socialism.

*Punch* did not consistently attack or defend these trends in public life. Still, there are signs it had a feeling of guilt about betraying its radical past. It rather irritatingly assumed that to ask an awkward question was a disloyal act, so that there was too much about agitators and too little about the rights and wrongs of their agitations. The politics of *Punch* were getting insulated from the polity by club windows. After all the discussions on the Staff it generally came down in a right-wing Liberal position and Liberals of this complexion were far more interested in the disputes between the religious denominations over education than they were in housing or the maternal mortality rate.

With the Boer war, Burnand's reign began to die away. From the point of view of having to look for new humours and incongruities and difficulties in ordinary life, a war is a godsend to a humorous paper, simply because ordinary life becomes diversified. You can add jokes about tents to jokes about houses. This does not —a captious criticism that was made after the next war—assume any point of view about war as such. A pacifist paper might joke about rations just as much as a fire-eating paper. The dislike of the British for military life more often takes the form of humour than of denunciation. In wars *Punch* shares a national experience and tends to make jokes with a wider appeal than in peace. Many of the jokes in the Boer war period were about the strength and weakness of the British officer and it is not perhaps fanciful to see some of the ground for the Esher committee laid in *Punch*.

The early Edwardian period had a lot going on but in public affairs the dominating question was Imperial Preference and Free Trade. It was difficult to be funny about either of these highly technical creeds and *Punch*'s best political jokes were about people rather than causes. Often it would use a social joke that had a relevance beyond the immediate incident but it comparatively rarely made these happy hits on politics. The foreign politics of the time were agreeably visual, with innumerable visits of crowned heads. Home politics could be dramatised only in Joe Chamberlain's eyeglass and his orchid, Balfour's lanky boredom, and the fight for the Liberal succession.

Social satire must be concerned very largely with the changes in the structure of society and those can be only movements up and down. Until the First World War, the movement satirised was mainly upwards ; a fall in status was too often due to commercial failure or sexual misconduct for it to be the subject of much laughter. Movement upwards, the contrast between manners formed at the bottom and displayed, owing to an intervening increase of wealth, at the top, is a traditional subject of satirical humour going back into the ancient world. It is defensive of the established order and brutally reformative of new entrants to it. The children of the *nouveaux riches* were beaten and teased into conformity with their station in the public schools : their parents were disciplined by exclusion, disapproval, unbelievable rudeness and the jeers of *Punch*. du Maurier, the most savage and the most influential of the baiters, did not often attack mistakes of social usage or even of language. Sir Gorgius Midas was a horrible man and it was a public service to slash at his display of money, his bullying of servants, his self-esteem and his variation of behaviour according to the status of his company. (The rich have now become so aware of the risk they run that they cautiously engage scholars of repute to guide them in their collecting policy. As the scholars sometimes persuade them to pass their collections on to museums, libraries and art galleries, the public benefit. There is nothing like a class of scared rich for providing amenities.) The society that *Punch* defended was itself a parvenu society—the descendants of the Whig manufacturers who fought for the Reform Bill. *Punch* rarely dealt with the landed aristocracy from the inside, except in the hunting field.

## III

Burnand went back for editorial inspiration to the early issues and tried, while making *Punch* funny, to revive its interest as a general magazine. More was made of dramatic criticism. Regular book reviews were started. There were more articles descriptive of events and special exhibitions.

W. H. Wills in the early numbers had written dramatic criticism that was sufficiently in the style of Jerrold and the others to seem merely an extension of the dispassionately disrespectful *Punch* attitude into another field. Then regular criticisms were dropped and, by the time they were resumed, they were either ponderous with Taylor or often merely humorous articles with Burnand, who inserted fragments of imaginary conversations between members of the audience. This was all to the good when so little of the paper was entertaining at all. Later it became unnecessary and *Punch* could have done with more rigorous appraisal of new plays. Book reviews, attributed by a horrible invention of Burnand to the Baron de Bookworms and his Baronites, varied very much as they were contributed by different men. On the whole they did not use bad books as an opportunity for humour. The tone was very high and mighty : we are prepared to be entertained—now entertain us. Some of them read like the kind of letters of complaint that readers sent to *Punch*. Yet they were fair and aimed at providing advice for the book-buyer and library subscriber. They were practical rather than theoretical reviews. There was very little pure criticism. Their strength over the years was the maintenance of a consistent standard. Once you knew that *Punch* was likely to recommend the kind of book you liked you could rely on its continuing to do so. It could be ruthless with pretentious novels, scornful of what it did not understand. Its coverage was much better on field sports, light novels, reminiscences and travel than on speculative or imaginative work. Generally its strictures were less reprehensible than its exclusions.

One of Burnand's happier strokes of resuscitation was to get Henry Lucy to take over *The Essence of Parliament* in 1881. Lucy was a political journalist of immense industry and experience. At different times his activities ranged from the editorship of the *Daily News* to parliamentary sketches for the *Observer*. His political articles in the *Gentleman's Magazine* had turned Woodrow Wilson to politics. He was an important figure in the Liberal " working " of the press. Prime Ministers sent him notes from Cabinet meetings and resigning Ministers were anxious that he should have their version of the facts. Neither Theodore Roosevelt nor the King of the Belgians read any other Parliamentary Report. Shackleton named a mountain in Antarctica after him. He knew everybody and his dinner parties were important as they were politically neutral and allowed opponents to meet socially. Important guests were invited to sign the famous tablecloth and the signatures were then embroidered. E. V. Lucas, who was not invited to sign the cloth, accused Lucy of being too coldly cautious. There seems to have been something a little chilling about him.

He made a break with the tradition of Shirley Brooks, who had far more political penetration, and turned the feature into *The Diary of Toby, M.P.* He wanted to drop the term *Essence* altogether, and nearly refused to take it on when Burnand told him that the Proprietors insisted on its retention because they considered it a valuable property. He made *The Diary* impressionistic and dramatic, economised space by the omission of articles and unessential parts of speech, and included fiction. Lucy invented the Hon. Member for

Sark. He put words into the mouths of M.P.s and some of the parliamentary witticisms that got into the books were invented by Lucy in *Punch*. For example, on a Minister listening to a dull speaker through his ear-trumpet—"Why waste natural advantages?"[7] He may have been canny in his relations with his colleagues but he was certainly outspoken in his reports. He had a sharp pen and a way of hitting off the peculiarities of members, as well as a terrifying memory. He could often quote the odd fact or speech which made the latest declaration ring false. Watts-Dunton said that he was the greatest living master of idiomatic English and was squandering his resources on political journalism. In many ways Lucy was the most consistent *Punch* contributor of his time and his *Punch* work, like his six autobiographical volumes, repetitive as they are, should be far better known. The neglect of him by historians is surprising. He treated politics rather as Horace Walpole did, as social comedy, and, if *Punch* were not to agitate for reform, then this kind of approach was obviously the right one.

Burnand also improved *Punch* layout. "Layout" has sometimes come to mean the arrangement of white spaces on the page. The Victorian *Punch* strikes us as being crowded and having little rest for the eye. For its time it was not badly made up at all: column-width varied and there was no feeling that the contents of the page had been forced into a rigidly subdivided scheme. Under Burnand there was an increase of illustration and, while this complicated the work of making up the page, it gave increased variety from the reader's point of view.

## IV

This is a convenient point to discuss verse in *Punch*. At first, the forms used were mainly those of popular ballads and there was an element of rather simple burlesque, imitations of sentimental songs with a bathetic last line and that kind of thing. Percival Leigh's Latin verses and macaronics were the kind of exercise that probably many readers had been flogged at school into performing with expertise. Content, however, still dominated form. Verses jovially described social and financial embarrassments or deceits played on young lovers by ageing spinsters, or the inroad of the moth in a restricted wardrobe. The metre and rhymes were to help it along, create a feeling of warmth and jollity and vaguely suggest a sing-song. There was quite a bit of verse but it was not very different in intention from the prose, merely doing a prose article the hard way. Its links were with the jog-trotting rhythms of the theatre and with journalism, always glad of different-sized verses to help with make-up. Thackeray's metres, however, had plenty of variety and sometimes a haunting music.

There was a rather different tradition in the universities, where light verse was treated as a problem in form, the harder the better. Attempts to reproduce classical metres in English, to adapt classical tunes to modern themes, go back many years. A rough-and-ready starting-point is the group of Etonians who produced first *The Microcosm* and then *The Anti-Jacobin*, in which attention was paid to metre and the reader informed of it. One of the group, Hookham Frere, later translated Aristophanes and his vigorous rhythms stirred up a whole movement. These young men were followed into the salons a generation later by Praed, the master of the light, elegant, sentimentally mocking verse that lived in albums, magazines and recitation. It was a measure of how slowly *Punch* became the *Punch* we know that this light verse tradition should have been so late in entering its pages. It required leisure, scholarship, patience and a precise frivolity. It was essentially an amateur product, and it was a long time before a man who was mainly a versifier could live off *Punch*. The young dons and bishops, chaplains and foreign office clerks did not need to sell their work and might have disliked the idea of doing so, while *Punch* men could not afford the time to polish and repolish. Even Brooks, who could write complicated verse faster than most men could write prose, never held it back for final revision. It was not till Burnand that one began to find the best light verse of the day in *Punch*. It was Gilbert who shook theatrical verse free of its puns and waggeries and what finally emerged as the *Punch* tradition may owe as much to him as it owed to Cambridge.

There are many pleasures to be gained from light verse. There is first the pleasure of watching expertise, as in watching a juggler. The versifier starts with a pattern, often a very complicated pattern, and assumes that his readers will recognise it. Then, making as many or as few difficulties for himself as he likes, he follows the pattern exactly. If he is producing a deliberate variation he exaggerates it, to show that it is not inefficiency but excessive skill. All verse patterns came to be used in *Punch* from the forward-pressing couplet or quatrain, to the formal epigrammatic couplet or even limerick. But most *Punch* versifiers were strongly influenced by the metrical preferences of Calverley and behind him the Cambridge tradition. The old French forms revived by Dobson and Lang and Gosse were comparatively rare. While the earlier *Punch* reader was unobservant of form and looked only for laughable content in verse, the late-Victorian reader increasingly looked first at the shape. When we wander through back numbers and grow puzzled or derisive at topical poems, it is important to remember that the *Punch* writers shared the educational background of their readers and that the basis of that education was an exact verbal drill in Latin and Greek. Everybody was used to looking closely at words and listening closely to rhythms. Light verse was a game in which the whole point depended on keeping the rules. There are, of course, other kinds of light verse and Auden's introduction to the *Oxford Book of Light Verse* widens the scope of the term with unarguable force, making the distinction not on form or subject matter but on degree of communication. He includes Byron and cowboy ballads because the whole community would have found no screen of specialised idiom interfering with understanding.

Light verse in the *Punch* sense, however, was esoteric. The writer's reward was not wide applause, but discriminating applause, and in time the arbiters were found, not in Cambridge combination rooms, but in the *Punch* office, which insisted that every contributor should reach certain standards of accuracy. This meant that the average *Punch* verse was much better than the average *Punch* prose. It was only gradually that this insistence on accuracy came to involve a reluctance to admit new metres.

The subject-matter of light verse in the late-Victorian and Edwardian period was either things in themselves serious, which in practice meant politics, or things associated with leisure or domesticity. The weakness was that too few light versifiers tried to make what they said as ingeniously funny as the way they said it. However, given that a humorist wanted to make a comment on some topic from the newspaper, if he proposed to spend all his space on making one point it was more enjoyable if he made it in verse, where there was something for the reader to do besides grasping the point, rather than in prose, where sparseness of material showed at once (except of course in the kind of decorated, complex prose *Punch* did not use.)

Under Burnand, *Punch* had finally abandoned savagery and even under the greatest political stress it never returned to the imaginative invective of Jerrold's time. Much of the political verse was probably considered satirical, though in the ordinary sense of the term it was not satirical at all. Satire is not simply expressing hostile opinions or even using sarcasm to do so. Very little political verse of this period was satire in the sense in which the term is used when speaking of Juvenal, still less in the sense which Ronald Knox defines in his introduction to *Essays in Satire*. A later generation faced with the need of working Percy Wyndham Lewis into the content of the term would perhaps be puzzled to understand whether it really meant anything to the late-Victorians at all.

Leisure in an industrial civilisation occupies a larger proportion of the minds of men than it does of their time. Late-Victorian humour came from the variety of leisure more than from the uniformity of work, and it is noticeable that later, when an attempt was made to extend *Punch*'s coverage to include work as well as play, much of the fun came, in fact, from the fringes of work, the morning tea-break, the staff Christmas-box, and the annual party.

Leisure has after all produced exquisite minor art, *fêtes champêtres* and fans and fireworks. At first leisure in *Punch* was either the formal entertainment, like the musical *soirée* or long dinner-party, or else field-sports. du Maurier and Leech were often concerned with social comments on some personal inadequacy revealed in a setting of sport or society. Leisure was not related to relaxation or gaiety.

The addition of boating to hunting, shooting and fishing introduced a gentler, lighter verse, the expression of states of happiness. The water lapped against the punt. Birds, trees and girls were pleasant but unexacting to look at. The passive versifier noted more of his environment than the hunter. Though there was little keenly observed nature verse, some of the most attractive verse in *Punch* stemmed from the Cambridge tradition of moving along a river either very fast or very slowly. The holiday, whether a drowsy afternoon in summer or a strenuous canoeing expedition with amusing predicaments, light-hearted fun and all the mild comedy of personal relations, produced a minor art of real distinction which has been overlooked, as sporting pictures once were, or as the prose of clerical malice still is. In this verse-world there was more flirtation than love, more irritation than hate. The wildness of the landscape was never more than the wildness of a river bank. (*The Wind in the Willows* is *Punch* by adoption). There was one pose of laziness, another of unremunerative activity. These were productive poses. It was a pity that there was also sometimes a Philistine pose.

R. C. Lehmann was the dominating figure in the new school. He was a great-nephew of Mrs. W. H. Wills and his relations included sculptors and singers ; his mother was a Chambers of Edinburgh. He was President of the Cambridge Union and a leading oarsman, very important in rowing politics, a noted coach and an authoritative writer of manuals of instruction. In later life his house at Bourne End was a centre of rowing society. He was called to the Bar and won a prize awarded by a newspaper for the handsomest barrister, but he did not build up much of a practice. He pursued a number of careers in short bursts of enthusiasm. He was a keen radical politician and for a few years an undistinguished Liberal M.P. Off and on he dabbled in journalism. He owned the *Granta*, which for some years was a nursery for *Punch* writers, including Barry Pain, Anstey, Seaman and Milne. When Morley invited Lehmann to edit the *Daily News*, he threw himself into the work. He had a good mind and a good memory. He knew men and affairs ; his staff liked him. His second daughter was born soon after his appointment and it was suggested that she should be called Dahlia after the *Daily News* ; however, he called her Rosamond. Like most of his enterprises, his editorship did not last. Archibald Marshall's account in his reminiscences of being Lehmann's secretary illustrates to some extent his strength and weakness. He was fairly well off and did not have to do anything unless he wanted to. For a man of his mental energy he was singularly unenterprising about providing himself with anything to do. He would sit for hours in his big library and read nothing but newspapers. He would take the dogs for a walk before lunch and again in the afternoon, and that was his day until the evening. This combination of ability and casualness, of fervour and inertia, comes to be very characteristic of *Punch* men. The short spurt, the poem or article, suited Lehmann's talents perfectly.

When he joined the *Punch* staff his views were sufficiently near to those of the Proprietors to preserve him from political molestation. Burnand was quite content to hold the balance between him and the Tories like Tenniel and Seaman. Lehmann was a hot-tempered, generous man whose verse was above all light-hearted. There were more expert manipulators but nobody who developed the new field of *Punch*'s activities more coherently and made more simple, moving, gay melodies from the enchantments of youth and summer and family life.

There are great spreading chestnuts all ranged in their arches
With their pinnacled blossoms so pink and so white ;
There are rugged old oaks, there are tender young larches,
There are willows, cool willows, to chequer the light.

Each tree seems to ask you to come and be shaded—
It's a way they all have, these adorable trees—
And the leaves all invite you to float down unaided
In your broad-bottomed punt and to rest at your ease.[8]

It is interesting to notice the difference between this kind of invitation to lounging and an enervating invitation to day-dreaming like O'Shaughnessy's *We are the Music Makers*.

Lehmann as a light versifier had a range far beyond the admirable looseness of his lyrics. In an article about R. M. Leonard's *A Book of Light Verse*, Lehmann disclosed his own beliefs : "It may be playful or tender, but it must not be spiteful or mawkish. It may be humorous or regretful, but the humour must not be mere buffoonery and the regret must not become a bitter lamentation. . . . Refined without affectation, polite without servility ; often conventional, but never dull. . . . There must be no rough inversions tearing the words from their due order merely to suit the exigencies of rhyme or metre. . . . And as to the rhymes themselves, they must have the appearance of being absolutely inevitable." [9] In his political verse he fought for Radicalism as Radicalism was understood in the Nineties. He wrote vigorously and gaily and often in retrospect he seems to have been on the right side without any profound knowledge of the Radical case. Only the very greatest satirist can overcome the difficulty that once the public fact is forgotten nobody is going to bother reading political verse with contemporary references in the footnotes. As so often happens in the history of *Punch*, the work that seemed important to a man at the time because it was a political act to write it is of no literary importance now. It is the Lehmann afloat that is remembered, not the man who wrote metrical comment on newspaper leaders in the library of the House of Commons.

Owen Seaman, Burnand's other new verse star, lacked Lehmann's charm and also his very definite poetic character. Seaman was an oarsman but he was not the laureate of boating like Lehmann. Equally politically-minded, he had a creed that tended to be a rather negative resistance to change, combined with a strongly-felt preference for the politicians of his own side. His strength was less in feeling and observation and gaiety and more in knowledge. He knew more about metre than Lehmann who, for all his versatility, was not an expert prosodist. When Seaman was young he had read widely and where he read he noticed. He never allowed a slack line ; he never allowed an ambiguity. His verses fell into two main groups. There was the formal poem or public exercise and here, especially later when he became Editor, Seaman felt bound to be as marmoreal as possible. Marmoreal verse may have suited Rome ; it did not suit England. All one can say of Seaman's formal exequies and hymns of homage is that they were tasks carried out none-the-less carefully for being misconceived. The classical influence in them was strong and sometimes they read as though they were intended to be the English translation of Latin poems or even to provide exercises in Latin verse composition.

Seaman's other main type of poem was the mocking comment on speeches, generally foolish speeches, or other news items. Though in time these became mechanical and in his decline unreadable, at first they had a bite and a rather ruthless gaiety that was impressive. He used his considerable knowledge to draw uncomfortable comparisons. He often had a damaging quotation up his sleeve. He could work out logically the full implications of a foolish statement. While he was still keeping up with books and plays and events and talking to plenty of different kinds of people his verses were good knock-about political journalism. Few men could possibly produce the amount of work he did and keep consistently fresh and vivacious. He is as much entitled to be judged by the best years of his poetry as he is by the best years of his editing.

There is one further point to be made about Seaman as a writer of light verse. In any study of the history of *Punch* it is difficult to judge work by both contemporary and non-contemporary standards. Sometimes we can see what contemporaries saw in a man, even though we cannot see it ourselves. Sometimes no effort at all will recapture the frame of mind of the original reader. Seaman's public was wide and enthusiastic for many years. If you read some of the light verse of the decade before him and then come upon him as he was when he was fresh and confident, you realise how very much better he was than most of his rivals. His verse was nearly always extensive. He wrote oratorically, taking time to make his points and space to drive them home. He wrote easily, polished intensely, and thought nothing of producing thirteen quatrains for his weekly poem.

He liked the slower metres and this added to the general air of deliberation. Marble must not race. He was an expert metrist, but curiously unadventurous in exploring new metres. The key word was often held back to the end of the stanza and then was frequently slang or some mild incongruity. The sudden shorter line, taken over from Calverley, had the effect of making, as it were, two streams of thought run through the poem, the more frivolous getting the shorter line. Parenthesis and relative clauses used either homely or incongruous illustrations or added more personal barbs to the outraged civic conscience of the major denunciations. Seaman's rhyming was in the fashion of the day, elaborate. The ingenuity in finding rhymes palled and so did the sacrifice of wit to a startling line-ending ; but there was in this late-Victorian frolic in verse a kind of juvenescence. Rhyme had been used for so long as an invisible and preferably unobtrusive emphasis or mnemonic. Light verse, depending on the exaltation of the trivial, reinstated rhyme. Unfortunately, whereas emphasis on metre produced new tunes, the rhymes remained too often merely quaintly laborious. The really ingenious rhyme needs very plain surroundings to set it off.

F. Anstey was primarily a prose writer ; in light verse he used the observant rather than the fantastic side of his mind. *Mr. Punch's Model Music Hall Songs* were based on carefully listening to the kind of thing that roused audiences. They were admired for their accuracy. To-day one is tempted to imagine that they are actual songs. The music halls of Anstey's day were numerous and the turns were numerous, and most of the turns were singers ambitious to be associated with a particular success. Before the mass reproduction of variety material, stars would sing the same song for years. Their fans were quite content that they should, as it was their only chance of hearing it. It was the thing to do to wander about London in and out of the music-halls, drinking in the bar and chatting with friends during the duller items, attending to the stage when some favourite performer was on. There were a large number of stars, who did several Halls a night, perhaps one of the big West End Halls and some of the local ones : London was still a congeries of localities. Men-about-town prided themselves on knowing some of the more obscure Halls. Anstey was a specialist appealing to fellow specialists.

The typical late-Victorian pleasure was the pleasure of recognition rather than the pleasure of being startled by novelty. The world was all right as long as Herbert Campbell was singing *They're all Very Fine and Large*. All Victorian reminiscences emphasise the importance of ritual, of the first shop on arrival at the family holiday resort (always the same resort), of the customs that gathered round weddings and christenings and funerals. This liking for the predicted explains some of the features of earlier *Punches* that are puzzling to-day. In our frantic belief that if a thing has been done once in a comic paper there is not much point in doing it again, we use up material at a tremendous rate and inculcate bad habits in readers. All *Punch* contributors long for the return of the time when one joke and one form could last you a lifetime. It was this comfortable repetitiveness that made it possible for Anstey to classify his imitations and to depend on his readers to co-operate. Many of the songs were presented in a framework of criticism. In most of his work Anstey was hostile to the pit and the gallery. He pilloried what he considered unlovely attitudes, like being against dukes or dropping aitches or going on strike ; but there was quite a lot of patronising affection in his reports from the music-hall as well.

NO. IV.—THE IDYLLIC[10]

The following example will not be found above the heads of an average audience, while it is constructed to suit the capacities of almost any lady *artiste*

SO SHY!

*The singer should, if possible, be of mature age, and incline to a comfortable embonpoint. As soon as the bell has given the signal for the orchestra to attack the prelude, she will step upon the stage with that air of being hung on wires, which seems to come from a consciousness of being a favourite of the public.*

I'm a dynety little Dysy of the Dingle,
(*Self-praise is a great recommendation—in Music-Hall songs.*
So retiring and so timid and so coy
If you ask me why so long I have lived single,
I will tell you—'tis because I am so shoy.
(*Note the skill with which the rhyme is adapted to meet Arcadian peculiarities of pronunciation.*

SPOKEN— Yes, I am—really, though you wouldn't think it to look at me, would you? But, for all that,—
CHORUS—When I'm spoken to, I wriggle,
Going off into a giggle,
And as red as any peony I blush;
Then turn paler than a lily,
For I'm such a little silly,
That I'm always in a flutter or a flush!
(*After each chorus an elaborate step-dance, expressive of shrinking maidenly modesty.*

E. J. Milliken's '*Arry* poems also reproduced things heard; they attacked the Cad and to modern taste are themselves rather vulgar. The hatred behind them was less controlled than du Maurier's; but it was not aroused simply by a threat to throw the writer's exclusive Eden open to the hoi polloi. They were attacking something evil in itself. 'Arry did not know the value of what he conquered. He was beyond such taming as even Sir Gorgius Midas responded to. He would destroy, and destroy without the passion that might build replacements. He would be responsible for ribbon development and for hooliganism. He was not poor. He had quite a lot of expensive pleasure. He was not pitiable, like some of du Maurier's butts. He represented vulgarity and pretension and it was an illusion that he was particularly English. Starting in the Autumn of 1877, the *'Arry* papers began rather low down the social scale and, as Spielmann points out, attacked vulgarity in higher and higher spheres in the same dialect, a mistake from which Milliken was either not adroit enough or too lazy to extricate himself. Modern editing has made one conscious of this kind of problem, which seems to have affected Victorian writers very little. Herr C. Stoffel of Nijmegen published a philological volume on the *'Arry* papers from 1883 to 1889, and it may be that their value is mainly linguistic, though Milliken said that his use of slang was not scientific. In a letter quoted by Spielmann, he said, "*'Arry* the essential cad is not a creature to be laughed at or with."

### 'ARRY AT THE SEA-SIDE[11]

But now, I am off to the Pier, Charlie. Boat's coming in from
Boolong,
And I wouldn't miss that not for nothink. The wind blows a little
bit strong,
And there's bound to be lots on 'em quisby, some regular goners,
dessay ;
And it *is* sech a lark to chi-ike them, the best bit o' fun of the day.

Old jokers in sealskin caps, Charlie, drawn over their poor blue old
ears,
Pooty gals with complexions like paste-pots, old mivvies gone
green with the queers ;
Little toffs with their billycocks raked, jest to swagger it off like,
yer know,

But with hoptics like badly-biled whelks. Oh, I tell yer it's all a prime show. . . .

## V

During the editorship of Burnand there was far more variety of content and of standard in prose than in verse. This was not one of the great periods of English prose. There was no prose technique of the period to compare with the light verse technique and articles stuck pretty generally to a straightforward exposition of the subject matter. *Punch* was much better written than most papers. It is just that under Lemon and in our own time the writing is better still. In the early days of Burnand the outsider was welcome. It was upon a foundation of occasional writers that *Punch* rested and this foundation was both a strength and a weakness. It meant that all kinds of experience could provide copy for *Punch*. It also meant that the professional qualities of drive and variation were lacking. It was unfortunate that some jokes of domestic triviality which could be managed only by the better writers so often attracted the less practised pens, which would have been much better off with more *outré* subjects. On the whole *Punch* gained far more than it lost by the encouragement of the man who wrote *Punch* articles just because he wanted to.

Some articles started from something in the news, some from something in the individual experience of the writer. Some articles were fictional in form, even though this might be merely to provide the framework of an imaginary conversation in the course of which the comic idea was developed. One common type of article took some stupidity from a speech and applied it with absurd literalness. There were burlesques of types of newspaper article and burlesques of particular series of articles appearing at the time. Sometimes the bulk of a *Punch* issue derived directly from the newspapers. The dramatic form, whether in burlesqueing plays, reproducing conversations, or for low-life documentaries, was very popular with writers, partly because it avoided connectives and long introductions. Although there were still little paragraphs of varying length scattered about, often based on political puns, there were fewer of them. It was not till towards the very end of Burnand's Editorship that the scattered jokes were collected together in *Charivaria*.

The straight essay was rare before E. V. Lucas. The humour of unconscious humour was used only occasionally, but it was always there ready, generally in the form of the funny old book article or the English phrase-book article. Once Burnand had invented the article of personal incompetence and misadventure it attracted much too large a proportion of the writers. Everybody who had ever been bad at anything seemed to think they could recover their prestige by being funny about it in print. As with other kinds of work, the clutter of inferior stuff masked what deserves to survive. Some of the funniest articles ever published have described the difficulties of daily living. There is no reason whatever why an article about a husband and wife at breakfast or about a tennis party at the vicarage should not be funny. Marriage is a large part of most readers' lives and at breakfast the couple are together whereas they are normally parted for most of the day. In the average English village, and until fairly recently the bulk of the population lived in villages, the vicarage was a social centre for the middle class and a tennis party was a normal occasion for meeting in the summer. Nobody complains that Molière was always using the family sitting room as the scene of his comedies or that the Restoration dramatists overdid the gaming house or the piazza of Covent Garden.

In the Eighties, Burnand was still keen and active and his own work was gay, vigorous, and not confined to punning. *Another Little Holiday Cruise* [12] was a good piece of reporting. Burnand was describing a yachting holiday in the Hebrides and the jokes and puns were fixed on a firm foundation of descriptive narrative. He had a Dickensian eye. " We are shown to our cabins. Mine is palatial. It is situated ' aft ' and has the curious appearance of having been built in perspective. The cupboard-doors, the drawers, the lockers and washstand are all slanting towards the point of sight." Again : " Crayley is the other passenger, our ' Fourth Party,' a thin, delicate-looking man, who changes in different lights—(*Happy Thought*—He might bring himself out as a natural entertainment, called 'The Human Chameleon.' Shan't suggest this to him, as, on a short acquaintance, he mightn't like it. Doubt if he would like it any better on a longer acquaintance)—and presents himself in various aspects, from twenty-seven up to fifty, and of whom no one ever sees more than half at a time, as he has a way of doing everything sideways, so that he is always in profile."

The characters of the four yachtsmen and of some of the crew were struck off with a masterly casualness. The jokes, newer then than now, still seem sharper than other people's. The places visited were picked out economically with vivid detail and the detail, like the comparisons, was humorous. The puns were kept under and the rattle of reference to contemporary events, the theatre and the gossip of the Town provided more than a convulsive joviality. An episode in which a piano-tuner was taken for the pilot did not suffer as much as one would expect from the fact that the pay-off was visible to all but the most unsophisticated right from the start. Indeed, and this is where one's respect for Burnand grows yet again, there remained the possibility of a double twist, of the man's turning out to be the pilot after all. Burnand did not, as so many writers of pay-off articles do, think that if the last line were funny there was no need to be funny before it. Like all the best *Punch* men, he realised that the reader was there all through and that though his enjoyment might not be complete till the end, he could reasonably expect to be entertained at each separate stage.

R. C. Lehmann's prose had the virtues I have already mentioned in his verse. It is important to distinguish his work from that of his imitators. In his day he invented something, the article of relaxed tone that joked about domestic occasions. The fact that forty years later infinitely inferior writers were producing Lehmann's type of article week after week does not reduce his originality. He could hit quite hard as a political satirist, but generally he wrote in *Punch* about holidays or home life. His combination of ability and casualness suited the deliberate avoidance of fundamentals in Burnand's

*Punch. Conversational Hints For Young Shooters,*[13] like the rowing poems, dealt with experiences common among a much narrower society than Lemon and Jerrold had aimed at. The assumption they showed of being addressed to an inner circle and their even, assured tone made them the classical models of the new *Punch*. This was how a gentleman should joke to other gentlemen about field sports. This was university education among a class to whom it was neither an economic necessity nor an opportunity for satisfying the higher curiosities.

*Mr. Punch's Prize Novels,*[14] one of the series with which Lehmann made his mark, was rather slapdash but it had a cheerful bounce whatever its deficiencies in similitude. The Kipling allowed Lehmann's political feelings to appear and was all the better for it. His radicalism was anti-imperialist and the disapproval that kept him firmly in opposition to the Boer War was apparent in his contemptuous attitude to the imperialist literature that preceded it. In the Haggard burlesque, this attitude had the curious result of making what is incidental in the original the focus of the imitation. The Haggard characters and narrative are almost unrecognisable. Some of Lehmann's most attractive articles were the ones in which he was most closely followed by Milne, the casual husband-wife discussions. These continued quite late and showed no diminution of power. (What gave each piece of Lehmann's more domestic humour its quality was that the material was only a part of the writer's total subject-matter. The man who can or does write only one type of thing will show this narrowness in each example. The versatile man will bring freshness to each example of every type that he attempts.)

The degree of tension and density of humorous writing under Burnand were those of contemporary entertainment. To-day on the variety stage this slackness survives and is popular. Behind the American cult of speed and attack there still lives on the English tradition that humour needs a strolling pace, that it depends on a slow build-up and aims at an amused grin. After the taut styles of Jerrold and Brooks came a period when taste preferred the extensive, the ruminative and the accumulative. In this century, serious prose and verse tightened up a generation before humorous prose and verse ; but it is too rigid reading to condemn Lehmann, for instance, because he did not belong to the schools of either Hazlitt or of Percy Wyndham Lewis.

F. Anstey, sometimes called by his full name of Thomas Anstey Guthrie—the " F " was originally a compositor's mistake for " T " which Anstey decided to adopt—was a self-contained, amusing, enigmatic little man, long remembered in *Punch* circles for his entertaining stories and his kindnesses to children. His autobiography suggests that having some small private means allowed him to refuse to compete. Bad reviews of his work he accepted as reasonable and he was much too easily convinced that his humour dated. In later life, his adaptations of Molière, like his curious versions of Dürer drawings, showed a mind obstinately original in small things. He suffered from an early success that imperceptive critics wanted to see repeated. *Vice Versa* was written very young and his later books, in quite different styles, were insufficiently powerful to force readers to revise their idea of him. (It needed a Dickens to escape from being type-cast as the man who wrote *Pickwick*.) Anstey was a popular member of the Staff, who dropped out gradually as he began to fear that he was repeating himself.

His novels were generally farces fulfilling James Agate's definition by exhibiting ordinary people in extraordinary circumstances. An initial invention, often some magical device, led to a series of brilliantly-constructed situations in which late-Victorian types, drawn with the greatest care, were puzzled and perplexed and tormented. Anstey has something in common with Labiche. In *Punch* he wrote some narratives in a loose form ; but no closely constructed serial has ever run in *Punch*, perhaps because of its large casual sales. This is a pity. Magazine readers have shown themselves quite capable of following a plot from week to week and fiction would have provided a whole new range of comic possibilities. Anstey did a tremendous amount of work for *Punch* and it is a pity that he would not use that side of his invention which produced his farcical novels. His comic talent could not compare with Burnand's for vigour but he had style and gaiety and an invention perfectly controlled at a lowish level of power. Anstey under-rated himself badly, but at least he always worked within a carefully maintained framework of quality.

His best known series, which merged into sub-series with separate names, was *Voces Populi*.[15] These were reports in dramatic form of things overheard. He went to an unemployed demonstration or the theatre or the zoo and, taking a few overheard remarks and a few characters, he produced a little playlet in which the humour was that in the original experience. It was almost a kind of letter-writing. Rarely, probably too rarely, he used the dramatic form for a short story or fantasy or as a vehicle for detached jokes. It was the accuracy of the *Voces Populi* which, like the accuracy of the music-hall songs, amused and impressed. Anstey said, " All I have consciously tried for was to present commonplace characters and conversations and incidents as humorously as I could, and with as little exaggeration or misrepresentation as possible."[16]

There were complaints that the *Voces Populi* were new-fangled. This was absurd, like many complaints of its kind. No paper has had more loyal readers than *Punch* and, alas, no paper has been afflicted with more stupid ones. The dramatic form was used years and years before Anstey. Shirley Brooks used it brilliantly. *Voces Populi* will always be of interest to the social historian, and, compared with some of the material that Elizabethan social historians have to use, it will provide considerable entertainment for students. To modern taste some of Anstey's other contributions, with their greater comic tension and density, are preferable. The very merits, the accuracy and immediacy, of the *Voces Populi*, have made them fade fast and they are now, perhaps, in the trough between acceptance as humour and acceptance as historical evidence. Read, not for laughs, but for interest, they should enjoy a second and considerably longer life.

Another successful form that Anstey used, was Baboo English. The grandiloquence of imperfectly-learned English when used by an Oriental accustomed to more florid language is less familiar now, presumably as language-teaching in Asia has improved. Anstey caught the Oriental student at his prime. He showed him in Bloomsbury making attempts to adapt himself to a half-comprehended English life. Because the humour was partly verbal it wears better than some of the straight reproductions of things heard. There was no racial superiority, no colour-bar in Anstey's humour. The Baboo's enthusiasm was ridiculous and had to be ridiculed. Twenty years later all kinds of patronising and hurtful reticences would have prevented the publication of the series, twenty years in which Britain had grown more wounding to its subjects overseas. There was a wonderful burlesque of a society romance as written by a Baboo, called *A Bayard from Bengal*,[17] which shows Anstey's wild humour at its best. Like all *Punch* prose-writers Anstey left masses of dead among the files—all that work and then in a week it's done. A tremendous amount of good humorous writing got overlooked because the suppression of authorship prevented the reader from building up any coherent picture of a man's work outside his main series.

An agreeable example of the more imaginative and light-hearted Anstey was his *Vi-Kings Essence*[18] remotely suggested by an Ibsen production.

" ACT I . . . *A rocky coast on the island of Helgeland.*

*Enter* SIGURD

SIGURD Bluish-white is the rock—though all round it is blackest fog. Ha ! I see a ray of faint light. In it will I take my stand. (*He does. Enter* ÖRNULF)

ÖRNULF Give place, Viking. In this play mine is the finest part. Therefore need I more light than thou.

SIGURD Nay, though must even find a ray of light for thyself, outlaw ! . . .

KÅRE (*a peasant, enters and throws himself at* Ö*'s feet in abject terror*) Grant me protection ! On my tracks is HIÖRDIS. One of GUNNAR's house-carls have I slain, because he flouted me for a thrall.

ÖRNULF That is the least that *any* gentleman could do on being flouted for a thrall. Here cometh GUNNAR. Leave this to me. I will arrange it with him. (GUNNAR *comes in*)

GUNNAR What, SIGURD ! my foster-brother ! This is indeed an unexpected—and ÖRNULF, *too* ! Well wot I what thou hast come about—that affair of HIÖRDIS.

ÖRNULF Open am I to an amicable arrangement, for a good riddance in sooth was she !

GUNNAR No wish have I to haggle, greybeard, but right willingly will I pay the damage, whatever it be.

ÖRNULF I will but charge thee my out-of-pocket expenses. Now make thou peace with KÅRE here, or else, most reluctantly, shall I be compelled to—"

The most famous contribution of the Burnand period was *The Diary of a Nobody* in 1888.[19] It was written by George and Weedon Grossmith ; many people, including Rosebery, thought it was by Burnand, an interesting reminder of the intelligent contemporary view of him. Though *The Diary* is now regarded as a minor classic of English fiction—stage adaptations recently have leant on affection for its well-known characters and period charm—it first appeared with an editorial note showing its aim was to burlesque memoirs by nonentities. In the early years of the century, under the title of *Extra Pages*, *Punch* printed quite a number of stories by well-known writers under their own names. These included Barry Pain, Somerset Maugham and Frank R. Stockton. Perhaps the most unexpected contributor to these pages was Henry James, whose *Mrs. Medwin*[20] appeared under his own name in four instalments in 1901. It was a little tale of an American woman in London who sponsored social climbers, and of her disreputable brother whose attraction for one of the great hostesses was used to make her accept an undesirable client. It was not The Master at his best. What on earth did the readers make of it ? Its texture was so different from that of the surrounding columns. It must have seemed even more oblique, less intelligible, half a century ago. All the same, it was a brave, wild stroke of editing and it was a pity that *Punch* did not strike out in this way more often.

## VI

Under Burnand's editorship there was a steady increase of illustration, from the time when apart from the cartoons there were just a small number of star contributions in a predominantly verbal paper to the time when the text for many readers was merely "something to keep the pictures apart." Burnand's increasing dilatoriness was complained of as making topical drawings out of date, but on the whole the artists seem to have been fairly satisfied with him. They submitted rough sketches and, if he approved them, they produced finished drawings, which were not paid for until publication. He would make up the illustrations for the pages a month ahead and then go off on holiday. He would sometimes send suggestions from the office to appropriate contributors. He did not consider he could be expected to have much technical knowledge. Like the average reader, he felt he could judge the realism of the drawing. There is a legend that the first Art Editor, F. H. Townsend, was appointed in 1905 by the proprietors without telling the Editor. The legend has been criticised on the grounds that Burnand had so fiery a conception of editorial independence that he would have flared up and insisted either on the Art Editor's being removed or on resigning himself. Perhaps the proprietors intended this. It is said that when the Directors invited him to meet them for any business discussion he simply replied that they knew perfectly well where he could be found. Little seems to be known about his personal relations with Townsend.

Townsend was a shy, kindly man who thought that nobody could tell really whether anything was funny or not. He used to say "Sometimes comes funny, sometimes doesn't." [21] He was conscious, perhaps too conscious, of his literary limitations. His conception of his job was that his main duty was keeping the inner ring of artists fully employed. There were not enough small pictures to train new men and when the inner ring had been provided with work there was not much opportunity for a young man to settle down to make a career of drawing for *Punch* as the rates were comparatively low and to live a man needed a weekly commission for at least half a page. There was a tendency to keep men on too long, as there was no pension scheme, and then when they had to be replaced it would be found that there was nobody coming along. One result of this was an artistic time-lag.

Down to late in the Nineteenth Century a handful of the *Punch* men had been very considerable draughtsmen and they had generally grown up in fairly close relationship with the leading " serious " artists. Then serious drawing changed and eventually humorous drawing with it, but not in *Punch*. The successors of the great men, instead of drawing in their own way, tried to imitate the generation before. Of course one cannot reasonably expect a close relation between the development of " serious " drawing and of drawing in a popular magazine ; but a time-lag of more than ten years seems unreasonable. Yet even as late as the middle Thirties *Punch* drawing had changed surprisingly little from the early Seventies. Townsend probably thought about *Punch* art in very much the same way that Burnand did. The only difference was that he drew himself and in a way that he would not have drawn if he had received no training : one of his modern successors has said, " He drew like an angel." He did not regard it as any part of his duties to train *Punch* artists. His job was to select work. The expertise demanded from the modern Art Editor, with so many technical problems of reproduction caused by the multiplication of media, was only just beginning to become urgently necessary.

A refusal to look at the work of other artists sometimes ended in a refusal to look at the world at all. Tenniel's insistence on drawing statesmen or machines as they were when he had first seen them was paralleled by the treatment of rural women or Kensington children, who, even after the First World War, were only superficially different from those in drawings of sixty years before. A few artists prided themselves on accurately recording changes of fashion in dress or hair-styles but many blandly assumed that a few inches more or less on the skirt was all that was required.

Nobody could draw like Keene and no good draughtsman would have tried. It is true that Keene himself was influenced by Menzel, but he was essentially a skilled hand that owed perfect obedience to a wonderful eye. It seems to be a pretty general rule that great draughtsmen bear very little resemblance to other draughtsmen while lesser men work best while they follow what is the vital movement of their time. The great man can be Ingres or Courbet; the lesser man has to be an Impressionist in an Impressionist period and a Post-Impressionist in a Post-Impressionist period. Burnand's and Townsend's artists too often tried to be imitations of Lemon's artists. The most successful example of discipleship was probably Gunning King, a follower of Keene, whom Kenneth Bird considers under-rated. His rural backgrounds may have been outdated when he drew, but his vision of them was contemporary. He was a good mid-Victorian illustrator forty years on, as in the famous "*Sometimes I sits and thinks; and then again I just sits.*"[22] *Punch* artists had less and less curiosity about what their colleagues in other fields were doing, and this isolation was paralleled by the curious jokes in the paper about "Modern Art," which changed very little until the end of World War II. One difficulty that must in fairness be mentioned was that, from the Nineties of the last century to the Forties of this, contemporary art was far less representational than ever before or since. The illustrators were left high and dry. It was not until after 1937 that the humorous possibilities of early Twentieth Century art were seized, and then they were seized nearly a generation late.

As Lucy pointed out, the invention of the electric telegraph was increasing the importance of topicality, and the gap between the decision on the cartoon and its publication became more serious. In 1895 Swain was getting the cartoon-drawing from Tenniel about five p.m. on Fridays. It then had to be photographed upon the wood, engraved and delivered to the printers by Saturday evening.

*Punch* has been caught remarkably few times, though occasionally printing has had to be stopped and the cartoon changed after the issue has been put to bed. Sometimes the unfortunate artist has had to prepare two cartoons. One bad bit of luck was the guess that Gordon would be saved in time. All too often the cartoons have had to be diplomatically vague. It was said in the office that the only safe title to a cartoon was *For this relief much thanks*. Anything not covered by this title could be dealt with by a picture of *The Walrus and the Carpenter*. The political power of *Punch* had declined only very, very slowly, and to some extent the influence of Lucy supported and reinforced the power of the cartoon. As late as 1897, a cartoon questioning British " Forward Policy " on the North-West Frontier drew a letter from Lord Roberts arguing the case and asking to be allowed to talk over his views with Lucy or with the Editor if he would kindly allow him to do so. Cabinet Ministers and Field Marshals still thought it worth taking trouble to have *Punch* on their side.

While Tenniel was doing one cartoon and Sambourne the other, the similarity between their aims narrowed the range of the paper, and when Tenniel retired in 1901, he left so strong a tradition behind him that for half the Twentieth Century *Punch* continued to print cartoons which ignored the development of caricature completely. Leech had died financially embarrassed and the Prime Minister he had attacked rather condescendingly gave his family a Civil List pension and his son a nomination for the Charterhouse. Tenniel's position was very different. Lucy tried and failed to get a knighthood for him out of Salisbury in time for the *Punch* Jubilee ; he succeeded with Gladstone. Tenniel was reluctant to accept the honour but was persuaded by the argument that it was really given to *Punch*. When he retired in 1901 he was given a public dinner with Balfour in the Chair. He spent nearly two months composing and learning his speech but broke down after a few words, moving his hearers more than all the eloquence of the other speakers, though he brooded until his death over what he considered the most humiliating failure of his life. Among other tributes on this occasion to the man and the paper, the Duke of Devonshire described Gladstone's bringing a copy of *Punch* into the Cabinet council and laughing over the cartoon.

Bernard Partridge was a new man with an outside reputation. He was brought on to the paper by Burnand on the recommendation of Anstey and du Maurier, who admired his work as an illustrator. Son of a President of the Royal College of Surgeons, he was educated at Stonyhurst. He entered an architect's office and then a firm of stained-glass designers, where he studied drapery and ornament. He began working on church ornament under Philip Westlake. For some time he could not decide finally between the theatre and art as a career. As an actor under the name " Bernard Gould " he appeared in the first production of *Arms and the Man*. He did all kinds of editorial drawing for *Punch* such as illustrating dramatic criticism. He did *Social Cuts* in the tradition of du Maurier and was a personal and professional disciple of his. He belonged, that is to say, to the tradition of reproducing reality, not of distorting it. The point of the joke underneath, generally a social point, was reinforced by the social accuracy of the drawing. (His illustrations to the reprint of Anstey's *A Bayard from Bengal* showed considerable comic invention.) He was one of the first artists to adapt himself to the new methods of reproduction, and as he realised that delicate variations of tone had gone for ever with wood engraving, he made the best of process with his striking blacks ; but he complained bitterly : " I do not keep drawings while *Punch* is so abominably printed—I think worse than any illustrated paper in England—except perhaps, *Scraps*, *Snapshots*, etc. and there is no earthly inducement to do one's best work. If one *does* do a respectable drawing it's murdered in the reproduction or printing or both : and all one can do is to produce work that will fairly well bear the rough treatment of the *Punch* printing press. I have tried taking trouble to do better work, but the result is lamentable. And it seems hopeless to agitate for reform. Paper, surface, machining—all are unable to grapple with the difficulties of modern ' process ' which poor old penny *Pick-Me-Up* mastered so well long ago." [23] His world of swells and formal clothes and sharply-defined features is the world of the great black-and-white magazine-illustrators of the end of the

ILLUSTRATION TO ANSTEY'S
*VOCES POPULI*

*8th August, 1891* *Bernard Partridge*

century. It is a familiar world to anyone who, as a child, turned over a family collection of magazines.

So much of his early work has been forgotten that his real talent has been neglected. When he succeeded to the second cartoon he seemed to feel it his duty to be purely a servant of the Table. He did not want to become a cartoonist and felt himself unfitted for the post. He modelled himself on Tenniel, who admired his draughtsmanship, and he dutifully produced cartoons for nearly half a century, but the waste was sad. He believed a cartoon needed " a simple statement of theme, with a corresponding treatment making an instant and direct appeal to the reader ; a sense of drama and of humour with powers of draughtsmanship and facility in portraiture, catching the essentials of a face in a few mocking lines ".[23a] In a letter of 1939, he wrote : " I am under no illusions about my work, which I know to be really very second-rate stuff. The subject matter is not often of my own conceiving and as to the execution it resolves itself into a strenuous stand-up fight against a rigid time-table . . . so that I feel I am little more than a hack draughtsman." [24] Partridge inherited from Tenniel the tradition that the principal cartoonist was a grand old man. He managed to become one quite young. He survived until long after grand old men had become unfashionable but he is remembered as being courteous and full of reminiscences that he would offer diffidently, slightly surprised if his listener assured him he was not bored. His knighthood in 1925 was deserved and appropriate. He was an utterly reliable craftsman, never wrong on a uniform, never late, always worrying about the job. He never quite lost the old-squire floridness that marked those who had acted with Irving. His cartoons were theatrical, whereas Sambourne's, and still more Raven Hill's, were dramatic. He liked a massive figure, coming down to the footlights and performing some feat at once classical and muscular, like hurling defiance. Once he was instructed to draw some politician as Ajax defying the lightning, with a small Ajax and a vast sky. He produced a towering figure with his head almost on the edge of the page and a little lightning just visible between the legs.

As he grew older he simplified his work, and showed brilliant ingenuity in edging discussion at the Table away from any cartoon that involved more than two figures. He had some of the simplicity that the older generation of artists shared with actors. It went with concentration on a job. He liked living in style, with elaborate formal entertainments—at one time his dinner parties were the longest in London. He was too courteous to protest against changes but most of his life was spent in a period of very rapid change. The fall in the value of money must have hit him badly, for *Punch* rates were never raised to give the same relative predominance to *Punch* men as they had enjoyed among journalists in the Seventies and Eighties and prices for his originals cannot have remained high. Yet no bitterness disturbed his unchanging execution of the commissions laid upon him. The worst excesses of the Twentieth Century were reflected in composition learned from teachers who thought in terms of frescoes of scenes in Roman history. The *George V Memorial Number*, which consisted largely of Partridge cartoons, showed the cumulative results of this curious procedure and did some damage to *Punch*'s prestige. I can remember an awed foreigner who refused to believe on this evidence that the British could regard *Punch* as a humorous magazine. At the suggestion that the adjective was not "humorous" but "satirical" he threw up his hands in defeat. Yet if the name Partridge conjures up an image of the grandiose, the competent and the lifeless, it must be remembered that he embarked on a new career against his better judgment and out of misplaced loyalty, so that the blame for the wasting of his very considerable gifts must lie with others.

The embellishments of *Punch* have always been one of the features that, while not consciously noticed by many readers, help to build up the general effect. The initials and borders and frontispieces and headings have provided opportunities for realism or grotesque invention unlimited by the need for a quotable joke. The illustrations to the criticisms and the serials have also given a chance to the man who is primarily an illustrator. Sitting in the stalls and catching a likeness on a first night is a knack, though some artists, given the dramatic criticism to illustrate, have pursued the actors into their dressing-rooms or based their work on photographs. On the whole, the space given to illustrations in the notices of plays has been devoted

**BLUFF AND IRON**

*The Old Chancellor: "Not my methods exactly, but you seem to have nearly the same success."*

to resemblance. The caricature element has been slight. *Punch* dramatic criticism has usually tried to constitute a record as well as a valuation and it is the record that is illustrated. Of these illustrators in Burnand's time, Partridge was probably the happiest. E. J. Wheeler, who did hundreds of little illustrations to articles and sometimes to dramatic criticisms in the Eighties and Nineties, struck Spielmann as old-fashioned, but to-day one can appreciate both his period charm and a smooth grotesquerie that might sometimes be early Tenniel. After Sambourne, who was unable to meet Lucy's demand for drawing on the spot, Harry Furniss illustrated the *Essence of Parliament*. He was probably the most famous of *Punch*'s parliamentary draughtsmen but no better than some of his successors on a page where the standard was always high. During the years of his *Punch* work, Harry Furniss dominated the pages. He was all over the place with jokes, illustrations, dramatic criticisms, headings and parliamentary sketches. He was a very experienced pictorial journalist who could work fast and get a likeness easily. It is said that he would chat to a man and caricature him on a pad held in his pocket. He knew everybody and built up the same kind of position in the House as Lucy. He was a good mimic. (It would be interesting to know how many men who can catch a likeness on paper can also imitate.)

He was an amusing companion, a tremendous worker and an expert in his field. Fiery-headed, fiery-hearted and cool-brained, he could be very good fun at the Table in a noisy kind of way, but then some fancied slight would turn him to a mean violence. He was cantankerous, overbearing and pushing. He toured England with lectures on *The Frightfulness of Humour* and *Humours of Parliament*, delivered with imitations, and his colleagues were sometimes wearied by being expected to wait anxiously for news of the attendances in the obscurer Scottish towns. He got involved in most complicated quarrels. He was very conscious of having made a name before he came into *Punch*. He complained that Burnand had forced him to give up working for other Editors and then refused him an agreement, trying to turn him into an outsider, working on sale or return. This repeated the pattern of Lemon's failure with W. S. Gilbert, and at least Gilbert was not a member of the Staff at the time. Furniss got up from the *Punch* table one day, said he would be back in an hour and never returned. He left, partly because his unstable nature needed change, partly because he could not work in a team, partly because he wanted a paper of his own, and partly over an incomprehensible quarrel with the proprietors about rights. The copyright of his famous drawing of the tramp who is writing a testimonial to soap manufacturers—*I used your soap two years ago; since then I have used no other* [25]—was sold by the firm to Pears for advertising. (There had been a previous row over it as Keene had insisted, quite humourlessly, that the tramp was intended to be him.) Heaven forbid that any *Punch* contributor should not hold strongly that all possible rights should be retained by an artist, however many he may have taken money for; but anybody who has read the correspondence between Furniss and his employers will find himself thinking that the artist was being dictatorial and slick and the businessmen patient and disinterested.

His own magazine, *Lika Joko*, called after one of his *Punch* pseudonyms, started briskly but never managed to attract the loyalty of other *Punch* men, though he had one or two promising beginners, including E. V. Lucas and C. L. Graves. *Lika Joko* lacked much distinction beyond his own work, and that could not support it for very long. He lost his Gallery Ticket on leaving *Punch* and was refused one for *Lika Joko*, which, as his reputation as a political caricaturist was carrying the new paper, proved fatal to it. Furniss made a lot of money but lost most of it writing, producing and acting in films in England and America. He worked for the Edison Company and on his own, and took a formative part in film journalism and controversies, fighting for the recognition of the importance of a well-built scenario and of constructing the story in terms of a visual medium. He had the streak of genius and ruthlessness needed in the early days but he was hysterically resistant to advice. He lived to be old and complacent. His autobiographical volumes are still readable because of the strength of the personality behind them. He had an appetite for life. His fierce interest in old plays, old clubs and old characters bring the London of *Pink 'Un* days vividly to life. Somebody ought to collect a volume of his best sketches as a companion to the history of the period. The

*30th July, 1887* *Harry Furniss*

DR. SPEAKER BIRCH AND HIS YOUNG PARLIAMENTARY FRIENDS.
GIVING IT THEM ALL ROUND.

influence of connoisseurs of drawing has restricted the reproduction of sketches from the late-Nineteenth Century primarily to draughtsmen with aesthetic quality. Historical illustration has been neglected. Nobody bothers about compiling a Victorian collection of views and portraits and maps of the kind that helps the imagination to recapture Tudor or Stuart England ; although Furniss was not a great draughtsman he did give the look of his time. Crafts, like inventions, often reach their highest polish after the rise of the development that supersedes them. The great days of coaches overlapped with the beginning of railways. The great days of the clippers came after steam had begun to replace sail. The great days of graphic journalism followed the invention of the photographic processes that killed it.

After Furniss, the next important illustrator to the *Essence of Parliament* was E. T. Reed, best remembered for his series of *Prehistoric Peeps*,[26] a new line in humorous art that has been imitated so much and had so much influence on advertising that it is hard to realise how original it was in its day. Reed was a very competent all-round artist, though he entered *Punch* as an amateur student encouraged by a chance remark of Linley Sambourne's to a friend that the Editor was looking out for a new man to do some comic work as Keene was dying. Reed brought something new into *Punch*. Instead of the low-life realism of the Keene tradition or the high-life realism of du Maurier tradition, Reed revived the original tradition of grotesque, but not fanciful, invention. He was a better Newman or Hine rather than a Doyle. He had a versatility in devising series that was badly needed. He was a reminder, as Burnand had once been, that after all *Punch* lived on comic ideas. His *Contrasts*[27] (*tricoteuses* and society women at a trial, etc.) often stung far more sharply than the work of the recognised satirist du Maurier. He joined the staff and worked up a number of Sir Frank Lockwood's legal sketches. Spielmann says the fluctuations in the quality of his work sometimes led to rumours he was leaving. However, one thing an editor of humour has to learn is the mysterious ebb and flow of merit in all but the very greatest of his contributors. Premature writing-off has lost some valuable talent. *Prehistoric Peeps* show how right *Punch* was to retain him, if this were not merely inertia—one never quite knew with Burnand. The accuracy of the palaeontology helped a good deal at the time. Fossils were still emotionally charged. It was a generation since *The Origin of Species* and there were still tensions to be released. Reed's work on the *Essence of Parliament*, though he did not make such a hit as Furniss, is a very agreeable surprise when examined in bulk. More modest, less melodramatic than his predecessor, he not only got likenesses, but some comic pressure behind the pencil transmitted itself without any of the mechanical distortions of the ordinary political caricaturist. His solid shapes, his dark foregrounds

*24th February, 1894* *E. T. Reed*

PREHISTORIC PEEPS.

*"No Bathing to-day!"*

against lighter backgrounds, springing out of the paper like a silhouette, pointed towards the hard poster-techniques of early Twentieth Century comic art, towards the methods of Tom Browne and the hunting artist Cecil Aldin.

In Burnand's early years the circulation of the paper depended heavily on du Maurier. For years English upper-class families rushed to see what du Maurier had done each week. *Punch* was one of the few experiences that children shared with their parents, and as they grew up they developed the same fund of good will towards du Maurier as an old music hall performer relies on during his later career. The success of the novels which he turned to when he feared his sight was failing began in America and spread back over the Atlantic. du Maurier was a strange, embittered man and a deep feeling that the novels were not as good work as he should be able to do soured him further. Every commercial triumph, every work overpraised, hammered home to him the difference between the young fellow-student of Whistler and the elderly best-seller. His colleagues were glad for his sake that the horror of a blind and poverty-stricken old age had been lifted and they shared in the reflected glory that *Punch* drew from his literary celebrity but they preserved the somewhat detached view of extra-curricular success which had needled Thackeray many years before. Burnand wrote to Lucy, " *Trilby* is, *as far as I have read it*, a decidedly clever as well as an interesting and amusing book, the freshness of the style being marred by the introduction of the *Commonest Cheapest* slang of the present day. . . . Had Thackeray had a bastard son in literature and had that bastard had another bastard in literature I think it possible that the last in this line might possibly have written *Trilby*." [28]

du Maurier was a man of genius hating himself for living comfortably on his talent. Easily depressed, disliking to be reminded of unpleasant things (which included politics, the dull and the new) and yet capable of terrifying pictorial nightmares, he showed hints of the abyss in unexpected places in his social cuts, and in the force behind inventions like Svengali. He avoided any meeting of minds in which his precariously-poised detachment might be shattered by the thrust of argument, though one of his two closest friends was Henry James. He lived in what was recently called " the smart art world " ; but there is no *Punch* man in whom cleverness and success masked potential greatness more. He was a Thackeray who produced *Trilby* instead of *Vanity Fair*.

The next big development in *Punch* art was Phil May. He was something quite fresh and it took time for *Punch* to absorb him. To the end it found him rather indigestible. May had been brought up hard in Leeds. His father was the son of a squire, but, after unsuccessfully entering George Stephenson's firm, he became a dabbler in water colours and business. His mother was the daughter of an Irish theatrical manager. May grew up against a background of family difficulties. As a cheerful urchin he drifted from job to job, always drawing. He first wanted to become a jockey. Then he did bits of acting and stage designing. He ended up begging in London. He tried to break his way into the art market with drawings of stage celebrities, made a little headway, fell ill and was thrown back to the beginning again.

It was his marriage at twenty-one that saved him. Relying on the strength of his wife, he began to get work and made enough of a name for the *Sydney Bulletin* to give him a job. Those years in Australia gave him a healthy climate, professional and social success and steady work. On his return to Europe, he wandered about sketching and did some book illustrating until *The Graphic* took him on. Now everybody wanted his work, which, among other advantages, was very easily reproduced. Like Keene, he was much admired in France. In 1892 he launched his first *Annual* and kept up the series until 1905. He turned up in *Punch* in 1893. It took two years for Spielmann to persuade Burnand to put him on the Staff. He was already established when *Punch* adopted him but, as with other contributors, the disappearance of many journals for which he worked creates the illusion that his work was restricted to *Punch*.

May worked very fast and would execute a delayed commission while the messenger waited for it. He squandered his vast earnings on cadgers and the invaluable originals of his drawings were given away and lost, though sometimes, after one of his Sunday afternoon receptions, Mrs. May would visit the guests and try to get back from them the drawings her husband had pressed them to take. He was usually paid in advance and never had any money, though he could always get a fiver at the *Sketch* by doing a drawing at the counter and cashing it like a cheque.

May drank heavily but not bitterly. He was a kindly, sociable person. Though he looked like a stable lad, he was much more musical than horsey. His face was deadly pale. He had beautiful hands. He lived in a fever of Nineties Bohemianism. Though he has been linked more with the *Pink 'Un* than the *Yellow Book* he was in fact a witty and intelligent lover of the arts. If London's Bohemia was genuinely the meeting place of the artistic and the raffish, May was one of the very few true Bohemians of the period. He died of a wasting disease caused by early malnutrition and hard drinking. At his death he weighed five stone. He was only thirty-nine and in the light of that some of the stories are not quite so funny—Mrs. May's waking up in the morning to find the hansom-cabby sleeping in the bed too, and all the rest. Though he was a single and exceptional break in the respectability of *Punch*, once the old boozing days of Lemon were over, he left a legend of the connection between drink and humour, a kind of " We won't go home till morning " spirit which, since the paper being produced was *Punch*, had no real literary expression.

Though May expressed his reverence for Keene [29]—" Keene is the Daddy of the lot of us "—and said " All that I know as an artist I learned from Sambourne," [30] he had little in common with either of them, though he " used the same bold, parallel lines of shading following the surface planes as Sambourne." [31] At first he did not join lines as skilfully but he gradually simplified this method, using a flatter and simpler tone throughout. He was something new, and it took time for people to realise that he occupied a place in the revival of book illustration in the Nineties corresponding with Keene's in the revival of the Sixties. It was not realised at first that he was a good artist as well as an amusing and prolific one. The basis of his work was an impression of certain kinds of appearance, especially the appearance of the slums in his youth. This impression was so strong as to resemble a photograph printed in the mind. It was summarised, with the important lines selected and put down fast. To an early Editor who asked, " Couldn't you finish up your drawings a bit more ? " May replied, " When I can leave out half the lines I now use, I shall want six times the money." [32] He converted the restrictions of pen-and-ink into strength. It seemed incredible that so few lines could do so much work. Phil May was one of the fathers of modern advertising design. He was the extreme

*Little Guttersnipe (who is getting quite used to posing): " Will yer want me ter tike my Bun down ? "*

reaction from du Maurier's crowded rectangles, from the kind of drawing in which the artist tries to leave signs of his labours in every square centimetre of his space. May made his paper work for him. Some of his pictures contained quite a lot of detail, but even so it was always the minimum detail. For lightning sketches, and for the odd sketches that led to the more elaborate work, he could begin anywhere and never hesitate. His more ambitious work was done slowly and built up from studies of models. His simplifications caught the eye. A Phil May picture sparked out from the page. He learned slowly and his spontaneity and speed were the result of constant practice.

He was mainly a descriptive artist and often there is really no detachable verbal joke. From his own experience he knew the humour of the slums and drew it. Often drawings that were straightforward representations, like a *New Yorker* "spot," were taken as funny on the general principle that guttersnipes and drunken charwomen were funny *per se*. May hated having to work to a caption and though many of his best jokes have become famous *as* jokes he would probably have preferred to be able to have a caption or not, as he liked. This lack of literary fulsomeness may have been another reason why many *Punch* readers at first welcomed him coldly. There was nothing much in Phil May for the stupid or unobservant and, like Keene, he was considered low. Once they got used to him, the younger readers liked him and he certainly attracted a new public who followed him to *Punch* knowing his other work. The Table was slightly wary of him, never knowing how he might behave or what adventure he might try to sweep them into. He was lovable but alarming and gradually he dropped out of the *Punch* sociabilities, very welcome when he appeared and for as long as he chose to stay, but a visitant from another world. He used to pinch a copy of the menu as evidence for his wife.

Under Burnand, and indeed under his successor, the joke drawing varied very little. There were always the oddments that fitted into no class but helped to give the paper variety and life, but the basic forms were few. There was the adaptation to various incongruous cases of some suggestion by a public man. There were dialogues between superiors and the inferiors, with the inferiors making mistakes. Superiors included parents and District Visitors ; inferiors, children and the Irish. Countrymen made mistakes when

*8th June, 1904* *F. H. Townsend*

**EXPLAINED.**

*Our Village Cricket Club, after the Opening Match*

*The Young Squire (who, at school, made a century against Harrow) : " I say, Spinner, I don't yet understand that first ball of yours that took my leg stump. Was I late, or should I have played forward ? "*

*Spinner (our demon left-hander) : " You couldn't 'ave done nothing with it, Sir."*

talking to gentry but scored off cockneys. Then there were written cross-talk acts, sometimes of considerable length, between two men in a club or two ladies at tea. Much more at this time than earlier, the typical *Punch* joke was the kind of joke that other papers published without illustration and *Punch* prided itself on the superiority of its jokes to others of the same kind found elsewhere.

The joke of social reference that throws light on changes in society was restricted to the upstart joke though this was given a bit of rest after du Maurier, who had worked it to death. Changes in society were regarded as outside the control of the individual and he could only attack them for happening or try to mitigate the rawness of those who benefited from them. There were seldom attacks on the financial dealings by which new wealth managed to buy country houses and set up as a judge of horseflesh, but only laughter at the corrigible mistakes of imitation squires. The illustration was always competent and it was always lucid. The total effect of each drawing by such steady contributors as G. H. Jalland and Reginald Cleaver varied on the whole with the quality of the joke.

F. H. Townsend was in a way the archetype of *Punch* artists of the period, an extremely efficient art-school artist who made a picture that was always recognisable and accomplished but rarely memorable. Townsend's brother-in-law, Fred Pegram, was his equal as a naturalistic draughtsman. Where, at least in rural backgrounds, Townsend derived from Keene, Pegram's tighter technique was nearest to early Partridge. As so often with *Punch* art of this period, the weakest point is the psychology of expressions. There seems to have been nothing in the comic drawing of the period to correspond to Watt's portraits, and Pegram was slightly affected by the oddly common *Punch* difficulty over making characters stand naturally. Even if his jokes and his milieu became increasingly stereotyped, his draughtsmanship as late as the early Thirties was still capable of giving a thrill of pleasure, and it is unfair that he was sometimes confounded with the competent hackwork in the midst of which he used to appear. G. D. Armour was no mean descendant of Leech. He was a sporting artist whose horses gave readers the pleasure of recognition, rather as Russell Brockbank did later with his motor-cars. (It is interesting to notice that in tackling a motoring subject in 1913 Armour, instead of trying to transfer his usual methods from one form of locomotion to another, produced something just like an early Bert Thomas.)

Generally, art under Burnand marked time. The big men died off and were replaced by lesser men. There were slightly fewer good jokes being printed at the end of his reign than there had been at the beginning. The standard of drawing was decent and adequate rather than inspired and the one new recruit of genius, Phil May, was accepted only grudgingly.

CHAPTER SIX

# ORTHODOXY AND POLISH

## *Owen Seaman's Editorship, 1906–1918*

OWEN SEAMAN'S work for *Punch* is still a matter of argument. Malcolm Muggeridge considers that he started a steady decline in the quality of the paper. Like Burnand, he certainly went on too long, but equally like Burnand, he is surely entitled to be judged on his best years. When he took over as Assistant Editor in 1902, and still more when four years later he became Editor, he pulled the paper together fast. Burnand had let the reins fall into Arthur à Beckett's hands and, while remaining genial, had become increasingly remote. He would disappear to his home at Ramsgate and the first that anybody knew of his return was the heavy thud of his boots, which he was accustomed to remove and throw outside the door of his office. Visiting contributors would find him looking rather lost and eating shrimps out of a paper bag and would be put off with slightly evasive expressions of hope for their welfare but very rarely any promise of work. Contributions left with him in person might never be seen again.

Seaman had been a schoolmaster and some kind of don up North and immediately he had taken executive control he proceeded to impose discipline upon the contributors. Slovenly work, and there was far too much slovenly work, was cleared out briskly and new men were brought in. Lucas and Graves had already been introduced by Seaman. Seaman's career was odd and its oddness had so much effect on the development of *Punch* that it cannot be ignored. A member of his family has pointed out the deep insecurity he felt as a result of his origins. In later life the most hysterically genteel *Punch* man since Leech, he shared with him, quite unnecessarily, a sense of family shame. Leech's family were shabby spongers, Seaman's family had worked hard and ably and made money, but they had made it in trade. His father was a ladies' haberdasher who had been apprenticed to an uncle, one of the partners in Stagg and Mantle, and then worked up a business of his own. When he prospered, he took his family to live in a largish house in one of the better suburbs, remote from the shop. Seaman went to Mill Hill, with its traditions of sober nonconformity and mercantile solidity.

His family continued to prosper and good teaching at Mill Hill developed his academic abilities. Incredibly, at seventeen he won a scholarship to Shrewsbury and entered the sixth form direct. A year later he was Captain of the School and one of the leading athletes. This belated leap up the educational ladder brought out his dour tenacity. Nineteenth Century public school boys were outspoken supporters of their parents' (often recently acquired) dislike for the stain of trade. Even after he had won a scholarship to Clare, gained the Porson prize for Greek iambics and made some mark, both academically and athletically, at Cambridge, the stigma followed him. All his ability, his social vivacity and his grace still let him merely peep over the gate of the promised land. The sometimes fantastic snobbery of his later days, his consequential and pompous manner, can surely be forgiven him once one realises the kind of treatment he had received from his personal inferiors during the formative years of his life.

Seaman was a clever man but without any bent for professional scholarship. He taught for a short time at Rossall and Magdalen College School, of which he just missed becoming Headmaster. In 1890 he became a Professor of Literature and lectured on classical and literary subjects at Armstrong College, Newcastle. He was called to the Bar but did not practise. He lived at a time when clever young scholars wrote political leaders and he wrote them too. It was only after some false starts that he found in political journalism and humorous verse something that he could not only do well but could make into a career. To the end he was never quite a journalist, however competent he was at writing fast and forcibly. He was something of the schoolmaster and something of the don. Like other clever men who do not settle in a university, which is specially organised to deal with clever men, he was more donnish than dons generally are.

Seaman made his name by his parodies. He described himself as " a self-made parodist ; apart from the influence of Calverley." He took parody very seriously : " In its highest form, parody is a department of pure literary criticism. It is often the way that humour has of paying homage to serious achievement ; of conferring its recognition of something beyond its own range, which it can honour but not emulate." [1] His parodies were nearly always metrically accurate and reproduced the general effect of their subjects' diction. Seaman missed greatness as a parodist through rigidity of outlook and lack of psychological intuition. He could never get inside a man's mind and write, as it were, outwards. He was apt to parody the same writers, especially Austin and Swinburne, over and over again. (It has been said that he hoped for the Laureateship and that personal disappointment reinforced public spirit in his incessant attacks on Austin.) On the whole, the earlier the parody, the greater the gaiety and the likeness.

As well as his light verse he wrote a lot of dramatic criticism, always of an evening's entertainment seen from a stall rather than of an art form, though it is fair to remember that the revival of the English theatre came after his tastes were formed. On the whole, his dramatic criticisms were, within their limitations, readable and sensible. When he became Editor, his early hopes of producing solid volumes of literary criticism financed by humorous journalism vanished, though after retirement he worked on some Browning lectures. At the Table he obviously found the atmosphere created by Burnand and Arthur à Beckett too loosely jocular for his taste.

Once he had power he began to tighten up the writing, to remove the puns, the digressions, the irrelevancies and to substitute for a casual, rambling pace something nearer to the style of the better kind of popular lecturer. He worked primarily by letters of detailed criticism. These poured out on contributors. He seemed to be able to take the most hopeless contribution and find something to say about it. He would write several letters about a single poem or article and even the stars felt lucky to get a contribution into print with only minor alterations. When he went to country houses for the week-end he would withdraw for hours to work at his mail like a Cabinet Minister. Burnand had increasingly refused to read anything. Some people always got in, some never did ; he did not much worry. Seaman changed all that. He edited everybody hard, and naturally new appointments to the Table, over whose contributions he had no power of veto, came from those contributors whom he considered profited most from his teaching.

The evidence on this question of veto is confused. Burnand, in a letter to Furniss at the time of the row, claimed he had complete freedom in using or rejecting or cancelling the articles of the literary staff.[2] A. A. Milne said that it was Seaman's wish to keep ultimate control of his work, as well as the proprietors' doubts of his political competence, that delayed his appointment to the Table.[3] There seems to have been a kind of intermediate stage ; trusted contributors were given special envelopes in which they sent their copy direct to the works, and it came under the Editor's eye only when in proof. At one time these envelopes were awarded to comparative newcomers, after three months or so. A letter of 1894 [4] says that at that time the privilege was restricted to the Staff. Sometimes all non-salaried possessors of these envelopes are described collectively as the " outside staff." These constitutional obscurities are of some slight importance. There was some resemblance, at times conscious, between *Punch* and a very good school, and granting or withholding marks of distinction and trust had psychological effects sometimes sufficiently violent to dry up or drive away a valuable contributor.

Seaman's humour was less robust than Burnand's, though it had more bite. He was not very interested in producing laughs. It says something in his favour that he printed more different kinds of humour than Burnand. In his early days he was quite prepared to take something that was good of its kind, even though it was not a kind he really liked. However, during the earlier period of his Editorship the prevailing types of humour were not so far outside the range of his response that he was severely tested by including them. The qualities he wanted in his paper were lucidity, regularity, intelligibility and soundness. He considered that the reader, by paying for a copy, became entitled to understand everything in it and that therefore all the jokes must be aimed at the maximum possible readership. There must be nothing for minorities, nothing too subtle to appeal to the oldest and stupidest : " We can't edit a paper for twenty readers." [5] In time he became obsessed by the fear that the paper would be unintelligible and jokes were driven home with maddening insistence. As an example of his heavy-handedness, rather than of *Punch*'s attitude to the arts, the following may be quoted : " Certain excitement was caused in journalistic and artistic circles by the news of the arrest of M. Hostrowisky, who has been a contributor to several papers in Paris under the name of Guillaume Apollinaire—*Reuter. His assumed name (so different from that of his birth) seems to have been ' writ in water ' (mineral).*" [6]

In several ways he shifted the centre of *Punch* appeal. There were closer links with the schools and universities, less close with the stage. He liked country gentlemen and clergymen and barristers and sixth-form masters and senior Civil Servants to contribute. He gave a good deal of time to charitable committee-work and the official world found it worth while to dine him and try to get him on its side in good causes. Marie Corelli said that she was never tired of saying that he was one of the finest speakers in England. The paper had always been serenely uncommercial in using space to print Obituaries of those who had served it ; it was equally willing to use its space on crippled children and service orphans.

Seaman's training in exact classical scholarship not only contributed to the maintenance of technical standards in his own verse and that of others, but gave him a good eye for misprints. *Punch* proofs were checked more and more carefully and the smallest point of doubt was scrutinised and argued over as if the future of the paper depended on it. Seaman's standards were almost impossibly high, but they were a link with a family proprietorship of professional printers. Although probably not one reader in a hundred consciously remarked the accuracy of *Punch* printing, it contributed to the total effect of reliability. The standard preserved under Seaman was maintained to such an extent that a few years ago a reference to a single misprint during the whole year was made in a speech at the annual Staff dinner and aroused thunders of amused recognition. (When it had been noticed that the Kaiser's crown in Tenniel's *Dropping the Pilot* was not the Imperial German Crown the presses were stopped and the right crown substituted after a few thousand copies had been printed.)

Reliability included political reliability. Seaman always considered *Punch* to be a neutral, non-party paper, standing in Olympian detachment above the petty conflicts of the day. As A. A. Milne says in his autobiography, *It's Too late Now*, he regarded a man's politics as deducible from his social status. If they did not agree the man was a traitor. One of the proprietors still retained the family's Liberal faith. He was treated with great deference but also with a bewildering assumption that as a gentleman he would, of course, be Conservative like Seaman. When Seaman had established himself firmly with no rivals near the throne, the cartoons became increasingly right wing, and the Liberals, who included Lehmann, a Liberal M.P., were driven gradually into an uneasy acquiescence. In the long run this was unhealthy. On Burnand's retirement *The Times* had emphasised the importance of keeping *Punch* bipartisan. The cartoons had always traditionally been the product of a heated debate between opposing views. Nowhere was the force of Seaman's personality shown more strongly than in the establishment of this political domination. He liked to be able to rely on the soundness of his contributors, of whom he required " a degree of presentability such as was only conferred, it was thought, upon the whiter students of the larger colleges at Cambridge." [7] Nevertheless not all his appointments bear out Milne's criticism. After a few years he had the ablest staff on the literary side that *Punch* had ever had.

The average was very high, though there may have been no equivalent to Thackeray or Brooks.

Milne, who worked closely with Seaman as his Assistant Editor until the war, says: "He was a strange, unlucky man. All the Good Fairies came to his christening, but the Uninvited Fairy had the last word, so that the talents found themselves in the wrong napkin and the virtues flourished where graces should have been. Humour was drowned in Scholarship, Tact went down before Truth, and the Fighting Qualities gave him not only the will to win but the determination to explain why he hadn't won. There is a story of him as a golfer, making an excuse for every bad shot until he got to the last green, when he threw down his putter and said: 'That settles it, I'll never play in knickerbockers again.' It could have been so delightfully said—but it wasn't. He had, truly, a heart of gold, and if it had been 'concealed beneath a rugged exterior', as it so often is in novels, it would have been more patent to the world than the veneer which was so nearly gold allowed it to be." [8]

The heart of gold to which his temperamentally-opposed second-in-command refers was shown not only by his humanitarian engagements. Although he never realised that contributors did not all have independent means or that it made a difference whether a particular article were in that week or next, he had an avuncular interest in their welfare. He enjoyed entertaining the young. He made them feel that it was kind of them to spend an evening with him and he entertained them sumptuously in food, wine and anecdote. He was a gay old bachelor, a devoted uncle, and his well-regulated social life was oiled by his high spirits, his courtesy and his concern. When he was made a baronet in 1933 (he had been a Knight since 1914) he replied to congratulations with:

> I thank you from a swelling heart
> For being glad that I'm a Bart.

This suggests the shell had not thickened as much as some of his detractors suggest. There may be something in the suggestion that his identification with his paper—he gave the impression of believing it would stop when he did—was so complete that he insisted on receiving the consideration due to its Editor. He undoubtedly became a great trial in the office. One member of the staff who was appointed at the end of his editorship remembers him only as a back. As he proceeded about the premises, he would wait stiffly before the innumerable doors, which the junior had to dive round him to open. In private he seems to have shown a warmth, a simplicity, a levity and a deep kindliness which it is tragic to realise he would have considered it improper to display in the pages of his paper.

The early years of the century were a period of great variety in political writing. Shaw, Wells, the Chestertons, Belloc, Saki, F. E. Smith and Winston Churchill were writing and talking about politics with a brilliance and vivacity unheard since the early days of Disraeli. Seaman might have been the expression in light literature of the Tory Revival but his belief that *Punch* should behave like an Institution tended to make him behave like one himself. From the point of view of a satirical paper faced with just the right environment for a second birth this was a pity, and yet it was an honourable and somehow oddly touching failure.

There is no *Punch* editor, not even Tom Taylor, who seems less sympathetic to the modern historian at first sight than Seaman. Then, as acquaintance with the man grows, as his editorial work is examined more closely and above all as the memories of those who knew him personally are compared, he becomes a figure capable of arousing respect and even affection. If only he had taken over from Burnand ten years before and resigned twenty years earlier. . . .

## II

The shock of the Boer War, the Conservative split on Imperial Preference and the rejuvenation and even temporary cohesion of the Liberals produced one of the great British governments, one perhaps slightly over-praised since. The regrouping and reorganisation of the working class in the Eighties and the political and economic debates of the Nineties led to the growth of the Labour Party and the first uncertain steps towards a Parliamentary merging of Trade Unions and Socialists. This meant that always behind the Liberal reforms was seen a menace to which they seemed to be handing over power. The railway and coal strikes, like the Suffragette outbreaks and the drilling for civil war in Ireland were more terrifying as a symptom than in themselves. In the exciting years of the constitutional crisis and the threatened civil war in Ireland, *Punch* rejected both Tory extremists and Ulster loyalists. Increasingly often it was content to express facts in the cartoons rather than to urge politics. In the last two years before the war broke out, *Punch* gave the impression of receding from politics. Perhaps after the intensity of the great debates there was a slackening of public enthusiasm for parliamentary subjects.

The shift from opposing new fashions because they were ugly and inconvenient, as Leech had opposed the crinoline, to opposing new fashions because they involved change was very gradual. Undoubtedly the fear of revolution sharpened Seaman's resistance to changes that were quite neutral politically. It was safest to oppose changes in language because it was after all behind the barriers of language that Seaman's generation and type preserved their past. Milliken's *'Arry* poems had been detailed because this unpleasant cad was being observed with a disgusted gusto and his speech habits were part of the evidence against him. Opposition to changes in the language became quite hysterical with the American influence and it was due not to concern for the purity of the language but to concern for the maintenance of what that purity symbolised.

The pre-1914 period had a relish for ideas. It was the age of Einstein and Freud and the Post-Impressionists and Vorticism and Cubism. It was the age of Yeats and Pound and Wells and Forster. Looking back there is a danger of over-estimating the area of contemporary consciousness occupied by the men who now seem to have been the most significant. On the whole, highbrows and criminals wear best, and there is a danger of dismissing the ninety-nine per cent of the population who did not read Little Reviews as being Philistine, which is grossly unhistorical. *Punch*'s book reviews, which wavered a bit under Burnand, became a steadily influential feature of the paper under Seaman, who removed the Baron de Book-Worms from *Our Booking Office* and introduced the Staff of Learned Clerks—a jest that in later years many readers probably imagined dated from the mid-Nineteenth Century. They lasted till 1949. Families made up their library lists and bought Christmas presents on their advice. They were considered reliable, which meant they were consistent. Seaman insisted that reviewers, whether Lucy or Milne or outsiders, should be clear-cut and not afraid to attack shoddy work. The stance of the reviewers was that of consumers, not judges or worshippers. They were in a club library or lady's drawing-room picking up biographies and travel books and light novels and reporting frankly on whether they held their attention. Sometimes the tone was prosy, as some young lady, possibly the daughter of a country house in which Seaman had week-ended, was admonished in ripely skittish tones, but most of the reviewing was straightforward and without the personal note of some of the articles.

Unexpectedly *Our Booking Office* noticed Christmas crackers. Generally there was one review in verse, easy, conversational verse well fitted to deck-chair reading. It was above all in these dextrous epistles—the accent is infectious—that one sees the superiority of *Punch* to other surveyors of general reading. Nothing was loosely praised or condemned and in concentrating on entertainment-value other values were unobtrusively maintained. The use of the first person singular gave immediacy to the reviews and emphasised that they were reports on experience. From those that were obviously Lucy to those that were obviously Milne there was a wide range of discussion. Comment was sometimes acute : of Leacock's *Nonsense Novels* [9] the reviewer said, " There is genuine gold here on every page, but I do not feel quite sure that Mr. Leacock knows when he has come to it."

There was an entertaining review of a novel about Egypt by Hall Caine [10]—" If Mr. Caine cannot claim to be inspired he has certainly spared himself no pains "—which used the method of deadpan reproduction of the plot, then less common than now. In fact *Our Booking Office* was always inspired by Hall Caine. He was " a bloodhound on the trail of pathos, who stretches octopus tentacles of coincidence and out of the pigeon holes of memory plucks like a hawk every topic of recent interest." [11] In 1913 a reviewer trounced P. C. Wren for abandoning works like his *Indian Teachers' Guide* for fiction :

> ' A poorer tale I've never seen
> Than *Dew and Mildew* (Longman's, Green).' [12]

On the whole books were not noticed in order to make fun of them, valuable sources of humour though bad books be. In a stately and unhurried way the books that came into the office were worked through. It was the Assistant Editor's job to enter them in a large ledger while Seaman picked up each in turn and mentioned any personal connection he had had with the author. In time the gap between publication and notice was so great that an author's first book, it is said, might be reviewed on the publication of his second. Though social status or personal knowledge might sometimes get a novel reviewed, the review itself was always honest. *Punch* had long ceased to cover the Arts systematically which, judging by many of the incidental remarks on the subject was just as well. Perhaps this *Glossary For the Opening of the Royal Academy* of 1908,[13] by R. J. Richardson, seems more penetrating to-day than it would have, say, a quarter of a century after it was written. Block dismissals of *Punch* are always dangerous.

## ART

An Artist is a person who paints what he thinks he sees.

An Amateur is a person who thinks he paints what he sees.

An Impressionist is a person who paints what other people think he sees.

A Popular Artist is a person who paints what other people think they see.

A Successful Artist is a person who paints what he thinks other people see.

A Great Artist is a person who paints what other people see they think.

A Failure is a person who sees what other people think they paint.

A Portraitist is a person who paints what other people don't think he sees.

A Landscape Painter is a person who doesn't paint what other people see.

A Realist is a person who sees what other people don't paint.

An Idealist is a person who paints what other people don't see.

The Hanging Committee are people who don't see what other people think they paint.

A Royal Academician is a person who doesn't think and paints what other people see.

A Genius is a person who doesn't see and paints what other people don't think.

A Critic is a person who doesn't paint and thinks what other people don't see.

The Public are people who don't see or think what other people don't paint.

A Dealer is a person that sees that people who paint don't think, and who thinks that people who don't paint don't see. He sees people who don't see people who paint ; he thinks that people who paint don't see people who see ; and he sees what people who don't paint think.

FINALLY

A Reader is a person whose head swims.

Seaman, like Burnand, was often his own dramatic critic but the principal dramatic critic was Milne. Shaw showed how good a school of playwriting dramatic criticism can be. Milne was very good on entertainment, a little apt to miss the point of serious drama. His writing was much lighter than Seaman's, though Seaman was a much better-read man and what he said was often more intelligent than what Milne said. Milne's inability to deal with *Androcles and the Lion* illustrates this.[14] " Mr. O. P. Heggie was remarkably good as *Androcles* and Mr. Edward Sillward was a delightful lion. They had a particularly funny turn with the Emperor (perfectly played by Mr. Leon Quartermaine) in the last scene, which might well have been encored. . . . Mr. Shaw is quite funny in *Androcles and the Lion*, but if he had any purpose other than this I did not see it." Seaman was more perceptive on Chesterton's *Magic*.[15] Compared with other dramatic criticism of the time *Punch* was sensible and agreeable to read. If Seaman stood for purpose, Milne stood for leisure.

Once Seaman had collected his team he rather lost interest in recruitment. Milne, the Assistant Editor and in many ways chief innovator, greatly improved the newspaper cuttings with comments, or " pars," which became one of the most popular features of the paper. They considerably eased the work of making the issue up. Seaman would lay out the articles in long galley-proofs and then fill up any space at the end of the columns with innumerable cuttings. For some years *Charivaria*, after its beginning in 1902, was contributed by a Jewish lawyer called Walter Emanuel. As the old paragraphs that it replaced had been contributed by many different hands this was a pity, though Emanuel maintained a fairly high standard of work. On his death in 1917, C. H. Bretherton did it for a time and then the feature was assembled by the editorial staff from material submitted by outsiders. As it consisted of separate jokes and, after 1907, occupied the front page, it came next to the illustrations in quotability and remained a feature probably more popular with the readers than it was with the Staff, who felt that some of the outside contributors to it got by rather easily.

## III

Of Seaman's recruits the most important was A. A. Milne, to many readers the key figure in the *Punch* of the pre-war years. He took the domestic article from Lehmann and light verse from Cambridge and he streamlined them. His father had been the owner of a preparatory school whose most successful old boy was probably Northcliffe. When before the First World War, Northcliffe tried to buy *Punch* and through an intermediary offered Milne a princely salary to edit it, he was as astonished at the young journalist's prompt refusal of the glittering offer as he was at the proprietor's refusal to take part or even interest in the negotiations. A precocious mathematician, Milne did well at Westminster, soon becoming less interested in work than in expressing himself through cricket and social life. At Cambridge he made his name on *The Granta.* He settled in London as a busy free-lance. His first *Punch* cheque was 16/6 for three contributions. When Lehmann protested on his behalf, the proprietors replied that the honour of writing for *Punch* was considered to be sufficient reward at first, but that when the honour began to wear off he would get paid more. Quite soon he was appointed Assistant Editor by Seaman, though not with the full powers that Seaman had exercised when he held the post himself. The two men were temperamentally opposed, which was probably good for both of them.

Somehow, after Milne had been writing in *Punch* every week for a few years, the older prose writers began to seem tired and heavy. His stance was that of the middle-class letter-writer and diner-out, and the basis of his most characteristic work was the working up of ordinary experience. He did not produce only loosely-organised series about domestic life and amateur games, he wrote burlesques of plays, and less successful burlesques of current literature. He was an efficient reviewer but he did not read enough to make his imitations more than parlour tricks. He tackled most of the kinds of article that other men tackled and this, together with his verse and his editorial work, gave him an even broader base than Lehmann. He called his collections of articles by names like *The Sunny Side* and *The Day's Play*, recognising there was a shady side and a day's work. As editorial policy dictated that these darker aspects of life should be ignored or else reserved for the traditional dullness of iambic pentameters, he wrote about what was left and this included the most characteristic product of the Twentieth Century—leisure. The Milne world was a real world though it was not the most important world. Meredith pointed out that comedy was possible only in societies where there was social equality between the sexes. Beatrice, Célimène, Clara Middleton and Ann Whitefield lived in *milieux* in which sparks flew between equally-charged poles. However, if the sexes have equal opportunities and equal freedoms they do not have common goals. Comedy springs from the entanglement of strivings. It is more ruthless than tragedy, because tragedy can end in reconciliation and pity, comedy only in defeat. The flannelled flirtations of Milne's characters were mimic warfare.

It is the Milne of the Saturday afternoon on the cricket field who is remembered. The characters of the house party were reflected in their cricket and their conversation. The match was both negligible and all-important. References to mid-week work were flippant or incredulous. The narrator was not much of a cricketer but he earned his place in the team by his repartee. His typical pose was sprawling beside a girl, watching and commenting. She was an athlete's sister, one of those tremendous girls who would later select one of their brother's friends and be a wife to him, but at present was luxuriating in companionship. In the evening there would be a dance at which the narrator would behave with purely verbal dash in the conservatory. Although the centre of this social life was a house, not a week-end cottage, one feels that the owners had not lived there very long. Most of the cricketers and amateur actors worked in the city. A journalist was a bit of a queer fish to all these barristers and stock-brokers, and had to be rather better at pencil games, and also to show that his career diverged from theirs only after he had completed his education. If it be objected that this was a Philistine and illiberal life, it can be fairly pointed out it was a deliberate abstraction and not a complete whole.

Milne succeeded in writing article after article of bright chatter but Seaman blocked the freedom to express his deeper feelings and his radical politics and there seemed no future for anything but more and more bright chatter. He turned to the theatre, where problems of construction interested him. He went to the war and wrote, returned from the war—nobody was very interested. Good editing might have turned the post-war politically-passionate Milne to account. He might not have made a good Editor but he remained potentially an invaluable contributor. If only with sobering years the mimic warfare had been followed to its conclusion, if the derisive, harsh side of him had been allowed to speak in the pages as it spoke in the time of Jerrold and Leech and it was speaking in other periodicals, if only the natural curve from the high spirits of youth to the astringency of age had been followed, he might have been among the half dozen greatest *Punch* writers. As it was he drifted away.

E. V. Lucas, appointed under Burnand but very much Seaman's man, was a considerable figure outside *Punch*. He came from a Quaker family that included Lister and Roger Fry, but his background was humble and he did not go to a University. He must have been one of the most industrious "quality" journalists who ever lived. He produced guide-books, books on art galleries, a standard edition of Lamb's letters, anthologies, novels, poems, and volume after volume of essays. He had very varied editorial experience and he was working chairman of Methuen's. He kept up his reading, walking, sight-seeing and social life without giving any feeling of rush. He lived, in fact, the ideal life of the light essayist—a man who found it as easy to talk by pen as by tongue. More than any *Punch* man he adopted a mask for his work. He wrote, as he once said, in a style that made his readers think he had a long white beard. His literary personality was light, charming and kindly. He appeared as a lover of Georgian week-end cottage life, a bit of a scholar, a bit of a dog-lover and a stalwart defender of what he considered the better human impulses. In private he was a cynical clubman, liking to entertain peers to sumptuous meals with champagne and brandy, very bitter about men and politics and the decadence of modern art. He was a great trouncer of "outspoken" books and was rumoured to have the finest pornographic library in London. Personal recollections of him vary widely. Some people remember endless benevolence, even if it did sometimes verge on a schoolmasterly desire to organise other people's lives. Acts of perceptive kindness are quoted to suggest that the sardonic exterior was misleading.

His theory that because of the turpitude of the human race he must write always in the sunniest way did produce a good deal of very readable stuff, though it also allowed him to divert attention from the world as it was. He was nearly always wrong about literature and the arts, and after all a Blimp with the airs of a scholar is less attractive than a Blimp with the airs of a colonel. His *Punch* work covered a great range, from sheer high spirits to light essays. He provided a valuable contrast to the rest of the paper. Lucas had a power of living and remembering, with writing merely secondary, and thus balanced the humorists who escaped into imaginary worlds. If sometimes he got sentimental—dogs, children and Sussex brought out the worst in him—for week after week he never fell below a reasonable standard of vigour and readability. His work wears surprisingly well. No writer of the period was more attacked by the necessary rebels, because of this element of a silly old man posing by a second-hand book shop. That particular war is won now and it is time to sift through the enormous bulk of his work.

Lucas joined the Table in 1904 and acted as Seaman's deputy as early as 1906. He was quick at the work, unlike Seaman, and also unlike Seaman understood the importance of praise. His political views in the pre-war years, like Milne's and Lehmann's, were radical, but gradually Seaman wore him down into silence. He formed a curious partnership with C. L. Graves. Comparison of the work which they each did separately shows that by far the greater contribution to the partnership was made by Lucas. Both of them had read widely and had the old journalist's sense of what was going on in the papers. They produced enormous numbers of joint articles and a number of popular humorous books, illustrated and partly inspired by George Morrow. A typical Graves-Lucas piece started from a news story about a wrecked menagerie train in West Virginia[16] where an elephant had lifted the wreckage and other elephants squirted water on the flames. They described similar help from animals : a woman trained a tortoise to act as a paper-weight : " as she was a woman much addicted to literary pursuits and invariably worked with her windows open, you can well imagine that the task was no sinecure."

Lucas could bring a fresh lunacy even to the mock *Answers to Correspondents* column[17] that is so common a humorous form. The man who wrote asking the cost of becoming a marquis was told that the market price was a hundred and fifty thousand pounds. He was advised that America did not confer titles but that a dental degree was not difficult to obtain at Milwaukee. Then there was the case of the man who lunched with an uncle who considered himself a judge of wine. The champagne was badly corked, but the nephew did not dare say so for fear of offending the old gentleman, who praised it : the waiter was grinning. The advice was to rise suddenly as though to fling his arms round his uncle's neck in a spasm of affection and to sweep the bottle and glasses off the table. " We admit that the restaurant would remain unpunished, but then that is a restaurant's *métier*."

E. V. Knox was one of the remarkable family who grew up under the shadow of Bishop Knox of Manchester, the Evangelical leader. The boys were all clever and gay and adept at the kind of scholarship that uses a combination of memory and quickness of wits in play. They were good at Latin acrostics and prided themselves on knowledge of Sherlock Holmes. Ronald Knox, don, Catholic convert, religious satirist, translator of the Bible and popular journalist never contributed very much to *Punch* but he turned up at intervals in its pages and showed the value of the tradition of academic fun. Wilfred Knox, the Anglican theologian, lived in his own world, a scholar and mystic. E. V. Knox at Rugby was scholarly and detached. He left Oxford without taking his degree (many years later receiving an Honorary Degree) and, after a couple of years as a schoolmaster, became a journalist. He was first printed in *Punch* in the last year of Burnand and soon became a frequent contributor under the pseudonym " Evoe." Apart from his verse, which I will deal with when I treat the verse of the Seaman period as a whole, he wrote most things from dramatic criticism and book reviews to articles of personal misadventure. He wrote Milne and he wrote Lucas but his most characteristic work was parody and " crazy " humour at a time long before it had become common.

He was almost the last of the school of whom Leigh had been the first. Neither was a scholar in the sense of adding to knowledge professionally but they regarded reading as a normal activity and remembered what they read. Evoe sometimes struck strangers as being interesting to talk to in the way that the older type of don was interesting. It is a pity that the life of the study did not more often come into his prose articles. Perhaps it was another case of Seaman's discouraging editing, of his belief that *Punch* was limited by the unnatural and excessive limitations of its readers. Evoe occasionally kicked over the traces and wrote about causes and beliefs and books, and he wrote very well.

At times he was rather too elaborately surprised that there were little people living in new suburbs whom any comparison based on Lemprière would astound. (Evelyn Waugh has criticised Ronald Knox for the assumption that everybody likely to read him would share a background of nannies and holidays abroad.) There was too much iteration of the oddness of having to use the Tube, of having to work for one's living, of having few and inefficient servants. However, under the rather factitious boredom and the pose of the young-man-about-town hampered by financial stringencies, was an enthusiasm and gaiety, of which at times he seemed rather ashamed. Some very ordinary article about the minor trials of life would suddenly have its surface broken by a kind of mad poetry and it was at these increasingly frequent moments that the differences between Evoe and other *Punch* writers suddenly appeared.

P. G. Wodehouse wrote for a comparatively short time in the early years of the century ; his comic exuberance burst out all over the place. He did not invent new kinds of article, but wrenched accepted forms to his purposes. The strong individuality, the fertility of comic detail and the life in his articles made them different from other people's. However, *Punch* lost him for many years.

It is impossible to give much impression of an article by extracts. A good *Punch* article is as complex as a good music-hall turn. Variations of pace, the placing of a repeated proper name, juggling with two themes of different weights and sizes may lead to complicated effects of which the reader is not fully conscious. This unseen mechanism will completely distinguish two articles on the same subject. It is never safe to dismiss a *Punch* article by topic. The difference between what is sometimes thought of as " the typical *Punch* article " and what *Punch* published at its best is a literary difference. A few odd paragraphs torn from an article can illustrate little more than phrase. It cannot illustrate structure and above all it cannot illustrate timing.

There are, very roughly, three main *Punch* traditions, distinguished by the contributor's distance from reality. There is the direct tradition, in which the writer remains on the same plane as that in which he received the stimulus ; this results in good, plain prose, and a strong belief in the duty of humour to amend. It is to this tradition that Jerrold, Brooks, A. P. H. and perhaps Malcolm Muggeridge belong. The central *Punch* tradition uses reality as a jumping-off point for producing laughs. It takes a personal experience, often a predicament, and works it up, or it takes a book or a newspaper series and guys it in burlesque. It will invert some slogan of the day and work out the consequences. This may be a flight from reality but so is a good deal of generally acceptable literature. Often it lands in an equally valid reality, that of art. The central *Punch* tradition produced some very good work in which part of the reader's pleasure was in enjoying the way the thing was done. Thackeray, Burnand, Anstey, Lehmann, Milne, Evoe, Anthony Armstrong, Eric Keown (with important differences), H. F. Ellis, Basil Boothroyd, Alex Atkinson, Anthony Carson and Claud Cockburn are some very different examples of this tradition. The farther side of it from reality come those who write out of a dream-world, using fragments of reality to make new patterns, the poetic or " crazy " humorists. These, oddly enough, include some of the parodists, who see one section of reality with exceptional clarity, perhaps because they enter the dream-world of the book and then write out of the centre of it. Evoe belongs to this class as well in the work that seems to me his best. I cannot think of any Nineteenth Century *Punch* writer in this tradition, though of course it included a few of the artists. Modern writers in this group include Richard Mallett, R. P. Lister, T. S. Watt and Simon Crabtree (Michael Wharton).

## IV

The most usual model for verse writers in these years was Seaman, who was not a good one. It was bad enough when he began imitating his own best work ; it was appalling when other people imitated bad Seaman. Down to the war he could still be vigorous and light-hearted. Quotation would be unfair, because his best poems took space to develop the theme and are therefore too long to quote in full ; truncated versions would emphasise his weakness rather than his strength. Also, he was best when most topical, when the verse had been stimulated by some incongruous detail in the day's papers, and historical commentary would have to be disproportionately full.

His leading disciple was C. L. Graves, brother-in-law of Earl Grey and uncle of Robert Graves, a busy journalist, particularly on political and musical subjects, and for many years Assistant Editor of *The Spectator*. He contributed to *Punch* for very many years and was Assistant Editor from 1928–36. In retirement he wrote a curiously old-fashioned history of the paper which he loved. His kindly, upright character, with its strong views on political and literary propriety, comes through in the manuscript. One can feel the qualities which made the younger men who worked with him call him "a dear old boy." Unhappily, to be honest, there is no leading *Punch* writer whose work appeals less to modern taste, except perhaps "Dum-Dum," Major John Kendall. The quintessential C. L. Graves may be seen in one verse out of seven on the tea shortage :

> Although, when luxuries must be resigned,
>   Such as cigars or even breakfast bacon,
> My hitherto "unconquerable mind"
>   Its philosophic pose has not forsaken,
> By one impending sacrifice I find
>   My stock of fortitude severely shaken—
> I mean the dismal prospect of our losing
> The genial cup that cheers without bemusing.[18]

Dum-Dum's strong point was taking newspaper cuttings of a line and a half and expanding them into at least half a dozen verses. He liked metres with long lines and slow movement and specialised in surmounting awkward rhymes. The kind of thing that both Graves and Dum-Dum could do needed genuinely clever men to do it and when they began their skill would have been appreciated by readers who felt they were writing light verse better than they could themselves. However, as the years rolled by they continued to write the same kind of verse and what had been talent degenerated into a quite mechanical repetition of old tricks. When Seaman, Graves and Dum-Dum were all snarling at their age in bastard classical metres in one issue, it is no wonder that *Punch* began to be dismissed as a fœtid back-water—a kind of club library in which angry old men snorted in verse.

It may be objected that this is a summary dismissal of contributors who were very popular in their day. Their popularity narrowed as their contemporaries died off. It is impossible to point out what went right with *Punch* and to persuade people to look at the *Punches* of the period again without making some attempt to discover what went wrong. One of the things that went wrong was a decline of curiosity, sharpness and tang.

The verse of Evoe was far more varied than it appeared at first sight. He continued to use the characteristic metres of the Seaman school, though he handled them with far more delicacy, but he gradually brought in all the principal existing verse forms. His themes in verse, like his themes in prose, ranged from the typical O.S. or C.L.G. oracular politics to verses from the point of view of the man to whom things happen. However, as well as the humours of public comment and private incompetence he had a much more original streak of lunacy. Almost the first appearance in modern *Punch* of nonsense was hidden away among the decorative embellishments of Evoe's verse. Seaman claimed to like irrelevance but was in fact temperamentally unable to appreciate the fantastic and illogical and poetic. Sometimes Evoe's tone was a wearied disgust, sometimes a private amusement at faddists. The danger of laughing at faddists is that occasionally they turn out to be pioneers and then your laughter looks stupid, unless, and this is the point, it is imaginative laughter. Both *The Clouds* and Socrates have survived.

Evoe's background, like that of other contributors, provided him with more memories of pleasure than of pain. He was discriminating over food and landscape and much influenced by nursery and schoolroom memories. Occasionally hot indignation transformed one of his versified leaders and what had been a political exercise suddenly became quick-moving, lucid and savage. On the whole he avoided emotion and there was a refusal to extend his strength, a refusal to compete, that left a feeling of power in reserve.

Here is a fair sample of early Evoe, *A Protest from Parnassus*[19] (In Apprehension of the Daylight Saving Bill) :

> I that have sung you what windblossoms blow lowest
> Down in the valley where dances the fay,
> Am I to rise when the lark is a soloist,
> Merely to humour a Government, eh ?
> Am I to make my melodious madrigals
> Out on the lawn at an hour when the thrush
> Shortens the glee of the worm and his glad wriggles
> Rather than roam when the nightingales gush.

This burlesqued both ' spring poets ' and light verse. The easy " -ay " rhyme was thrown away while preposterously difficult words like " soloist " and " madrigals " were rhymed. The central idea was farcical and the detail was fun. Basically it was the same type of light verse as other *Punch* writers were producing but it was better. A favourite theme of Evoe's was the contrast between the picture created by the later romantic poets and actuality. This was dangerous ground but he often crossed it superbly. The lament for the difference between the grandeurs of childhood and the restrictions of maisonette life filled *Punch* louder and louder with a clamant self-pity that has no place in satire. Evoe, almost alone of the *Punch laudatores temporum actorum*, succeeded in making comic verse out of the threatened ruin of a class.

*Inspiration*[20] had as a subtitle " A Suburban Rhapsody." The theme was a simple one. The rhymer had gone to sit in a deck-chair in the garden to write inspired verse, and he was interrupted by the voices of nature itself. The setting was a kind of disgusted evocation of domesticity—mealtimes, plumbers, Eliza Jane, trifle, " the tradesmen's fusses." One verse ran :

So sweetly the bird sang. Great thrills ran through it.
  It seemed to say, " The glorious sun hath shone,
Flooding the world like treacle wrapped round suet ;
  Why should we harp of age and dull years gone ? "
Time seemed to be no sort of object to it—
  It just went on and on.

The bitter comparison made a wry but genuine kind of poetry. The disgust that was real was the core of a disgust that was assumed. Treacle and suet might not have been a very precise image but this was 1914 ; it communicates a little to us that was deliberately not communicated to contemporaries.

One frequent verse writer of the period who should be mentioned was " Algol " (C. H. Bretherton). He was a busy journalist, whose verse journalism appeared in many papers, a link with the rest of the humorist press. Humorous papers shared artists with *Punch* but at this time few writers. He aimed at a lower level of scholarship than Seaman and his fellows and reflected a kind of world that was coming into the drawings, the world of the suburban householder, the Little Man, who gardened rather than hunted, struggled on a daily journey to work in London and took part in social events altogether less classy than those attended by du Maurier. An interesting example of his relation to the older *Punch* tradition were some verses called *Coal.*[21] These began with a profusion of classical imagery and it only gradually appeared that he was using his gods and heroes mockingly. Instead of the usual sneer at the miner, or even the half-hearted sympathy, he argued in favour of an alliance between the consumer and the miner against the coal trade.

Oh, if we twain together might conspire,
Would we not grasp them by the scruff and fire
    Coal merchants, barons, dukes and millionaires,
And run the business to our hearts' desire,
    Paying no dividends on watered shares ;

Blessing State ownership and State control,
You for high wages, I for cheaper coal.

In the period down to 1920 there were many versifiers who appeared frequently but were so completely and indistinguishably inside the Seaman tradition that there is nothing much to say about them once the Seaman tradition has been discussed. The whole point about it is perhaps that only its creator could do much with it. But there have always been odd contributors who don't fit in anywhere, like Jessie Pope. For example, *The Tempestuous Petticoat* :

Gossamer petticoats, frothy frivolities,
  Thrilling with pleasure we greet you again ;
Long have we missed your ebullient qualities
  While at the top of the cupboard you've lain ;
    Ruches and rucks
    Gathers and tucks,
Dear to our ankles your sorcery still is ;
    Extra large feet
    Shrink and look neat
Framed by your fluttering tumult of frillies.

Sisters, have done with the cult of the sinuous,
  Struggle no more to be straight up and down,
Aim not at figures austerely continuous,
  Curveless in profile from slipper to crown.
    Paris declines
    Skimpy designs,
Skin-fitting toilettes, in weight a few ounces,
    Granting instead
    Garments that spread
Fringed by a flutter of filigree flounces.[22]

Or Eleanor Farjeon. Here are two of her *Nursery Rhymes of London Town* :

### BEVIS MARKS

Bevis marks the blackboard, Bevis marks his socks,
Bevis marks the time o' day by the City clocks ;
Even if a pin drops Bevis says, " Hark ! "
There's nothing worth mentioning that Bevis *doesn't* mark.[23]

### NEWINGTON BUTTS

The bung is lost from Newington Butts !
The beer is running in all the ruts,
The gutters are swimming, the Butts are dry,
Lackadaisy ! and so am I.
Who was the thief that stole the bung ?
I shall go hopping the day he's hung ! [24]

One interesting contributor was Rose Fyleman. *Punch* reacted against the horrors of modern life by retreating in many directions and one favourite direction was fairyland. Sometimes twice on a page there were pretty little poems about fairies and elves and trees with key-holes. *There are Fairies at the Bottom of Our Garden* [25] appeared first in *Punch*. Why there should have been this connection between recollections of classical mythology, grunted disapproval of most things that had happened in politics or society or art since the late Seventies and fairies, I do not know. It is as baffling as the *Punch* passion for country place-names. In a period in which more and more people lived in towns and what remained of the country was being ruthlessly destroyed, *Punch* often wrote as though the average contributor had just wended his way over the last hill before the inn of his dreams. As late as 1924 *Punch* contained this incredible note : " The Editor begs to acknowledge with respectful gratitude a Valentine of early spring flowers sent to him from the Fairy Queen, through one of Her Charming Majesty's agents. (Anonymous.) " [26] However, the point about the Fyleman poems is not that their subject matter was coy but that the versification was neat.

## V

Art under Seaman, which until just after the war meant art under Townsend also, altered very little. It derived from book illustration, at a time when literal illustration was going out of fashion. The pictures had to be brought to Seaman covered over, with only the captions showing. He judged their suitability for the paper on the caption and the covering was then removed for him to see whether the picture illustrated it. There is a surprising variation of competence within the same tradition. Seaman and Townsend printed people who drew very well indeed in the comic tradition and also people who could hardly draw at all and did not compensate for incompetence by comic invention. The contributions of Wallis Mills, banal in caption and amateurish in drawing, once again illustrate the important historical point that far too often editorial decisions to publish bad work have been remembered, while editorial decisions to publish good work have been forgotten. Claude Shepperson, for example, was unnoticed for thirty years until he was elected A.R.A. It is still possible to find a certain amount that is elegant and enchanting, not only for its period flavour.

Whereas thirty or forty years before, the jokes in the text had been rather badly behind the jokes under the pictures, in Seaman's time, with the exception of the work of a few leading contributors, it was the writers more than the artists who were exploring new fields of humour and showing awareness of change in their world. An artist like H. M. Brock, who helped as much as anybody to build up the characteristic *Punch* flavour, presented the reader with recognisable scenes, rather perhaps as the reader himself might have presented them. In those days, many *Punch* readers looked for familiarity in an artist, where their descendants look for strangeness. Seaman hated change but he did tell G. H. Armour in 1929 that people were more interested in motor-cars than in horses and complained about his " types." However, Armour's pictures after this were as frequent and as horsey as before. Perhaps Seaman thought that the middle-class was dividing into lovers of field sports and lovers of animals and that the balance was turning against hunting.

An interesting example of only partially-realised talent was Lewis Baumer. He was in a way the leader, and certainly the most

*27th March, 1912* *Lewis Baumer*

*Breathless Lady (to energetic partner): " Gently—Mr. Hopkins—please do remember—it's Lent "*

popular, of the social commentators, using " social " in the old rather than the new sense. His tennis-parties and tea dances and bright young things and crusty old men and carefully-reared children depicted one aspect of one movement in English history as completely as Leech depicted another. Whether looking back we decide it was a good thing or a bad thing, it is stupid to ignore the fact that one of the most marked trends in early-Twentieth Century English history was the growth of the domitory area and the development in it of a culture, or at least a sub-culture, based primarily on leisure activities and marked by the evolution of a taste that developed from a tension between conspicuous consumption and conspicuous restraint. Baumer did not tell the whole story, but he told a good deal of it and, even when his work became spiritless and his jokes repetitive, the loss of vitality reflected the deracination that was probably unconsciously his theme. Though for many years he was a very typical *Punch* artist and a man of whom critics were complain-

*19th March, 1913* *George Morrow*

*The Phœnix (preparing for his centennial transformation).* "PARDON ME, SIR, BUT COULD YOU OBLIGE ME WITH A LIGHT?"

ing when they attacked the paper, he was capable of real comic invention as, for example, in the short series of burlesque films that he did in 1916.[27] These were not only funny in caption but funny in themselves. The shapes were funny.

Completely fresh and the biggest scoop for years was George Morrow, who began contributing in 1906. Morrow as a draughtsman was individual but not outstanding. It seems impossible that he would ever have won prizes for correct composition at school. He was a cheerful, bohemian Irishman, a member of a rackety family, several of whom, in particular Edwin Morrow, were also contributors. George Morrow was primarily a man with a sense of humour. His soft, diffident voice with its subtle and poetic lunacies (he claimed to have dreamed that the King was at a banquet and said to him, "I see the next course is lobster, I shall have to go and change into my Admiral's uniform."), the versatility of his talk, his all-too-little writing and the work he did in inspiring as well as illustrating humorous books written by Lucas and others distinguish him from the ruck of humourless certificated drawers from casts. Morrow in his prime, which continued far longer than with most humorous artists, could draw a simple little figure with a face that was funny *per se*. In his more elaborate compositions there would often be a head in a crowd that was obviously a Morrow head, yet it was funny in a different way from other Morrow heads. Some of his finest work was in single-figure story illustrations.

However, his reputation rests mainly on his big series. Like E. T. Reed, he was linked with a fairly mechanical framework that caught the popular imagination, and the fineness of his comic sense was under-rated. Much of his work was straightforward anachronism. Towards the end of his long life it consisted almost entirely of the "Rationing in Boadicea's Palace" type of joke. Repute always narrows. He was never entirely or even mainly a historical artist. *Entertainments At Which We Have never Assisted*,[28] which depended on the literal application of some phrase or title, was just as characteristic of him as a historical subject. He covered almost every kind of humorous invention, except the social cut. For years he did the *Royal Academy Depressions*,[28a] one or more pages of ingenious comic perversions of Academy pictures. As many of these leaned more heavily on subject than on painting, there was nothing philistine in guying the subject-matter. It is a pity that *Punch* did not do much parodying of painters' styles until recently. Morrow once drew a picture of a factory where one of the processes was rolling oats.[28b] As a joke he drew an operative rolling one single oat on the machine. The blockmakers took this oat to be a blemish and removed it, so that the drawing as printed showed no oat all at. Discovering this, Morrow requested that his single oat should be stamped on to every single copy sold. For issue after issue in Seaman's time, he was one of the two artists who were trying to make people laugh with both drawing and caption. His versatility and his variety make some of the later draughtsmen look tired and repetitive. Perhaps some of them may have rather looked down on him ; but he often carried the paper on his shoulders.

The other essentially comic artist who gave *Punch* its character

*5th November, 1913* *George Morrow*

**ANOTHER WORLD'S WORKER.**

*The artist who paints the black halves on " restored " pictures*

was " W. Bird," a pseudonym of Jack B. Yeats, W. B.'s painter brother. His humour was irrational, wild and precise, his drawing much criticised as incompetent. He broke all the rules and his genius still draws readers back to volumes in which nothing much else appeals to them. He was not exactly a representative of the modern art of the day, as he was in his serious painting, but he owed a good deal to it. His deliberate comic use of the freedoms the rebels had won showed almost the only loosening in the arid perfectionism of *Punch*'s pages. It is fair to point out that Townsend and Seaman continued to print both Morrow and Bird, though many readers must have brought pressure on them, attacking Bird's drawings as not representing reality with exactness and his jokes as obscure. We are all at the mercy of our period, but to me much of Bird is still funny, and refreshingly funny, and his attempts to cope with the more routine kind of *Punch* joke are saved from dullness by the mad certainty of his line.

It is interesting to realise that to the backward view the contemporary ranking of artists is almost reversed. Who would have thought half a century ago that all the competence in rendering thatches and trees and hoofs and uniforms would be dead, while a few scrawls and distortions shone and developed. The object of publishing a humorous paper is not to record changes of costume. The history of expression, of the English face, was not illustrated by *Punch* in this period. We enter the characters' homes, but not their minds. We spend a good deal of time with their children (J. H. Dowd was the Armour of the nursery.) However, it is only fair to point out that as illustrators men like Townsend were at the head of their profession. It may have been a curious ambition to want to make the paper of Leech and Tenniel into a weekly exhibition of English black-and-white, but at least the ambition was fulfilled. That particular tradition remained genuinely alive longer in *Punch* than it did outside.

It is quite impossible to mention all the competent artists, much less all the frequent ones. It is a penalty of playing safe, of doing what everyone else does, that there is nothing much left later on. With few exceptions, the best *Punch* contributors were quite unlike one another. Of the important artists of the pre-war and war period who have still to be mentioned, Ernest Shepard departed least violently from convention. It is important to realise the relationship of his work to say, Shepperson's. He started from a sound knowledge of how to draw and an interest in middle-class life in its less strenuous aspects. Shepard's work was distinguished by movement. Compare any of his drawings of any period with the usual *Punch* drawing. He does not seem to have depended on a studio pose or a diagrammatic composition. One feels the studies for the pictures were made on a wind-ruffled sketching-block. He was preoccupied with the freize rather than the group. Above all he was thinking in terms of the dance. With Shepard the rest of *Punch* began to look static. How heavily other men's dowagers sat on chairs, their horsewomen on horses or their judges on benches.

*8th January, 1919* *W. Bird*

*The Fare.* "I DEFY YOU!" *The Driver.* "WHO ARE YOU?"
*The Fare.* "I AM A RETIRED TAXI-DRIVER."

Even where the scene in Shepard was a conversation one feels that there was a wind in the room and that someone had just moved and that someone else was about to move.

One fundamental issue in the modern *Punch* must be touched on. If you're afraid of something, the thing to do is to fight it or to run away. To stand where you are and try to think the menace out of existence rarely produces much in the way of art. Where the endless delineators of suburban summers falsified was by suggesting that all life was like that when it obviously was not. The stronger artist will render an area of reality with disgust or delight in accordance with his judgment of it, or else he will take deliberate flight. Shepard's illustrations to poems, sometimes to poems that were very sentimental, were not only much better-drawn than most of the representational artists could manage, but informed by a passionate belief that the only justification of flight was disciplined grace. Sometimes, as in Walter de la Mare (and with the right encouragement earlier he might have become something like a graphic de la Mare), the idyll departs from civilisation and gets deep enough into the primitive to be blown by the winds of panic. His illustrations to Milne's *When We Were Very Young* and *Winnie the Pooh* may perhaps be occasionally guilty of the prettification he was attacked for, though compared with other illustrations to children's books of the time they will be found strong and much less sentimental : but at least they appealed to children more than any illustrations since Tenniel's *Alice*. Shepard is one of the *Punch* men who have managed to do good work outside fashion and is probably more appreciated in the aesthetic climate of to-day than he was twenty years ago.

H. M. Bateman suffered, like Heath Robinson, from becoming associated with one line in his later work. He was a versatile comic artist in his early days and his pictures, with their determination to concentrate on being amusing, made for cheerfulness in the pages. At first they were firmly grounded in observation, the same kind of racy observation that the older music-hall comedians brought to their character-songs. Behind the drawing was an individual humour. One never felt with early Bateman that he was illustrating some joke sent in to him, but that the joke and the drawing were conceived together. Later the technique of telling a story in a large number of little pictures—one of these once covered four pages of an issue—instead of being in itself a funny idea, became merely a method of dilution. Eventually the same kind of situation and character was used so often that it became detached from any particular picture and lived independently as a kind of national folk lore . . . the Bateman Colonel or The Man Who . . . committed some solecism or other. At his best, Bateman was individual, funny and invaluable.

George Belcher was a Regency buck in manner and a close observer of the appearances of low life by vocation. His drawings were completely different from those of any of his contemporaries

*20th March, 1918* *H. M. Bateman*

THE COAT THAT DIDN'T COME OFF.

and, as one turns over the leaves of dead volumes, one greets them with delight. Kenneth Bird has described him as "Phil May in chalk." He found jokes with difficulty and preferred to have them provided for him. He had a sense of fun, but not much sense of humour. Sometimes he did not understand the joke he was illustrating. He was sent a joke that depended on being set in a fishmonger's and illustrated it with a drawing of a greengrocer's, explaining, when questioned, that there was a very good greengrocer's just by his home. He has been criticised for making his figures look like posed models and he was certainly not a Phil May in eye or curiosity. Yet somehow the pose did not matter. He

*11th February, 1925* *George Belcher*

*Lady (to Next Door, discussing departing lodger) : " I likes to part friendly, but I* did *just say ' Gawd 'elp the cat wot 'as to lick* your *plate.' "*

never produced anything that looks like an art school study. His charwomen were all much alike ; but he knew the old London well and laid his emphasis on the convivial and the fruity. It is as one of the few *Punch* draughtsmen of the period to reveal humour in character or to have a line humorous in itself that he lives. He drew the poor as a kindly gentleman who paid them to come and be drawn by him, not, like Phil May, as somebody sketching the neighbours. But he drew very well indeed.

" Fougasse " (Kenneth Bird) was trained as an engineer, like Sambourne. He was badly wounded in the First World War and made his name with military subjects. Clarity and speed were everything in his work and he was constantly trying to simplify. In later life some of his work became diagrammatic, like the Vienna Pictorial Statistics. He began fairly close to the orthodox illustrator of the humours of life like Bert Thomas ; but he rapidly developed a personal style that was perhaps the first introduction of contemporary advertising techniques to the editorial pages of *Punch*. It was a necessary movement, though it meant that the decorative element was thrown out with the linear padding. In early Fougasse a tree would be in a drawing for itself, for the opportunity it provided for filling the whole rectangle with a pleasing design. Later the tree would be there only if strictly needed to make a point, and then it would be an ideographical tree, not woody, leafy and alive. He relied on the reader's imagination, whereas the illustrators felt themselves bound to do all the work for the reader. Fougasse led the way to aiming at an active rather than a passive readership. Like Morrow, he was primarily a humorist. His jokes were better than other people's. It is probable that he became known for his captions before he was recognised for his revolutionary drawings. His humour was rooted in sympathy with life. He dealt with the recognisable in character, setting and situation, and later was to use radio and motoring as constant subjects. His weakness was that in choosing the rôle of the Englishman laughing at himself he often took themes that suggested satire and laughed too kindly. On the rare occasions he has hit hard he has cut deep.

When Sambourne died in 1910, Partridge moved up to take the principal cartoon and there was no discernible change in his methods or his merits. Partridge was succeeded as junior cartoonist by Raven Hill, a great admirer of Sambourne's. Though just as much an illustrator of an idea hammered out by the staff, he had a far stronger impact in the paper than his senior colleague. He took a vehement share in discussions—Lucas said "He knew every move of the political game and wished his knowledge shared" [29]—while Partridge was, like Tenniel, silent and withdrawn. Instead of painstakingly building the cartoon up, he dashed it off, once in an emergency in under half an hour, and some of his own

*20th January, 1937* *Fougasse*

*"There's a moose loose!"*
*"Are you English or Scots?"*

fierce political passion came through. In a generally fairly happy society, he was probably the most cantankerous *Punch* man since Furniss and this, while it made him a difficult colleague, saved his work from dullness. As you open the paper his meaning hits you.

When Raven Hill began to draw for *Punch* as a regular illustrator, he was already a busy pictorial journalist. *Punch* only very gradually became his main concern. He never held the same position as Partridge—it was Partridge who was knighted—perhaps because he was neither as monumentally static in his work, nor yet quite a strong enough draughtsman to strike out on his own. In his cartoons, profiles were firmly drawn. Motion was convincing. There were few of the props with which it was traditional to clutter up the scene. Every part of a Raven Hill cartoon was there for the purpose of some effect. As feeling rose, he rose with it. Evoe has said: "He has done some wonderfully forceful and vivid stuff, and was a great foil to Bernard Partridge. I think he reached a splendid peak of performance during the war." [30] His friend Kipling chose him to illustrate *Stalky*.

## VI

With the war the problem of fighting back or running away became more urgent. Soldiers fought back at the enemy as far as they could. They did not on the whole run away physically, but they naturally and properly ran away mentally, into dreams of life after the war, into hate-fantasies against the staff, conchies or the Kaiser, or into humour. The jokes may sometimes seem to us poor ones : the Western Front was not an area in which a high intellectual standard was possible. One cannot look through the war-time *Punches* without emotion or forget the background of black-bordered casualty lists and immense weariness. It was the function of the humorous press to circulate the better or at least the more printable jokes. At the outbreak of the war, Seaman had been doubtful whether there was any place for *Punch* at all in war-time. His natural tendency was to see public affairs dramatically and this made him unable to conceive of humour as emerging from the conflict. Once he could be persuaded that *Punch* had a function as a morale booster, he worked hard.

In the post-war pacifist period attacks were made on *Punch* for not opposing the war and the suggestion was made that the old Radical *Punch* would have done so. This showed ignorance of the fire-eating contents in the Forties and Fifties. Jerrold and Thackeray were often violent about foreign affairs. The Pope and the French, the neglect of the Volunteer movement and inefficiency in defence were always rousing the paper to abuse. In 1914 *Punch* took the same view as the overwhelming majority of the nation. Looking back, it seems difficult to imagine what other course could possibly have been taken ; but then the look of 1914 today is very different from its look in 1930.

LEADERSHIP SLIGHTLY LIGHTENED BY DEPARTURE OF TOM MANN FOR SOUTH AFRICA

*4th March, 1914* *Raven Hill*

THE NINE OLD MEN OF THE SEA.

RAMSAY MACSINDBAD. "WELL, WELL, IT MIGHT HAVE BEEN WORSE. THERE MIGHT HAVE BEEN TEN OF 'EM."

The tragic background was represented by the cartoons and many serious poems, of which John McCrae's *In Flanders Fields* [31] is the most famous. For the most part *Punch* made jokes about food and shelter at the front and at home, rather than jokes about death and destruction. In peace there may be a case for directing satire at the grim, but the time for anti-war propaganda is before the war starts.

For much of the war there was no conscription and pressure to volunteer was social. Ex-suffragettes distributed white feathers and *Punch* was full of jokes against the shirkers, without much discrimination between the coward and the man who was, in fact, being made best use of. Rarely was there any joke at the excesses of the recruiting drive. The other main subject for home-front humour was shortages ; in those happy days every joke about rationing was new. (I am told that First War *Punches* were carefully examined by gag-writers in the Second War for their rationing jokes.) The Land Girl with her sweet ignorance of the facts of life was a popular butt. This was one of the oddest examples of Seaman's narrowness. Only the daughters he met at tea-parties in Mayfair could conceivably have been as ignorant of farming as the typical Land Girl of the pictures. The rural working class had always been used to female labour on the farms and the rural middle and upper classes, if they had less experience of back-breaking work, had grown up in the country and helped with the harvest for fun. *Punch* had always taken an interest in hunting and the kind of girl who hunted could not suddenly have turned into the kind of girl who was flummoxed by a horse. Nor was the Land Girl of the pictures drawn from the town shop girls, who were more often shown as bus-conductresses, waitresses and, where they were most likely to be found, still in shops. The home-front and the battle-front met when a letter from home about some minor catastrophe was received in the midst of carnage. This situation crops up so often in the pictures that it must have represented a very frequent stimulus to disproportionate fury.

A good average war-time series was F. O. Langley's *The Watch*

*Dogs*. Langley did a tremendous amount of work for *Punch* over many years ; like Gilbert à Beckett he became a Police Court Magistrate. One of these letters home [32] began with a description of a bombed town in a " This desirable residence " style. Then came an affectionate description of a Town Major. There was an account of how he refused permission for the door to be taken from a wrecked building for fuel and then mentioned he had not yet put a picket at the back. The article ended with the reception of the first Jutland report, the depressing one, by a French peasant, and the query, " If that is how a French peasant took the first news, how do you suppose the German peasants are digesting the second and better version ? "

Of the artists who were particularly successful in the war, Bert Thomas, after Fougasse, was probably the best. His very individual line, broken as if he had dashed the idea down while it was white-hot in his mind, was rather like Bairnsfather's, though he was a far more varied artist and his jokes were generally better. He had some of the attack and speed of Raven Hill. His sometimes frenzied methods were effective for depicting action, less so for jokes that simply demanded some common-or-garden emotion like surprise. He drew a wider range of classes than most *Punch* artists. Of the writers, Milne did not, as he was accused of doing, treat the Western Front like a house-party. His war articles have been rather neglected in comparison with his pre-war leisure-hour stuff. They had the same versatility and gaiety and they dealt with the only aspects of the subject that could possibly be treated humorously. It is preposterous to suggest that a humorous periodical providing one of the few alleviations in the middle of blackness should have produced every number in the style of Remarque or Barbusse. *Punch* could not reasonably have been expected to keep up the standards of Wilde or Whistler in every joke throughout the war but it contained plenty of agreeable pleasantries, like its remarks about margarine, " *C'est magnifique mais ce n'est pas le beurre*," [33] or " America is anxious to see a settlement of the Irish question but there is no truth in the rumour that we have cabled to say that we will take on

Mexico if America will take on Ireland." [34] or " No indication that Bulgaria would surrender unconditionally appeared in the papers in the week before. A great scoop this for Bulgaria," [35] or the remark that the weather was so wet that that year it looked as if the Channel had decided to swim Great Britain.

A. P. Herbert had begun contributing while still at school but

*9th April, 1924* *Bert Thomas*

*Diner (to another complaining of soup being spilled over him) : " It's all right, Sir. I know the soup here ; it never stains after 8.15."*

it was the war that really gave him his chance. Wykhamist, son of a Civil Servant, ex-Librarian of the Oxford Union and Barrister, he was a magnificently-equipped *Punch* recruit.

Ah, what a night ! The cannon roared ;
There was no food to spare ;
And first it froze and then it poured ;
Were we dismayed ? We were.

> Three hundred yards we went or more,
> And, when we reached, through seas of gore,
> The village we were fighting for,
> The Germans were not there.[36]

This was a good average piece of light verse. The scansion was not ostentatiously adept but unobtrusive and serviceable. There was little fat that could be hewn away. There was a point to the verse, it was gay and above all it moved forward. The rhymes were so right and simple that they became invisible. A. P. H. wrote better verse than this. The point I'm making is that this could be found in the same *Punch* as the most dreary and mechanical work and, when people insist that all *Punch* used to be like that, the quotation from A. P. H. makes it clear that it was not. His light verse was disgusted but never evasive. He was as direct in verse as in prose. *The Secret Battle*, almost the first anti-war novel, came clearly from the same area of inspiration. The verse never laughed with a twisted smile at its own cleverness. The Gallipoli stuff, the lines about being wounded, the training-unit verses gave a picture of war in which both the Mess and the trenches got their due weight. Although most *Punch* war-time contributions were very officerly, in A. P. H.'s verse you never got the feeling that the army as a whole was out of sight of the Mess.

The war increased the appeal of *Punch* for the public. There were Messes and hospitals and odd times behind the line in billets. Mothers at home sent *Punch* to their sons at the front. Anything that recalled the old England in the First World War, like anything that suggested a new England in the Second World War, provided something for the strained to hang on to. At the Armistice *Punch* possessed an enormous amount of affection and good will. Is it not possible that some of the quite fantastically exaggerated reaction against the paper in the post-war period may have been really a reaction from wartime laughter that had itself been a reaction against fear, squalor and tension ?

It is a truism that war accelerates change. Undoubtedly Lemon and Jerrold and Brooks would have paid more attention to the changes it caused in the industrial pattern, in literature and the arts. The main criticism that can be made of *Punch* editing during four of the most crowded years of Britain's existence must be that there was too much " business as usual " and insufficient realisation of the wonderful new fields opening for a humorous paper. The future was to be with the tank rather than the horse, with electricity rather than with steam, with Picasso rather than with Dicksee. The truth of this criticism does not affect the fact that there was plenty of vitality and gaiety left in England and this vitality was reflected neither stodgily nor dishonourably in page after page of the war-time *Punch*.

CHAPTER SEVEN

# YEARNING FOR THE PAST

## *Owen Seaman's Editorship, 1918–1932*

TO THE modern reader the period after the First World War is the hardest to see clearly because each revolution in *Punch* has left behind it opponents and apostles. *Punch* in the past has suffered from indiscriminate praise and indiscriminate blame.

The history of *Punch* from the Peace Treaty to Seaman's retirement at the end of 1932 was strangely like the history of *Punch* before the war; the world had changed but not the paper. What has been said in praise of Seaman for his insistence on high standards of accuracy and clarity continued to be true. What has been said in praise of him for finding new blood was less true in the sense of searching for original talent, but he still kept *Punch* open to new men provided they wrote within the scope of his appreciation. The criticisms that have been made of his pre-war editing continued to be valid and must, indeed, be strengthened for two reasons. He was becoming ever more fussy and, although the climate of humour was changing much faster, he refused to accept or even to understand the changes.

It is difficult now to realise the hysteria with which *Punch* was reviled in this period and beyond. It stood for everything that public opinion in all Parties detested. It was not even wholeheartedly on the side of reaction. It was tolerant, avuncular and patronising. Criticism came from Right and Left, though every attack on class changes, Americanisation of English speech, modern art or the modern girl was received with clucks of approval in hunting lodge and rectory and in the sad sitting-rooms where the daughters of military men gave music lessons. On points like Epstein's " Rima "[1] *Punch* took the same view as the cheap press. It criticised change with neither profundity nor wit. For some time two or three items an issue were directed to the single point of attack : modern art was cruel to our feathered friends. The real Hudson was forgotten.

The readers on the whole confined themselves to continuing their subscriptions and writing violent letters of complaint at any change however slight, however necessary. The attacks, on the other hand, were as harsh as the attacks that the *Punch* of Jerrold had withstood. It was curious that later, when attention was attracted back to *Punch*, contributors who had been appearing in it for years were assumed to have been imported as the result of a recent campaign of improvement. It was also noticeable that outside writers of some distinction invited to contribute searched their memories of the paper as they had read it at their preparatory schools and produced articles of the kind that had been dying out thirty years before.

In a succession of revolutions *Punch* has reformed itself, tacitly accepting the truth of many of the criticisms made of it for over a generation ; but it would be a pity if, now that the war is won, the unnecessary casualties are forgotten. Obviously the late-Seaman Age cannot compare with the Age of Jerrold or the Age of Brooks or even with the Age of early Burnand. That settled, however, it is interesting to turn to the volumes and see what it actually published and how much of it is still good. Seaman did manage to keep his best contributors ; he was more successful at this than some Editors. He depended too much on his stars and he did not always see their full possibilities. Yet he did publish in text and drawings material of real contemporary merit.

As he aged, and he was always old for his years, he lay back rather grandly upon the cushions of his title, his position as Editor of what he considered the greatest paper in the world and his well-organised social life. He no longer needed to fight for supremacy against abler colleagues. Lehmann had gone. Milne had been politely advised that he had no future in the paper and a glittering one in the theatre. In appointments, the young were succeeded by the old. Lucas, who was becoming a sympathiser with the clubman side of Seaman and had lost some of his radicalism under the strain of hackwork and publishing, introduced as Milne's successor in the office W. A. Locker, a nephew of the author of *London Lyrics*, and Lucas's and Graves's old Editor in their early newspaper days. He was a very experienced political journalist of the late-Nineteenth Century type with a memory that was very useful in the office, a kindly, amiable old boy, who enjoyed producing a stream of little puns over his tea. The young men coming along had grown up in the acceptance of Seaman as an adult, a tremendous mixture of Victorian father and Edwardian uncle. The conflict between the generations, so bitter at the end of the war, never burst out in *Punch*, unless there was some element in it over Milne. Seaman was tough. None of the young men he school-mastered was the type to lead a palace revolution : and he may not have been a likeable man but some did find him lovable.

Generally speaking he did not believe in " being as process ", which Mr. G. M. Young has found to be the characteristic Victorian belief. He did not see *Punch* as an organism or plan ahead, looking to see the way humour was changing, learning from successes and failures in the past. He saw *Punch* as a National Institution and about as liable to change as the Nelson column. Its function was to act as a fixed point for a bemused public until the normal condition of stasis was resumed. The humour of incomprehension joined the humour of incompetence and sometimes one gets the impression that the paper was written by the half-witted and proud of it. Seaman's fussiness over details of metre, grammar and clarity meant that form could not follow content, that moulds were set ; but it did mean that *Punch* continued to be written in clear and precise English. It was the English of the clerisy and it may have lacked tang, surprise and vitality. Yet how easily the country's leading humorous paper might have been written in journalese. False delicacy can become a disease. There was always a danger that Seaman would spot some possibility of offence where none existed and also that what began as a sexual censorship might widen out to a social one until a point was reached at which anything that the silliest mother might want to keep from her ten-year-old daughter, such as that low persons dropped aitches or that contemporary artists sometimes distorted the figure, was cut. The resultant emasculation affected the humour-producing mechanism of the brains that served *Punch*. It was safer to do again something that had been done before. Once when George Morrow was Art Editor, he brought Seaman a drawing that depended on an octopus's flooding the surrounding sea with ink. Seaman liked the caption but looked worried and said, " George, eh, where does the octopus discharge the ink from ? " Morrow replied, " Well, Owen, I'm afraid it is from the, eh, anus." " What a pity. Then of course we cannot use it." " Eh, Owen, I understand that in an octopus the anus is between the eyes." " Oh, in that case, we'll take it." [2]

Starting from the assumption that lack of change was a good thing in itself, Seaman made only the alterations in the contents of the paper forced on him by need to replace the dead. The make-up of the paper varied very little from beginning to end of his reign. The radio was not criticised, for example. Film criticisms began in 1925 but only special films were reported. These reports slowly increased in frequency down to the end of 1928. Then they became regular, at first contributed by A. P. H. and Lucas, who began over the signature " F.F." Soon Lucas became the only film reviewer and, as he despised the cinema, he suited both Seaman and the kind of reader to whom Seaman wanted to appeal. *Punch* was sometimes funny about bad films and sometimes gave sensible advice to readers about what was entertaining but it was the late Thirties before it began to publish serious film criticism with Richard Mallett, whose regular film articles began in 1938. Occasional articles covered a circus or fair and there was a good deal about Wembley.

The two main movements in humour during the period were a

widening of possible humorous subject-matter—the funny bits in serious novels were funnier and one of the key books of the period, *Ulysses*, was comic—and the use of the full range of the language. Slang, American, French, Italian, puns, distortions, special vocabularies like those of the law or physics were all used to get comic effects. Perhaps a third movement may be found in the return to a dream world of illogical, " crazy " humour, which may be German-Jewish in origin but became established in the entertainment business in New York. James Thurber used all three developments. Seaman refused to admit any of them. He thought the English language was the kind of language one had translated into Latin at school. The humour of madness he claimed to enjoy but to exclude in the interests of slower-witted readers. In practice it worried him. The humour of character and situation and intrigue he seems to have imagined that he printed.

One sometimes gets the impression that the object of *Punch* was to supplement its readers' sense of humour, whereas the *Westminster Gazette* or the *New Statesman* complemented it. *Punch* has an air, at times, of providing jokes for those who found joking difficult. Sometimes men with a keen sense of humour were forced to write more broadly and obviously than came natural to them, because of the assumption that a sizeable proportion of their readers had a sense of humour that was sub-normal. It was not realised that to pander to these lost to the paper quicker-witted readers, for whom it would have been more inspiring to work. The more one thinks about this policy, the odder it seems. For a humorous periodical to be aimed at the unhumorous was as absurd as for a musical periodical to be aimed at the tone-deaf, but it is quite clear, by the tone of the correspondence from some of the older readers and by opinions expressed in conversation, that Seaman's *Punch* did arouse a frenzied and deadly loyalty among bores, the naïve and the prematurely old.

It is revealing to compare what was printed with what could have been printed. Mr. E. V. Knox considers that one constant theme in *Punch* history is the missing of the best men. Before 1914 *Punch* verse could have gained new inspiration from Belloc and Chesterton.

How inconceivable it is to think of Seaman's using Max Beerbohm. How inconceivable it is to think of Lemon's not doing so. In an interesting article on an exhibition of Beerbohm cartoons in 1925,[3] Seaman tried to be fair to a fellow Institution, but the praise was simply a restatement of reputation ; the disapproval, delightfully enough, was much better worded than Seaman's usual pontifications. He accused Max of being unimaginative, which may be true, though not in the sense he intended it, and then got into a tangle over whether Max's malice was a virtue or a vice. It is clear that Seaman did not quite like to say what he really felt, which was that attacks on people he approved of were bad taste, but those on people of whom he disapproved were good taste. There were two reasons why Seaman could never have used Max ; he could not distinguish between what was done and how it was done, and he could never have been certain that he was not missing the point and that that point was not made on the wrong side.

The *Essence of Parliament*, taken over by W. A. Locker on Lucy's resignation in 1916, sagged rather. Lucy was almost impossible to follow but his successors tended to make cautious little jokes rather than take a line of their own. It was no longer a feature unique in the press and unless *Punch* could add something to what was printed elsewhere there was not much point in giving space to it. Locker gave way to C. H. Bretherton (" Algol ") at the beginning of 1926. He was a good deal livelier than Locker and wrote in a mildly mocking style that was probably as far as Seaman let him go. The illustrations of A. W. Lloyd, who first made his name in South Africa, combined caricature of politicians and imaginary scenes, often based on taking a metaphor in a speech literally. They did not draw attention to themselves, but over the years built up a following that liked to have their mental picture of Parliament peopled and found the designs decorative and not distracting.

Dramatic Criticism continued to be shared. J. Thorp took over temporarily when Milne enlisted and stayed on. At Stonyhurst he had acted in school plays, which were re-written to omit female parts. In *Iolanthe*, he took Robin Goodfellow, the character who replaced the Fairy Queen. (The proud adaptor sent a copy of his version to Gilbert !) For a time he became a Jesuit trainee but drifted into fine printing, advertising and industrial design. He was a man full of enthusiasm, who first met Seaman over charitable committee work. One of his schemes was the Agenda Club, the activities of which included recalling the Gentlemen of England to their duties and trying to regularise the hours of Golf Caddies. He says in his entertaining reminiscences that his copy was never cut merely to fit on the page and he was never given any editorial direction on opinion. When he began Seaman said, " Say what you think but sometimes remind yourself that the actors earn their living at this business and give them the benefit of the doubt ".[4] Some of the plays were still reviewed by Seaman. Evoe did a good deal in the Twenties. Haselden, immaculate, quiet and witty, continued to illustrate with hit or miss likenesses, as he had done since before the war. Plays were reliably and sensibly dealt with by the *Punch* team. *Punch* now never published anything comparable to the famous American attacks on bad plays as it had in its past. Sometimes the quietness of the general tone made people miss the force of a condemnation when it did condemn. Moving with educated opinion behind it, *Punch* developed an interest in the serious theatre. It was not until Eric Keown started as a regular dramatic critic in 1932 that *Punch* began to be taken seriously by the theatrical world, but until he retired Thorp's opinion was at least worth considering well beyond the range of the " tired businessman's legshow " which was popularly supposed to be the extent of *Punch*'s competence, and Evoe's unpredictable flair would sometimes lift the Dramatic Criticism into a class of its own.

The pars continued to please readers by the wide coverage. From all over the world they were sent in and *Punch* provided the best, and for some time the only, collection of amusing misprints and inadvertencies. Seaman continued to insist that the point should be hammered home. In *Charivaria* the general form set by Walter Emanuel was retained ; this was a news item, real or manufactured, followed by a comment. The personal and the politically—or socially—penetrating were eschewed and the general tendency was to make jokes peripheral, about fashions and crazes and minor events. Some topics were used over and over again because the important things were too important to joke about.

Book reviewing in the later Seaman period varied very much. On the whole it was not as good as in the days of Milne and Lucy. The replacement of young talent by elderly correctitude which had to a large extent been forced on *Punch* by the war continued during the peace and the note of bufferdom that in the pre-war years had been occasional now became more obtrusive ; but it is a mistake to compare the *Punch* book reviews of the period with those in *The Times Literary Supplement* or the *New Statesman*. It is fairer to point out that they were far superior in vigour and common sense to those in most periodicals addressed to audiences that expected to be amused. It is absurdly unhistorical to criticise *Punch* for not devoting all its space to close analysis of work that was still not making its way beyond a coterie. If the test be where do you find the best discussion of *Ulysses* in the Twenties, it is true you will not point to *Punch* ; but to adopt this as a test, as has been done, is to pay an unintentional compliment. Nobody would apply a test like this to *The Bystander* or *The Windsor* or *London Opinion*.

## II

The politics of the early post-war period were confused by the general assumption that they had returned to pre-war alignments and procedures. The break up of the Liberal Party loomed larger than the rise of Labour. Asquith, whose influence on the future, the fairest test of a statesman, ended with the first wartime coalition, was still treated as a major political force. The struggle for power in the Conservative Party was not understood. The Irish remained for several years in the limelight but it was a different Irish problem. The Trade Unions were still regarded as something extrinsic to the polity and the idea lingered on that they were the creation of paid agitators and would somehow die away. The shock of the Russian Revolution, now often referred to as though it rocked the propertied classes immediately it happened, was long deadened by incomprehension—the earliest reports had suggested it would greatly increase Russia's value as an ally—and then seen as a desperate attempt by a gang of murderers to fasten themselves upon our comrade-in-arms until they could be dislodged by the " real " Russia, whose armies were backed in their intervention by us. It seemed at first more of a threat to monarchy than to property. There was little realisation of its economic aspect.

Seaman saw everything in terms of loyalties. This made him personally very loyal to his staff but it imported moral elements into purely intellectual disagreements, which added dramatic verve to the cartoons, especially Raven Hill's, but deprived them of real deadliness. You cannot win a war if you do not understand what makes your enemy tick and how he fights his battles. Both Right and Left have attacked the political direction of *Punch* in this period on the grounds that it lacked understanding of what was going on. With Lehmann, Milne and Lucy gone there was a decline in the political knowledge of the Table.

The General Strike seemed at the time the opening of a phase of revolutionary action, though it is seen now to have been the end of the post-war phase of industrial activity. *Punch* apparently believed that the fault lay with a small number of agitators and that the millions who joined in the strike lacked all those qualities of sturdy common sense and ability to think for themselves that on other pages of the issue would be attributed to Englishmen. Foreigners were still fair game, including America, to whose language, *mores* and criminals *Punch* continued to be rude. France was more difficult. Anglo-French relations after the War were embittered and it took the rise of Hitler to cause a rapprochement. *Punch* had been late in becoming Francophil and it was now torn between the love of individual members of the staff for French food, art and countryside and disapproval of French chauvinism. The mutual delight of

America and France in each other's company did not make fairness easier. There was a tendency to ride away from the problems of the future, like trade deficits and Asian nationalism and the shift from a north-country population engaged in mining, textiles and heavy engineering to a Midland and Thames-valley population engaged in chemicals, light engineering and the making of cars and planes. The reappearance of old controversies raised disproportionate interest. *Punch* was probably more excited by the lowering of the voting age for women or by Winston's Churchill's acceptance of Safeguarding as compatible with Free Trade than by the industrial development of Canada or the attempt to make the Labour Party into a Federation in which one unit would be the middle class.

The English mind was coming alive before the war, but the war itself speeded the process up. The Twenties, with their gaiety, interest in the arts and curiosity, seem recognisably the beginning of the age we live in now. It was a period in which contrasts of wealth were vulgar but it was the vulgarity of development, not the vulgarity of decay. The Twenties were brash rather than genteel. The period was *Bull Dog Drummond* as well as *Antic Hay* and *Vile Bodies*. Beneath all the fuss about whether girls should say " damn " and drink cocktails and wear skimpy clothes was a steady widening of responsibility. The Squire became conscious of the existence of workmen for whom his ownership of shares made him as responsible as he felt himself to be for the tenants of his cottages. The slum-dweller began to feel kinship with slum-dwellers elsewhere and to be prepared to work for the betterment of their lot together with his own. The development of communications meant a widening of the mentally-acknowledged community. It is sometimes forgotten that in the world of to-day, split in half as it is, the two halves each represent some victory over the parochial.

*Punch* tended to be obsessed with the Flapper, a perfectly legitimate subject for social satire. The Flapper seems pretty silly now until we realise she represented simply the Woman of To-day in the awkward age. The objection to the Flapper joke was not that it was imperceptive or reactionary or spiceless but just that there was too much of it. It went on and on. The reason for this was partly Seaman's belief that his readers were as fond of the predictable and continuous as himself, partly that the narrowing of the list of possible subjects led inevitably to excessive concentration on the few that were left. *Punch* needed more men from the provinces, more men who were in sympathy with the technological revolution and would have joked about it from the inside, more men from the Dominions, more men from the poorer schools and from no school at all.

One great difficulty that faced Seaman was the breaking down of the educational tradition that had produced him. Even at the leading Public Schools boys were studying history and economics and chemistry and modern languages and art. The classical drill was dying out even on the classical side and boys were going up to the Universities knowing more about Homeric archæology than about prosody. The Latin tag was no longer a *lingua franca* within the ruling class. This made Seaman feel in a real crisis of communication. What would be comprehensible ? There was no universal discipline to replace the Classics. Even if jokes could be made in scientific formulæ there was no guarantee that a reasonable proportion of the readers would understand them. The shared experience of the hunting-field, the drawing-room, the club and the village and the schoolroom on which *Punch* had relied for so long could not be assumed now. Public events could still be taken as general in impact, though there was a decline in the kind of political joke that depended on the reader's being at least on the fringes of politics. What private experience could be assumed? Seaman, perhaps unconsciously, decided that one shared experience would be a decline in standard of living. The class that read *Punch* was breaking up, and would enjoy jokes about having fewer rooms and servants, about cutting the new owners of the big house and adapting itself to the intimacies of adjacent gardens and borrowed lawn-mowers. Evoe had been working on these lines many years before, an example of his odd prescience. The new *Punch* line was quite different from the old social-climber joke of du Maurier. Then society was fixed and laughed savagely down at the family trying to get into it. Now the best people were going down and Sir Gorgius Midas was in their place.

Where Seaman failed was in not dramatising this ruin of a class. A satirical periodical might well have provided a kind of ghastly sunset, but he was too kind a man to allow his paper to hit the supplanters and he was too old-fashioned a man to sit down to think out what was happening and base his policy on understanding the weak points he could attack. He seemed to have been unconscious of the rise of a new potential readership, of the fact that there was growth as well as decay. *Punch* was saved because there were a number of men of very considerable talent who found it possible to work within the limits he set.

No other humorous periodical aimed at an educated readership and quality advertising. Once it was agreed that the Parliamentary Report, Dramatic Criticism, Film Criticism and Cartoons were to be semi-straight and often perfectly serious, *Punch* as a general magazine was in competition with papers that ranged from *The Tatler* to *The Spectator*, *The Sunday Times* and *The Observer*. In this group there was nothing else in which humour played more than a subordinate part. There were Competitions, often very amusing, in *The Saturday Review* and later in *The New Statesman*. There was an occasional light article, especially in Christmas Numbers. In the " glossies " there were some humorous illustrations, a column of humorous anecdotes, odd humorous poems and sometimes pages of rather mechanical caricature.

The avowedly humorous papers that lived by publishing light fiction and articles ranged from substantial collections of " holiday " stories, to flimsy, badly-produced weeklies which seemed to print the same drawing and the same short article in every issue. Basically, a good deal of this hackwork derived from *Punch*. The artists and writers were sometimes seen in *Punch*, and one could not escape the feeling that some of the contents were, in fact, *Punch* rejects. However, the jocular assumptions about how their readers spent their time were far from Seaman's.

The chief threat, to repute rather than to sales, came from American magazine-publishing and in particular from *The New Yorker*, founded in 1925. Harold Ross, its founder, had a high opinion of *Punch* and seemed at times to imagine that his periodical had taken features from it ; but soon he came to the conclusion that it was a completely different kind of magazine. *The New Yorker* was not so far from the *Punch* of Mayhew, gossipy, acid, metropolitan and very uncertain until the stars began to make their way in it. It took all New York life for its province. It was not, despite its English reputation, sexy, though it accepted, as *Punch* did not, that girls sometimes got on by using their figures more than their brains. It assumed not only superficial sophistication in its readers but some knowledge of what was happening in the arts and literature. It was middlebrow, but what may be called brisk middlebrow rather than stodgy middlebrow. It used far more pointed social comment in its drawings than *Punch*. It had longer stories and articles. It took over and developed the " crazy " humour that was popular in America and it let its artists distort and simplify. It cut captions down to the minimum.

Its arrival in London gave a standard for would-be supporters of humorous magazines to rally to. In the late Twenties and Thirties criticisms of *Punch* often ended with a claim to prefer *The New Yorker*. Not unnaturally, some of the older *Punch* men were driven into reaction by its challenge. If Seaman had only learned from the better features of *The New Yorker* and left what was silly or shoddy or plain dull in it, he might have rejuvenated *Punch* painlessly. It was the mid-Thirties before it had much influence on *Punch*'s contents and by that date the kind of reader who would have enjoyed a rejuvenated *Punch* was lost.

## III

The writers of the late-Seaman period included a number of new names and some old names in new forms. A. A. Milne made a new reputation with his children's verses, *When We were Very Young*,[5] which were gay in approach and skilful in construction. They took too large a share of the criticism that *Punch* received for " going all whimsy " about childhood.

In the Twenties, Evoe was one of the three or four writers who kept *Punch* alive. Some of his success was due to an inner gaiety bubbling out through a crust of scholarship and socially-imposed decorum. Where so many writers tried to vamp up a frivolity they did not feel, Evoe disciplined and checked his own. He joked as though there were something reprehensible in joking and this gives a curious obliquity to some of his humour. His parodist's eye, though he used it less as he lost touch with post-war literature, could still operate upon an advertisement or a newspaper article or a slogan. He was almost the first *Punch* writer to be fascinated by the streak of madness in modern Britain.

A. P. Herbert, long established as a direct and forceful poet, especially during the war, and a writer of most kinds of article, was the other main star of the Twenties. It is a point strongly in Seaman's favour that just as he published the drawings of W. Bird, who seems now to have been everything that he disliked, he published A. P. H., who said in print the kind of things that people said in private. As one looks through the issues of the period, A. P. H.'s stature grows. The decline of his reputation seems a temporary thing, based too much on one bad patch in a life of sustained quality. He was quite unlike any other *Punch* man of the Burnand, Seaman or Evoe régimes.

A good deal of A. P. H. can be dismissed as routine. He tried to write the typical *Punch* article and, like most men who have tried it, apart from its inventors, he failed. He had little talent for making bricks from the straw of suburban life and he lacked the kind of comic invention with which Evoe rearranged reality into wildly funny patterns. Much of modern life he simply did not understand. No *Punch* man was more likely to burst into attacks on modern art, long-haired yellow-bellies and the rest of it. Where he disliked he attacked and, as with all extraverts, his attacks sometimes embarrassed admirers by their ignorance, frivolity and narrowness ; but, unlike some of the men whose timorous hates weakened the paper, he was a man of genius and he is entitled to have his weaknesses disregarded. A. P. H. was the greatest English journalist of his time. He wrote magnificent plain prose in argument or comment and sometimes in description. He belonged to the same line as Swift, Hazlitt, Cobbett, Shaw and Orwell. He was one of the very few *Punch* men of this century to have created a personal style. A Herbert article nearly always had an individual voice, persuasive, infuriating but as sharp and recognisable as Shaw.

A. P. H. lived in the present : he was one of the few humorists who rarely used the past as material. He lived with enormous energy, wrote as easily and straightforwardly as he lived and was always readable, direct and relevant. At a time when the paper was turning its back on the world it lived in, he almost alone represented the greater sanity of fighting back. Whether or not he was wrong is, for this purpose, irrelevant. What is important is that he regarded right and wrong as worth fighting about. To many readers, *Punch* was A. P. H. He was genuinely a satirist, unlike many of the *Punch* men who are given this title by people who do not understand what satire is. When his indignation was aroused by some abuse, he might denounce it in admirably-written invective, but more often he picked out its weaknesses and laughed at them. Very often he used the *reductio ad absurdum*. Nearly always the evils he attacked were capable of improvement and in and out of *Punch* he has improved them. He has fought more reforms through than any living man ; he is, indeed, a survival of an obsolescent type, the Reformer. His miscellaneous journalism, his chairmanship of committees, his active social life, even his Membership of the House of Commons as Junior Burgess for Oxford University have all helped, but it was primarily through *Punch* that he aroused opinion and got things done.

A. P. H. fought whatever party was in power. He fought against the maintenance of wartime regulations, against the Licensing Laws, against resorts that interfered with bathing, against policemen who acted as *agents provocateurs*, against the survival of obsolete laws like the one that said you could not get married after 3 p.m. and the neglect of the Thames as a highway. His most important reform—though the total effect of his libertarian campaigns should not be under-rated—was the big change in Matrimonial Law. This was actually brought into effect by one of the most remarkable Private Member's campaigns in history, but the groundwork had been laid by persistent fighting in *Punch* . It says something in Seaman's favour that he published articles which must have aroused frenzied complaints from many readers.

A. P. H. was successful with a number of series built round characters, like Honeybubble or Poker. The Topsy articles, written in a breathless rush, were tremendously popular. The most original and successful form that he invented was the mock Law Report. The *Misleading Cases* [6] were sometimes fantastic odd bits of law logically extended until the result was absurd ; sometimes they were aimed at amending the law by ridicule. The variety of the basic ideas, the scholarship, the magnificent judicial English, far cleaner and finer than the real thing, the incidental fun and the directness of purpose behind them made them one of the great *Punch* series.

In verse, he soon left behind him the mock ode and classical allusions and moved towards the verse-epistles which really suited him. He always had something to say, and this made for verse that swung on instead of lagging about in the same spot. He was always trying new forms and he mastered nearly every one he tried, with a mastery unspoiled by ostentatious effort. As his work for the theatre widened, his rhythms became influenced by music. This inspiration from musical comedy and revue was the first big new influence on light verse since the adaptation of Aristophanic metres. You could not sing Seaman, but you could sing Herbert. Here is a typical chorus from *Ballads for Broadbrows*,[7] a late-Twenties attack on busybodies, the members of Town Councils and Prosecuting Societies :

> " Let's stop somebody from doing something !
> Everybody does too much.
> People seem to think they've a right to eat and drink,
> Talk and walk and respirate and rink,
> Bicycle and bathe and such.
> So let's have lots of little regulations,
> Let's make laws and jobs for our relations,
> There's too much kissing at the railway-stations,
> Let's find out what everyone is doing,
> And then stop everyone from doing it."

A. P. H. has been rather unfairly neglected of late. Some ill-judged attempts to lecture the Left without any clear alternative doctrine, a few grumbling, Blimpish verses, eccentric references to a world in which dancing at night-clubs seemed to be the full expression of the human personality, a certain ingenuous liking for the limelight and some thumping errors of judgment have distracted attention from the range and brilliance of his work as a whole. If his views have sometimes been silly, so were Shaw's, and, like Shaw, he is entitled to be judged by his best.

Lucas, to many of *Punch*'s post-war critics, was far more objectionable than Graves, who spoke from so remote a world that he was as invisible as the cover. Lucas was looked upon as an effete descendant of the Stevenson of a *Child's Garden of Verses* and the essay on *Walking Tours*. After some of the artists, he was the arch *bête noire*. Yet if one examines what he actually wrote it is difficult to see what all the fuss was about. He wrote very good nonsense, some of it dead beyond its occasion, some still lighthearted and inventive. His pre-war range of work continued but he concentrated on the light essay. It was a good thing to have one item in the paper that was intended to provoke interest and amusement rather than laughter. If Evoe was as far as *Punch* went in the direction of a clown, Lucas was the light comedian or even the serio-comic. The essays got a little insipid as he grew older and more gloomy and the world became even less to his liking ; but they were always readable, far more readable than much of the routine comic stuff. They had generally a basis of fact, something he had read or seen or experienced, and they often had good jokes in them of the kind that the better letter-writers make. They gave no feeling of straining to be funny. How grateful readers must have been for a writer who did not feel bound to try for laughs when he did not feel like it. Like de Quincey and Chesterton, to mention two bigger men, Lucas wrote so much he diluted his reputation ; but now that he no longer blocks the way of the young but can be read historically and without emotion—after all he was born nearly a century ago—he might be worth winnowing.

He cut down his essays when he became film critic, one of the reasons for appointing him, and a bad one. In a letter to the Managing Director, Philip Agnew, in 1931,[8] Seaman said, " I am scared of your suggestion to E. V. Lucas that he is too good to write about films. I suppose this is due more to your contempt for films than to admiration for his other contributions of which you have often complained. So long as he writes about films you are spared his other contributions at least once a week. Perhaps, however, he will produce something better now you have hinted that he must be more worthy of himself. . . . What I say about E. V. Lucas is very private. He has been awfully kind and called me in a letter the loyallest of editors, and he might not think these remarks confirmed his flattering estimate. I still think the reputation of his name is an asset to Punch."

One of the most valuable of the regular contributors was " Anthony Armstrong " (A. A. Willis) who made his name writing about the humours of the post-war Army but soon began writing articles of civilian life. He tried most of the ordinary forms of humorous article and showed the efficiency and versatility that later turned him into a successful general journalist. His strong point, one difficult to convey by description, was that he wrote the same kind of article as innumerable other contributors and wrote it better. He was gay and clear. His world was the Twenties world of chaps in country cottages and cars and golf clubs and night-clubs. He was sometimes nearer to Sapper than to Evoe and he did, indeed, later turn to writing thrillers. His great success as a playwright, *Ten Minute Alibi*, was a detective play. Like " Algol " before the war, he represented the point of view of the ordinary man, not of the man who was disgruntled by finding himself ordinary. He was awed by Seaman's erudition and irritated by his pedantry and remoteness from the ordinary man but he has described to me more vividly than anyone what it was that made Seaman loved by those who were not hostile to him.

" A. A." had an extraordinary facility in playing with simple apparatus, partly the letter-writer's art of working up the everyday. He worked so hard at being a free-lance that in time his subject-matter became increasingly limited to a free-lance's home, car and family. The Second War, with his creation of Pilot-Officer Prune, gave him the fresh experience that his talent needed. Read in context among other articles trying hard to be gay about bridge parties and trains to work and cutting the hedges of tudorbethan maisonettes, his articles can give an almost aesthetic pleasure by doing the same thing so much more neatly, and with so much more comic invention.

A recruit to the Staff who was long enough under Seaman's training to be considered in this period was Eric Keown, who restored the old connection between *Punch* and *The Granta*. He was an all-round journalist of the type of Brooks and at different times, as well as writing a stream of humorous articles, has been Parliamentary Correspondent, principal Literary Critic, Dramatic Critic and Social Investigator. Quite improbably tall and filled with an unruffled and courteous energy, he enjoyed life in its movement and its detail. He combined gusto and attention whether in social relations or sport or the arts. He matured slowly and his early work was light-hearted rather than humorous. Under Seaman and for a good time afterwards he was a very popular contributor of light articles. These were of two kinds ; there were what may be called routine *Punch* articles, which did not develop the type much beyond the point it had already reached, though they were done gaily and made his original reputation. They were certainly above the average of their unexacting kind. As well as these, there were much more original articles, somewhat tentatively offered, in which he seemed to be indicating his desire to escape from what had become the restrictions of a form and produce something much more individual and new. These often had a framework of straight reporting, whether of an experience or a book, with the humour bubbling out in the selection of detail and in the endlessly-inventive phrasing. In a way it is a pity that he did not pick up and fortify the light essay where it was falling from Lucas's tired hands ; it might have led him back to the use of the full range of burlesque and fictional forms, free of the overwhelming influence of the immediately preceding practitioners in them. As he gained experience, he turned increasingly to commenting on reality and to selecting the odd incident that illuminated it. His style, which had coped awkwardly with imitation Anthony Armstrong, emerged as one of the strengths of modern *Punch*. He seemed to have an inexhaustible supply of metaphors, each so right that it passed almost unnoticed. Nobody made faster reading and the smoothness and ease of the style, with its effortless variations of pace and accommodation to different subject-matter, have deprived Keown of some of the reputation he deserves. You have to re-read to see how it was done and then the richness of his gift of phrase is suddenly noticed like life revealed by magnification. As dramatic critic, his stance was the traditional *Punch* stance. He was the man who liked the theatre as he liked all the pleasures of life and expected to be interested and entertained and was prepared to be grateful for any real attempt to please. Where he differed from the older *Punch* critics was in his capacity for development. Actors have told me that he is now one of the dramatic critics who are taken most seriously by the Theatre. To-day he remains poised between his considerable knowledge of plays and books and a firmly held moral standard. The quiet deadliness of his condemnation—he prefers a gun with a silencer—is the more impressive because he likes life and prefers to enjoy it.

Two series that were completely different from anything before must be mentioned. Archibald Marshall's *Simple Stories* [9] used the *fausse naïve* brilliantly. There was a good deal of variation of approach underneath the simple and easily recognised style. He did not pall quickly, a good rough test of the amount of craftsmanship that has gone into a *Punch* series. It is interesting to compare the relation between form and content in the *Simple Stories* with that in Ernest Bramah's *Kai Lung*.[10]

*1066 and All That*,[11] by Sellar and Yeatman was a burlesque History of England, or rather a burlesque history textbook. It had two qualities that were rare in *Punch* at that time, exorbitance and accuracy of aim. The burlesque was wild, jokes and puns were piled thickly. Some of the running jokes were poor but their authors' delight in them was infectious and what, at the second appearance, seemed facile and silly by the twelfth appearance had established itself with the solidity of a Folly. Behind the wildness of the fun was considerable knowledge of what textbooks were like and a wonderful sense of what the average historical memory retained. The reader continually felt shocks of recognition—yes, I did dimly half-believe that Sir Walter Raleigh was executed for being left over from the last reign. Sellar and Yeatman's attempts to repeat their success in later series suffered from the fact that people said they were attempting to repeat a success. It was assumed that bolts had been shot. Their attempt to adapt the form was probably a mistake ; but some of their material was good and funny in a fresh way. Such discoveries as that the horse is the only animal you could knock nails into were simple and appealing.

## IV

There were fewer changes among the artists than among the writers, though the school of Baumer recruited D. L. Ghilchick, who did a very large number of social cuts, often based on some domestic topicality. The text was intentionally kept as the amateur's opportunity, while the pictures had to be professional. It was impossible for an artist to devote his life to *Punch* unless he could be reasonably sure of regular sales. The salary system had broken down. Hence space was reserved and the outsider could get in only occasionally or during a war. The first duty of an Art Editor was to see that the regulars had the half-page or full-page drawings that provided a livelihood. There were often only two small drawings per issue and this restricted the training ground available for new men. The odd reluctance to plan ahead that affected the literary side not too seriously, for there were always plenty of amateurs to provide at least literate bulk, was nearly fatal when it came to artists, and later on there was a short period in which there was difficulty in filling the picture-space at all.

Frank Reynolds succeeded F. H. Townsend as Art Editor from 1920–1930 without much increase of freedom. He had more knowledge of the technicalities of reproduction, increasingly important with the widening range of media. He perhaps lacked Townsend's sensitivity in personal relations, but he was a vigorous personality, and a cheerful, friendly, encouraging one. He suffered from Seaman's belief that his job was simply the preliminary sorting of the jokes. During Reynolds's long illness, George Morrow deputised for him and eventually became Art Editor, a post he held until 1937 but for which he was temperamentally unsuited.

Frank Reynolds had begun contributing in 1906, but he became frequent only from the War, and in the Twenties and Thirties he,

*11th June, 1930* *Frank Reynolds*

*Visitor.* "WHY, THAT'S THE THIRD WIDE HE'S SENT DOWN!"

*Village Supporter.* "AH! 'E BE A GOOD LENGTH BOWLER, SIR, BUT SOMETIMES 'E DO ZEEM TO BE A BIT OFF HIS WIDTH."

perhaps, contributed more than any artist to giving an issue of *Punch* its character. As Fougasse said in his Obituary Notice, " His line possessed a freedom and energy which make us recognise it now as the forerunner of much of the free style drawing of to-day. He played, in fact, an important part in the transition from the comparatively tight naturalistic drawing of the beginning of the century (a legacy from the old wood-engraving) to the freer and more fluid and very much less documented styles that followed." [12] His suburban householders and village sportsmen were always drawn energetically and he specialised in conveying emotion in backs. Although easily his most famous picture was the German family in the First World War having its morning hate—indeed, he tended more and more to use the Teutonic face for everybody—his best work was probably in some of his coloured pastiches in Almanacks and Summer Numbers. The ugliness of his work may have been a reaction against the prettification of *Punch* but some of it must be put down to the fact that he found one or two ugly faces and figures easy to reproduce and simply kept on, year after year, reproducing them. It is only fair to say that while his work has dropped out of fashion it has retained several admirers who, by the range and perceptiveness of their appreciation of draughtsmanship, deserve to be taken seriously.

Charles Grave, who began contributing as early as 1912 but did not become very frequent until the Thirties, when for a time he was relief cartoonist, did for ships and sailors and foreign ports what Reynolds did for suburban householders and village cricketers. His work was very popular.

The principal cartoonist continued to be Bernard Partridge, who kept his stately course to the end of Seaman's reign and for many years beyond. The second cartoonist continued to be Raven Hill until 1935. On the whole the established artists did not change their styles, one of the more marked developments being Fougasse's steady simplification. Some of them showed increased technical competence with practice; others continued after their drawing and their jokes had become tired and careless. Fortunately, in the arts there seems to be a high correlation between output and ability, so that the better men suffered least from the strain of a weekly contribution expected year after year.

On sheer bulk of work and on social closeness to the *Punch* circle G. L. Stampa merits mention. Short of being actually on the Table he was as much of a *Punch* man as any one has been. Roué, bohemian, raconteur, link with the days of Phil May and tremendous evenings in hansom cabs, he lived entirely in the past, refusing to have a newspaper or to recognise any change since . . . the date varied from conversation to conversation. He belonged with the gentlemanly racketiness of the Burnand period and it was probably a good thing that *Punch* in later, more austere times, should be reminded of its frivolous past. He spanned an immense period, from 1894 to 1950, and his work included, as well as jokes about street arabs and cockneys at the seaside and servant girls, the theatre drawings and initial letters. In early subject-matter he was influenced by Phil May and he has preserved the appearances of the Gaiety chorus-girl and the bohemian life of the time ; in method the influence of May on him was small.

The most definite breach with the past on the art side was the admission of modified forms of the kind of draughtsmanship already well-established in the lesser comic press. Looking back it is easy to see the stylised realism of these maisonette-owners, with their smiles and bulging eyes and sharp jaws and noses, as the transitional stage before the victory of the fantastic. W. L. Ridgewell and G. S. Sherwood looked brighter on the page than some of the far more versatile and accomplished delineators of appearances. Their jokes varied between the routine suburban-life jokes, though they were among the best purveyors of these, and jokes that depended on eccentricity or incongruity. At the time it seemed sometimes as though Ridgewell were given space as the odd piece of relief, the strongly individual turn that set off the rest of the programme. He did not seem likely to be a harbinger of a complete change of style in the paper ; but he was. Ridgewell did evolve and to the end he would sometimes do a realistic background that, but for period, might be early Partridge. Some influence from Bateman, some from Fougasse and a restless mind kept him on the move and his development, including the debit of a loss of visual delight, was connected in some way with the variation of style between drawings in the same volume. He was always casting back, trying something new, showing he had been looking at another man, turning to his

*7th November, 1934* *Ridgewell*

"*Wait a second, Sydney. I'm not out yet.*"

newest style and emphasising its characteristics. Sherwood stemmed from the later developments of Ridgewell, with an occasional backward glance to W. Bird. He could be very funny and, though less varied than Ridgewell, he was one of the more consistently successful amusers.

Arthur Watts had a very individual sense of humour, nearest, perhaps, to Sherwood's. He generally drew from a curious angle, as though looking down on the scene, and though this was, of course, a trick that staled by repetition, it made a pleasant change in the weekly issue from the normal "fourth wall" stance. Watts belonged to the men who followed Bateman in trying to look funny as well as illustrate funny ideas ; his houses and rooms were no less accurately representational in consequence. He seemed to find plenty to amuse him within the restrictions imposed on him and never gave the feeling that he felt them as restrictions at all. Possibly the Ridgewell-Sherwood-Watts school actually gained from the narrowness of the field within which a *Punch* artist had to work. Nicolas Bentley, a busy comic artist and illustrator, owed something to Ridgewell and Sherwood, and something also to the smart magazine and advertising type of artist like " Fish." He has wandered in and out of *Punch* over a quarter of a century and, at his best, is very sharply funny. He was one of the first of the younger generation to get into the paper when the ice began to break in the early Thirties, and he is one of the comparatively few *Punch* artists since who has succeeded both with the humour of incongruity and the humour of social criticism. As a draughtsman, his range was small, but he never, like some of the later " new humorists," gave the impression of abstracting in order to conceal incompetence, and his designs, with their sharp blacks and whites, decorated the page.

Seaman retired only under pressure of ill-health. Various attempts had been made to indicate that the time was ripe, including a very elaborate placing of dinner guests at one of the out-of-town *Punch* Dinners, which was supposed to hint that the Proprietors wished him to consider the matter. Seaman was not the man to take hints of this subtlety and the Chairman of the Company was deputed to approach him privately. During lunch he talked about the need for the old to take their rest and for the young to have their opportunity. After a good deal of this, Seaman suddenly leaned across the table and said in an agonised tone, " Lawrence, surely you are not thinking of retiring ! " His colleagues believed that he genuinely could not imagine *Punch*'s continuing without him. Even on his holidays in the South of France he had never stopped discussing what the office would be doing at that particular moment. However, he was too sick a man to carry on. His friends, and one can never understand his complex, infuriating and fascinating character unless one realises the quality of his friendships, were glad to see him returning to the idea of working on a full-dress study of Browning ; but a recurrence of illness cut his retirement short.

CHAPTER EIGHT

# RESTOCKED BACKWATER

## *E. V. Knox's Editorship, 1932–1949*

EVOE HAD been a contributor for nearly thirty years when he became Editor in 1932. He had not worked regularly in the office but had come in as a relief during holiday periods or when someone was ill. He was an established favourite with the public, both in the paper and through his volumes of reprinted work and anthologies. He was in no way a disciple of Seaman's, but he was in the difficulty that too rapid alteration would look like a censure upon the man who for a generation had run *Punch* as C. P. Scott ran the *Manchester Guardian* or George Edwardes the *Gaiety*. Fortunately his conception of editing enabled him to avoid too sharp a break. It has been pointed out by Kenneth Bird that in periodicals, as in schools and families, there is a pendulum that swings between discipline and freedom. Seaman was the strict Victorian father, very kind, very anxious that his men should live up to his own high standards of morals and accuracy and behaviour. He was always bearing down on contributors, and while this helped some it wore out others.

Evoe reacted against this positive editing, against the endless schoolmastering, against the formality. In some ways, the comparison that used to be made of Baldwin and Chamberlain works here, though the sequence was reversed. Seaman, like Chamberlain, saw some things very clearly. He supervised everything himself and he had an expert knowledge of the few subjects he considered important. He condemned where he did not understand. He had a carapace of certainties and a warm, shy heart inside. Evoe saw far more things than Seaman and far more kinds of things ; he saw things less clearly and he judged with less certainty. He was impatient of detail and believed in letting well alone, in choosing good men and giving them their heads.

The office, in which Seaman had worked incessantly, correcting set after set of proofs and writing long letters by hand, changed its character. It became casual, deliberately rather slapdash, a place for long conversations on any subject under the sun, for a good deal of snoozing and reading and day-dreaming. Sometimes there would be nobody in it, everyone being at a club or a pub or away in the country. Press night became an agony. Week after week it seemed impossible that the Editor would ever get down to the proofs. A lengthy dinner was given in turn by a small dining-circle collected in order to prevent Evoe from disappearing altogether. Then suddenly he would get down to work and the paper would appear for another week. This deliberate reaction from Seaman made a climate in which humour could flourish. One gets the feeling, as one never does of the previous régime, of good jokes arising spontaneously, of the pleasures of life about the office seeming more important than the business of producing a paper.

Evoe's strength was in creating this atmosphere among his immediate colleagues, the younger men who loved him, appreciated his gentleness and kindness, found his company stimulating and enjoyed his odd, oblique humour. He was often infuriating : the urgent article was hidden under a pile of papers, the decision required a month ahead was given when it was really too late so that a solution to the problem had to be fudged, and the major issue was left undiscussed while some fascinating by-way was explored at great length. As an Editor, Evoe had the defects of his qualities. His remoteness and casualness and his continuance of the traditional Editor-Proprietor relationship is illustrated by his habit of flicking cigarette-ends over his shoulder into the waste-paper basket : one would be much too bored to stub them out. After a few fires the management took away his wicker waste-paper basket and replaced it apologetically with a metal one. On the other hand there grew up with his staff the kind of relationship that would exist between the ideal don (and Evoe was a don *manqué*) and his pupils. An important quality was his integrity. Nobody got into the paper because they belonged to the same club or could bring some kind of pressure to bear. This integrity also applied to matters of scholarship. Evoe accepted Seaman's attitude to the classical tradition. Verse must be prosodically accurate ; it was a game in which the whole point lay in keeping the rules and it was a game to be enjoyed primarily by possible players. A colleague has remarked that working with him was a little like helping to edit the *Journal of Hellenic Studies*. Evoe believed that *Punch* had a valuable national function to perform and that its political influence was important, though he did not take it as solemnly as Seaman had. He varied between thinking *Punch* should be a National Institution and fearing that, if it were, it could not continue to be comic. However, these were fundamental and long-term decisions and could be postponed.

If, rather doubtfully, one can relate Seaman's *Punch* to Cambridge —and Thackeray, Burnand, Lehmann and Milne make a pretty strong tradition—one can relate Evoe's *Punch* to Oxford. *Punch* was a College, with the Table as Fellows. (Evoe was still sufficiently near to the early *Punch* to feel awkward about editing their contributions.) What mattered was what would matter in a University Press or a University Opera Club, the production of quality. Universities, like periodicals, can resist change only at the expense of increasing the pressure of the waves and the devastation of the final break-through. *Punch* was not subsidised from the rents left by a pious founder or from the grants of local educational authorities. It was one kind of strength that it managed for so long to behave as though it existed in the dream-world of the middle-class, in which standard of life had no connection with money. Evoe believed passionately in editorial independence, the policy on which the paper had grown up ; but he sometimes seemed as though he regarded any suggestion that the compositors and contributors could be paid only out of hard cash as an attempt to impose a commercial control on what was in its nature something like the British Museum or *The English Historical Review*.

At the beginning of the century, with editorial contents of sixteen pages, advertising seldom exceeded six pages. Herbert Heather, who built up the commercial side of *Punch*, was anxious to increase the advertising, but Philip Agnew was reluctant. When he gave way there was a steady increase of advertising. Advertisers pressed for the use of colour for the advertising pages of the weekly issues as well as in the special numbers. Before the First War, advertising revenue began to exceed revenue from sales, and no advertiser was going to buy space that nobody saw. From this point of view, quantity of circulation inevitably had to be considered together with quality of circulation. It was not enough that the kind of people read the text that the Editor wished would read it. Advertisers expected circulation figures and though, as they were not appealing to a mass market they did not want a mass circulation, they would certainly not pay for a declining circulation. As the advertising began to outnumber the editorial pages, the proprietors increased these from sixteen to twenty in 1919, then to twenty-four in 1922 and to twenty-eight in 1924, the growth of the advertising keeping pace.

One of the commercial advantages of *Punch* has been the brilliance with which it has created in its advertisement pages a kind of shop-window for the advertising profession. The arrangement of the advertisements and the firm encouragement of the best, and only the best, copy and art-work in them made *Punch* one of the few periodicals whose advertising pages had fans of their own. The position of *Punch* advertising was established by Roy Somerville between 1910 and 1922. The name of his successor, Marion Jean Lyon, who married Raven Hill, is still remembered with awe and discomfort, as one of the first women to blast their way into the advertising world and to rule over the clients as firmly as the Editor ruled over the contributors. This is not, of course, a history of a business but the history of a paper. It is necessary, however, to point out that the pressures to which Evoe was stalwartly resistant were not merely attempts to import a low, commercial element into a rarefied air.

Evoe made several editorial alterations in the direction of speeding the paper up. The long caption under pictures—caricatured as " Collapse of stout party "—went, though the big changes in the pictures did not come until the appointment of Kenneth Bird as Art Editor in 1937. He made the comments on the pars less ponderous and went some way in the direction of brisking up *Charivaria*, though not very far as it was still felt that this feature should be retained primarily for the older readers. He appointed Richard Mallett to succeed Lucas on Films and Eric Keown to take over the Theatre from J. Thorp, for a time with Douglas Woodruff. Keown also took over the *Essence of Parliament* in 1933. H. F. Ellis and Richard Mallett, who came into the office as Charles Graves gradually retired, did much of the editorial work. This meant that the editorial features were predominantly written by men trained up young on the paper and daily under Evoe's influence. The improvement of the magazine element in *Punch* and the evolution of distinctive *Punch* attitudes in it is one of Evoe's main legacies to the paper. In a sudden wild attempt to increase its popularity he introduced a crossword-puzzle, taking the major part in framing it. It was dropped after a few weeks.

Evoe cut down the prosier types of article. He liked much of the kind of humour of everyday experience that Seaman had liked, but he also liked the new crazy humour, the humour of irrelevance and wildness and poetry that Seaman had hated as an American invasion. He could handle the formal occasional poem himself but felt less often called upon to make pronouncements than Seaman had. His own political views, once Liberal, had become Churchillian Tory and, at a time when Conservatism was Baldwinian and appeasing, *Punch* seemed old-fashioned in its defiance of dictators and support of the armed forces. However, *Punch* became much less directly political under Evoe.

His weakness as an Editor was his refusal to plan. He did little to attract or retain contributors. If people cared to post in material, it would be used or returned. Hardly ever was anything amended. He disliked Seaman's idea of training men up. He did not believe in personal contacts and *Punch* became for most of its contributors simply 10 Bouverie St., a number and a street-name. His aloofness, like his inability to praise, came from a shyness that was partly the pose of the period of his youth, partly an odd kind of respect for the integrity of others—Editors should not probe or be probed—partly an inability to realise that communication was by word and not by thought, partly, perhaps, a kind of egotism. The result was that some men who had done good work and would have done more drifted away, chilled by lack of encouragement. The psychological mechanism that produces humour is delicate, and the humorist has both the comic's anguished thirst for applause and the artist's drive towards perfection mingled with self-doubts. A man who had, as he thought, done acceptable work for years might suddenly receive an article back with a letter, " Dear Sir, This won't do. Yours faithfully,". He took this as simply rudeness if he were of an aggressive temperament or planned discouragement if he were not. When his staff remonstrated with him Evoe would say that of course the man would understand the letter—which simply said quite clearly that the article fell below the high standard which the writer had set for himself by his other work.

With all his casualness, Evoe had one of the great editorial characteristics, flair, the quality that had enabled Lemon to see promise in one small drawing of Sambourne's and carry him for ten years while he slowly realised his potentialities. He seized on to " Pont," signing him up, an almost unprecedented stroke of policy at that time. From a few early Emett drawings he picked him to illustrate a number of poems by Walter de la Mare.[1] Somehow better contributors did appear. Somehow the range of contents widened. Evoe had a queer, vague sensitivity to what was going on and what might go on. The contributions fell off by Seaman's standards of meticulousness ; but there were many more kinds of contribution and men developed on lines of their own. Evoe's high-and-mighty attitude to the readers meant that his judgment was not influenced by the senile. He was prepared to risk disapproval by publishing stuff that appealed to a minority and to the young. Unfortunately, the young were ceasing to look at the paper and there was still enough that did not appeal to them to make a hasty glance at an odd copy unbeguiling. But on looking back over the *Punch* of twenty years ago one can see, beside the old growths, new growths, something *Punch* had not seen for many years. The central *Punch* tradition was reinforced by new men and the new men turned out to be more adaptable than the old. After all, the vitality, variousness and toughness of *Punch* have been revealed since.

Evoe's unpredictable reign, with its neglect of detail and wild swoops of invention, its odd mixture of turning away from life and penetration through it, was a latent period. He printed some of the best work that had ever appeared in *Punch* as well as some of the worst and it was from the best that the new branches budded. Sometimes the marking time was more apparent than the slow wheel. If institutions are more than metaphorically organic, then the shifting of emphasis, the re-education of readers and contributors, the refusal to be committed to temporary fashions in humour or politics while drawing nourishment from them, may be a necessary stage in growth. When Seaman went *Punch* did not look like having a future. If Evoe's Editorship had not left behind it something healthy and capable of growth, no amount of galvanising and altering would have saved the paper (changing a paper is traditionally in Fleet Street the penultimate stage before going bust). *Punch* was ready, perhaps over-ready, for big and apparent changes, but after Seaman it had probably needed more than anything a period of convalescence, of almost imperceptible but steady refashioning, and of cultivating the imagination.

## II

Evoe's Editorship was cut into three parts of roughly equal length by public affairs. He took over as the Slump was receding. Then came the rise of Fascism, the continued unemployment in the heavy industries and the rising national shame at poverty, bad housing, malnutrition and maternal mortality. The Conservative Party, by repeated narrowing of its governing circle, created the strongest opposition on its own side since the opposition of all the talents that brought Walpole down. Then came the Second World War, a war of movement, dramatic, arduous but varied, in which there was much more to write about than there had been in the war before. The Government became a Coalition, which is always hampering to the cartoonist. In the post-war years the first Socialist government to have a clear majority continued war-time measures as the framework of a peace-time world, which meant that Nationalisation and financial controls were discussed academically rather than violently. Foreign policy was not, on the whole, an issue between the Parties. The growth of Russia caused doubts that were slower to become general than we remember, and anyway people had had a surfeit of foreign policy for years.

It is difficult for a comic paper to be genuinely bi-partisan. One can hardly have two cartoons, one right and one left. In the Nineteenth Century *Punch* had been Liberal, though there had always been hot Conservatives on the Table and the discussions over the Cartoon were live debates. The younger men appointed by Seaman were mostly not interested in politics—one politician on the Table was enough—but accepted the Conservative view as a matter of course when they had to make a decision. It is probable that most arguments over the Cartoon were between right-wing and moderate Conservatism. When the cartoon ceased to be the result of hard argument and sharp disagreement it began to lose its bite. Instead of the object being to cause annoyance the object became to state agreement. Only in refusing to support appeasement did *Punch* take a line that would have annoyed any Conservative. Annoyance to Socialist readers was, in intention, avoided by making less and less reference to Socialism. It was not grasped that the out-and-out controversialist, like A. P. H., attracted left-wing readers while they were repelled by evasions and assumptions. An article which ignored unemployment and assumed that every right-minded man spent his Saturday afternoons playing golf was much more festeringly offensive than an article that went for the unemployed bald-headed by accusing them of being lazy. In the war no serious difference of opinion existed, except among fringe groups like the Trotskyites, or over strategy, in which the amateur always was fully aware that he might be proved wrong by the sudden release of well-hidden news. With the post-war Government *Punch* had to decide whether to be part of Conservative propaganda. It continued to put the Conservative case as mildly as possible in the cartoons and for the rest to devote its primary attention to leisure and domestic life without quite appreciating the criticisms of those who said this attitude was, in fact, implicitly political.

The intense Englishness of British communities overseas naturally made ties close between them and *Punch* and for many years most issues contained some contribution either inspired by memories of Britain in the colonies, or by memories of Asia or Africa in Britain. The poem of topographical nostalgia bulked large. The other literary result of the Imperial tradition was the article of native humour and far-flung misadventure. The efficient writers of the reminiscence of colonial administration were many and there is no one giant who can stand for the whole class.

## III

During the seventeen years of Evoe's editorship there were many changes in the personnel of *Punch*. The gap of the First War generation was marked. C. L. Graves still maintained some of the Seaman tradition ; but his health was failing and he was out of sympathy with the new régime and gradually receded. Lucas was past his best. Of the writers, only A. P. H. and Evoe himself represented the generation who had known England before the war. Under Evoe's Editorship, Evoe's writing showed renewed life. He performed the almost unprecedented feat of changing his style in middle age. His work became more varied and he moved away from the little golfing story or household incident towards comment, often admirably perverse, on some aspect of the news. The sentences became fuller, the tone more individual, the diction more subtle. Apart, perhaps, from the wonderful early parodies, Evoe was producing far finer work than he had thirty years before. A. P. H. became Independent Member for Oxford University in the 1935 election, a tribute to many things, but one of them certainly *Punch*'s permission to air his prejudices in public. In between campaigns for legal reform and an important campaign—*What a Word*—against business and official jargon, he reported on the House of Commons, largely from a social point of view. In the war he was in command of a boat on the Thames, and after it he rather sadly failed to understand the Labour Party.

H. F. Ellis, a classical scholar and rugby player, was a cheerful young man who came into *Punch* on the way out of Education. He had taught for short periods at a prep school and at Marlborough but he was obviously formed by Nature to be Evoe's closest follower. Like many in the central tradition he developed slowly. He was unadventurous in the use of forms and only gradually began to reveal the strong individuality of his humour. Clever, sensitive, oddly afraid of using his remarkable powers at full stretch, he wrote various kinds of article, the worked-up domestic experience, the rag of the newspaper item, the scholarly *macédoine*, the series built round a character—*Assistant Masters: Are They Insane?* [2] is a classic—and something rather difficult to describe, the article in which craziness was contained in a vessel of the usual shape and size and where the gleams of lunacy showed through chinks made by the careful selection of incongruous detail. He wrote much better than most humorists and whether he was writing about Rugger—he somehow managed to rewrite the rules, though not for *Punch*—or the French Cabinet his actual writing, which matured steadily, was often in advance of the subject-matter. Ellis has the extraordinary fertility in making jokes that characterises Wodehouse. There is, of course, a difference between isolated jokes, however thickly strewn, and humour that informs a whole. The difference between good Ellis and mediocre Ellis is often less in the quality of the incidental jokes than in the degree to which the shape of the article as a whole has been conceived cold, as a vehicle for incidental delights or in an initial incandescence of comic imagination.

After the war he wrote an article on *Washing-Up* [3] which might legitimately have been a somewhat savage parody of not only the typical *Punch* article but even of the typical humorous article. Instead it was a breath-taking example of expertise. He took a theme as hackneyed as Herrick's themes and by sheer quality made it seem new. It made a successful monologue when recited by George Benson in an Intimate Revue. To his colleagues it was a wonderful demonstration of what could be done just by writing. It was a proof that the dominance of subject was not as absolute as everybody had been saying and that even a subject as banal, as remote from the contemporary thought-world, as matter-of-course to a working-class reader as it was distressingly novel to a middle-class reader, could give intense aesthetic pleasure by the quality of its craftsmanship. In H. F. Ellis's hands the traditional *Punch* topics were no more hackneyed than the piano in Grock's musical act or Chaplin's cane. It is odd that his international reputation has grown so slowly. He is certainly funnier than some of the American humorists who have been pushed over here. In a way, he can be best summed up in a phrase of helpless inarticulateness once used by a reviewer of Evelyn Waugh, "His jokes are funnier than other people's."

Ellis was the man living in a definite society at a definite time, a little puzzled by it, a little resentful of it, a little shyly curious. He did not, like the older *Punch* writers, find anything funny in ignorance or incapacity *per se*. The minor *Punch* writer has often taken some perfectly everyday experience and shown himself to be subnormal in his reactions to it. The Ellis narrator was usually the reasonably competent man only too anxious to meet reality half-way, to use the inanimate for the purpose for which it was intended or to understand the information in his newspaper. Full of goodwill, conscious of being rather quickly exasperated, remembering the far more difficult subjects he had already mastered, he presented a standard of normality below which reality intermittently fell. The average *Punch* humorist of incompetence has been the little brother, aware that clever people could do things all right but cosily laughing at his own failures, knowing that a bigger brother will always come to his aid. H. F. Ellis was the man who had every reason to expect life to live up to its average and was soberly confident of being able to deal with it when it did so. His look of faint surprise was a criticism of the gaps in the average, of the occasions when life was not, shall we say, quite itself. He started from the same point as many other *Punch* humorists but he ended in a criticism of life and, I think, fundamentally, of its variations in quality. Slashing attacks on the black side are frequent enough in *Punch*. Cold examination of the spots on the white side is something rarer.

Richard Mallett was the son of a journalist and a free-lance from the age of sixteen, when his first *Punch* contribution was accepted. He came into the *Punch* office from *The Evening News* and did everything from reading the post to organising emergency editions in Manchester in case of invasion. He did a good deal of reviewing, took the Films over from E. V. Lucas and formed part of the small circle to which Evoe talked in the long evenings and which saw him at his best. "R.M.," as he signed, was *Punch*'s link with the world of the Arts, of Music and Literature and the higher Press. He read enormously and his fantastic memory was constantly drawn on by his colleagues. He was a curious mixture of scholar and journalist, fiercely individual, working away at common conceptions to test their validity, examining the ordinary clichés of daily life as though they were completely new.

Richard Mallett has been called, and that by an American editor, one of the best film critics in the world. No film critic was less affected by things outside the film. The whole of his remarkable attention was concentrated on it. The star vehicle of the week might not be reviewed at all, though he would have seen it and know every other film made by its writer and director and cameraman and small part players; he would have read the American reviews and the English reviews but if he did not think it worth talking about he would simply leave it out. This made him a reliable guide. He could be as witty as any film critic but he regarded criticism as essentially an act of judgment and something to be done lightly but soberly: otherwise there is a danger of gradually coming to fit the opinion to the verbal joke. He was one of the few film critics who, after taking a film as a whole, would discriminate between different aspects and sections of it. Over the years, sometimes bashing his readers, more often guiding them, he has built up a reputation for integrity, balance and penetration that is based on the weekly comparison between what he has said about a film and the film itself when it comes to the reader's local cinema.

His humorous work is difficult to map. It came roughly within the class of "crazy" humour, but the craziness was not merely the wild juxtaposition of incongruities that often serves for crazy humour, but an inversion: reality was not distorted. By linking observations of extreme accuracy he would produce an effect of wild poetry which really depended on his having seen things that nobody had ever noticed before. His observation was of behaviour generally but particularly of speech behaviour. He loved words, phrases, clichés and many of his mad combinations and recombinations were not merely ends in themselves but somehow illuminated the life from which they have been taken. His puns owed more to Joyce than to Burnand. He was unlike any other writer. He did not fit into the political framework of the Thirties because he does not fit into any framework. When England was reading the proletarian novel he was writing his prose poems—*Translations From the Ish* : [4]

COMPARISON

Like some clocks
He had a nice mellow chime,
But when he came to strike

He was hoarse,
Out of tune,
And several tones lower
In a different key.

NOTE ON AN ARCHITECT'S DESIGN

This is the sort of place
No gentleman's library
Should be within.

SIMILES

Her hair resembled
Varnished hemp,
Her hat and fur
Turkish cigarette-ash ;

And the little dog she led
Half a tarantula.

THE TWO RACES OF MEN

If ignorance is bliss
And knowledge is power

What's yours ?

Mallett worked a good deal from notebooks and enjoyed trying different forms for the presentation of his reflections. The articles about Aunt Tabitha and her Uncles managed to create a coherent lunatic world, to follow a theme through a wildly-twisting yet always *just* convincing argument and to introduce the widely varied observations and jokes which, placed with exquisite deliberation, send the mind scuttling here and there. The attitude behind Richard Mallett's humour was elusive. The demand that a humorist should have a point of view is a cliché : one never finds it argued. Certainly when a hack gets worn out it is sometimes because of reluctance to plough up new areas of the mind and this in turn may be due to the absence of any stimulus such as would be provided by a view of the nature of things ; but what is forgotten is that the drive to create farce is the desire for the applause of an audience. All the theorising about clowns that was so popular thirty years ago was simply a special case of the pathetic fallacy ; it ruined some of them and very nearly ruined Chaplin, who began talking about himself as though he were a kind of visual Eliot. Writers on humour do not laugh easily and they sometimes feel it necessary to produce over-cerebral explanations for non-cerebral phenomena. The element of pure clowning in Mallett was very strong. On the other hand he had a cagey, self-camouflaging mind and there were signs of a determined attempt to avoid the point-of-view, the trap of the stance. The cold dissections of clichés, the examinations of language —sometimes he seemed to be the comic spirit as semanticist—had an emotion behind them which was hatred of the falsities of easiness.

As a verse-writer Mallett was very accomplished, but he wrote it only occasionally. He was more important as a parodist ; I believe him to be the greatest English parodist since Beerbohm. Parody suits him very well. It is the point at which his critical faculty, his observation and his clowning meet. The early parodies, like the extraordinary one of *The Waves*,[5] carried on from the Beerbohm tradition : a writer was absorbed complete, from point of view to method of punctuation, and then some slightly but not violently incongruous subject was written about as the original might himself have written it. Later on Mallett invented, as far as I know, the criticism of a book in the style of a book, though he never completely dropped the older kind of parody. In these a Faulkner character, for example, would be given a new Faulkner novel to review and comment acidly on Faulkner's tricks, the comment itself being in Faulknerese. Implicitly and explicitly savage, Mallett hit much harder than most of the *Punch* men of his generation. His parodies were accurate to the smallest detail. Things nobody else noticed would be guyed in passing. The weakest point was an occasional neglect of the victim's mind for his verbal habits.

Parody has always been, of course, an obvious form for *Punch* and at one time the editor's note in *The Writers' and Artists' Year Book* recommended it to intending contributors. Between the decline of the old, verbalistic classical curriculum and the rise of the grimmer disciplines that applied rigorous criticism to English prose and verse, reading was normally too casual for parody to flourish. Only a Mallett, firmly indifferent to what the unworthy reader might be missing, persisted in getting it right. There has generally been more good burlesque than good parody in *Punch*, as might be expected. It was the absence of any link with burlesque that made Seaman's parodies sometimes dull ; it was the absence of psychological perception, of ability to get under a writer's skin that made them remote from their originals.

St. John Hankin, whether parodying poets or dramatists, produced good fun that was good criticism, but his likenesses varied in similitude too wildly for him to be put in the front rank of pure parodists. He was, however, what for most readers is more important, an extremely enjoyable one. Here is his Browning :

YET ANOTHER WAY OF LOVE[6]

You see this rose,
  Its calyx, its petals ?
Since fair it shows
  Could you forget, all's

Well with your heart to the heart's confusion
And the mind's disjointure. What's conclusion ?
Look on her blossom half white, half pinky.
Would you choose her, the choice yours, think ye ?

But if, depressed
With all this fooling,
Rose and the rest,
You 'scape your schooling,
And, stopping low to her sweet shoe's latchet
(Since truth's the truth if you can but catch it !)
You risk conjecture " Why yes ? " or " Why no ? "—
Lord love you, I'm hanged if *I* know.

Evoe at his best was superb. He had the scholarship, the skill with words and the fun. He liked to take a writer and extend his thought and his method until the parody became the most gradual *reductio ad absurdum.* He was particularly happy with the better poetry of the pre-1914 period. His Hardy,[7] for example, was not only funny but brilliant criticism. In the later period, one of the busiest *Punch* parodists was William Kean Seymour. Many of his targets were ephemeral and it is a little difficult to-day to judge the likenesses of some of his *Jackdaw in Georgia.*[8] He tackled too many writers in a short time to get really inside all of them. (A single Mallett parody has taken a year.) He did give, however, a series of lightning impressions ; in retrospect his eye for the features of a fashion seems more accurate than his eye for the idiosyncrasies of a man. G. H. Vallins usually, but not always, imitated older writers. It was pastiche rather than strict parody and really derived from an earlier tradition. For example, he applied Chaucerian verse to contemporary types like the Air Raid Warden.[9] The anachronism was perhaps too slight a peg for humour and the reader's pleasure came from the skill with which Vallins wrote in the styles of different men rather than from amusement.

Jefferson Farjeon was, perhaps, the best example of the inevitable effect of time-lag on readers. His *Smith Minor* [10] series was enormously popular with older readers, who wrote the schoolboy character sentimental letters and sent him tuck. Even Archbishop Temple engaged in a coy correspondence. The humour, gentle and sentimental, belonged to an earlier age ; but readers used to that tradition may well have felt entitled to be given some of what they liked. Smith Minor had at first a rival in Geoffrey Willans's Molesworth,[10a] but proved more popular, though Willans wrote far better and, while keeping to the schoolboy self-revelation, gained much more delicate effects. His other humorous work covered a very wide range of subject and treatment.

D. H. Barber was, perhaps, the busiest of the writers who carried on the tradition of the domestic anecdote. His characters, Sympson, Conkleshill, Edith and others were probably the only characters produced by writers of this school who built up a readership of their own. Unlike most of the *Punch* writers, he was essentially a " pay-off" man. The incident, often set in a seaside town or suburb, led up to a final surprise and depended on it. E. M. Delafield, the novelist, wrote conversation-pieces of village life which were accurate in observation and sub-acid in tone. They were always a professional job and carried the reader firmly and swiftly to the end. If they were all much the same in form and material, they at least had more minor variation than most similar articles. They were never prosy and never padded and were, perhaps, one *Punch* tradition at its fullest point of development. It was the world of village gentry re-housed on a smaller scale and working busily at village activities. It was a shrewd and humorous world, if a narrow one, and to the stock objection that all England was not like that, one can reasonably reply that a surprisingly large amount of England was.

Mary Dunn started from the same kind of jumping-off point as several of the rather indistinguishable band of feminine contributors who localised a substantial proportion of *Punch*'s pages in Kensington ; but her humour was bludgeoning and destructive, her effects broader. Her most famous series, the mock memoirs of a character called *Lady Addle*,[11] produced rather strained smiles but gave much pleasure to the irreverent. It was cheerful, hit-or-miss fun and the tone was loud. It made one conscious of how hushed and cloistered the tone in other parts of the paper had become. Lady Addle behaved as no peeress in Angela Thirkell would have behaved and her creator was allowed an occasional innuendo that it was perhaps assumed would be omitted by Companions reading the article aloud.

J. B. Boothroyd began solidly in the central *Punch* tradition, making his name with his *Home Guard Goings-On*[12] and *Letters to a Conscript Father*.[13] He quickly drew ahead of the field and began to establish his literary individuality. He got angry with the world and then worked off his anger by exaggerating his difficulties. He could fantasticate an experience until the article soared into a world of clear lunacy. At the same time he was developing other lines, deriving from the tradition of burlesque. His interest in the world of popular music and show business and his increasing interest in the world of journalism provided him with endless causes of irritation and hence humour. Down to the end of the Evoe period Boothroyd was still writing at one remove from reality, working up the experience or the "impression." By 1949 he had established himself as the best writer of the kind of article in which *Punch* had specialised for so long and soon he was making the other cultivators of this particular field look dowdy. Once again, as so often before, a man of unusual talent had come into what seemed to be an exhausted field, re-animated the tradition and by so doing killed off the vestiges of the past. Boothroyd also wrote a good deal of very neat verse, generally short versifications of satirical ideas, in which not a word or a line was wasted, a return to the topical or psychological quatrain of Shirley Brooks's time.

One of the professionals who made good on *Punch* was Angela Milne, a niece of A. A. Milne who signed herself "Ande." She has had a varied life as a journalist working mainly on feminine-interest features, a Civil Servant, a Land Army worker, a wife, a mother and a novelist. Her work depended at its best on the union of three talents, sheer ability to write verse or prose, extraordinarily close observation and fertility of fun. (It is interesting that both Ande and Mallett, two of the most observant of modern *Punch* writers, who disprove the cliché that *Punch* is blind to reality, should tend towards the fantastic and poetic in their humour.) The long series Ande did during the war under single-word titles must have contained the most closely-packed comic ideas in the history of the paper. This series played with the half-observed and the pleasures of recognising something you never knew you had noticed or imagined. The range of material was narrow, the amount extracted from it was astonishing. Ande was very neat in verse, excelling in chilling adaptation of ballad and didactic forms. A writer easily discouraged and at times suffering from sudden failures of judgment, she showed comic invention, subtlety and an eye for the oddities of her environment that made her one of the leading figures in the modern *Punch*.

Many *Punch* writers of this period reacted to life with evasion, but B. A. Young reacted with curiosity. Going everywhere and reading everything, a journalist of wide experience and a writer of radio plays, he took the oddness of fact as his jumping-off point. He wrote well and knew all kinds of things, including a good deal about science, usually ignored in *Punch*. He tried most of the forms used by the Lucas-Graves team and their successors, and by the war was established as a good, all-round writer, with an eye for material. The Army, in which he spent ten years, widened his experience, developed his style and confirmed his strongly Conservative views. He hit things he disapproved of and had the advantage of belonging to the right wing of the Conservative Party and thus disapproving of a good many things. (It is interesting to remember that though the paper under Evoe was very definitely Conservative, there were hardly any writers apart from Young whose work was an expression of Conservative beliefs. D. H. Barber, who later became a Conservative candidate, talked sometimes about the bazaar-and-meeting side of local politics but hardly ever about political questions themselves, and A. P. H. clung to the belief, not generally shared, that he was some queer kind of Liberal.)

The background of Bernard Hollowood ("Hod") was completely different from that of any other *Punch* man. He came from Industrial Staffordshire, with a tremendous interest in manufacture, industrial history and economics. He taught for many years, at all levels up to the University, and was a busy economic and general journalist before he began writing for *Punch*. He has been Assistant Editor of *The Economist*, has held a post with the Council of Industrial Design and has edited a very handsomely-produced journal, *Pottery and Glass*. He has written histories of business houses, worked in advertising, played cricket for his county, broadcast and appeared on television and been a Liberal Candidate. His gaiety and energy and common sense brought valuable qualities to the paper and on the Table he provided a slight variation from the usual political viewpoint. A bubbling fertility of comic fancy, emerging through upper levels composed of such materials as economic geography and a close knowledge of the American press, produced a kind of realistic crazy humour. *My Lifetime in Basic Industry*,[14] a series about the mining village of Scowle, was an extraordinary mixture of burlesque of the industrial novel, wild farce and close knowledge. Things like poverty and coal-dust, rarely present in the modern *Punch*, were used as material for fun that was oddly savage. The elusiveness of the writer's attitude was only partly due to the obvious fact that unless he were cautious the paper would not publish him at all. The firm grounding in folklore, the fact that the preposterous customs of the villagers were so like the customs that lingered in industrial villages before the rapid development of communications, the atmosphere of anecdote and working-class self-derision gave this series another dimension. (The too-little published Charles Greave also gave some of the raciness of the industrial north to his articles of fantastic reminiscence.)

One of the Hollowood's strongest lines was the application to economics of a humorous technique often used on other disciplines, the *reductio ad absurdum*. In a wonderful feat of jumping from one orbit to another he converted the great *Punch* tradition of academic humour to the newer studies, an important creative achievement, unrecognised and uncopied. He began to branch out into descriptive journalism with his very successful series on a visit to post-war America. His more recent work as Radio and Television critic and his occasional pieces on Sport show his efficiency in describing and judging as a spectator. In his best work, private fantasy and public affairs commingled, though the *Punch* tradition of the worked-up domestic experience did not suit him. His style, always clear, sharp and rapid could handle a subject but not carry it. Hence the comparative failure with the routine article, where only the diction and the cadence can distinguish it from others of the same kind. When he wrote imitation Boothroyd or Ellis, he failed. When he had the confidence to write Hollowood, he was first class.

Hollowood was also a prolific artist, often having a couple of pocket-cartoons in an issue. These were captions rather than designs. In incisive comment and in wild invention they linked *Punch* with the earlier *New Yorker*. In a period in which the superiority of drawing to caption has reversed the old order, the limitations of Hollowood's draughtsmanship have distracted some attention from the brilliance of his ideas.

Hollowood had one leg in the grittiest reality and the other in the crazy world which *Punch* writers began to enter shortly after the artists had shown the way. Colin Howard, for example, would start off as though he were going to produce a routine domestic article and would then diverge into a frothing foam of expanding absurdities. At his best he managed to create the kind of mounting comic tension of a good clown act. There was one article, for instance, that began with a gift of cheese to a young couple. A friend advised them to pour in a glass of port. Up to this point it seemed like quite a common type of domestic comedy. Then the cheese went dry, needed more, became dipsomaniac, was weaned on to cheaper drinks.[15] Invention built up the incidents into a wonderful cloud-castle. Like D. H. Barber, he came from the popular humorous press, but was unique in being able to switch from the loosely woven texture required for mass-audience humour to *Punch* work that was imaginatively close-woven.

H. W. Metcalfe brilliantly derived fantastic humour from incongruity between incident and tone. He had a naval character, who joined vigorously in rural life and addressed his servant in the language of a Victorian clubman, sometimes of a Victorian novelette. The effect was often very funny. The pace of the articles was brisk and this alone made them an agreeable change from the normally deliberate movement of *Punch* prose. The most consistently inventive of the fantastic humorists was T. S. Watt, and the most subtle user of language. He wrote from inside his own queer world instead of, as it were, creating a world to peer into from normality. He experimented freely, writing occasional verse of very considerable competence and trying both fiction and worked-up autobiography in an attempt to produce new effects by manipulating traditional forms. One of his most successful lines sprang from something invaluable to the humorist, an obsession. Sooner or later, whatever he was engaged on, Watt would bring in the Lake Poets. At first this was amusing, then it became temporarily tedious ; but he persisted and established his obsession. No *Punch* writer has operated more delicately or been able to do more with the quietly incongruous adjective.

I have devoted some thought to the question of how to deal with myself. Naturally, however catholic one's taste, one begins from one's own work and therefore the validity of one's judgments on other people ought to be tested by seeing how one judges oneself. There is a further justification for not gliding over the subject with mock modesty. This is, to some extent, a book about humour and about a rather specialised kind of journalism. I know from personal experience what engaging in it is like. I had wanted to write for *Punch* since the age of eight. This odd obsession, which I have since found I shared with other *Punch* writers, is both a strength and a weakness to the paper. The weakness is that there is a danger of hot-house loyalties, and jealousies of the casual newcomer. It can be a force against change. On the other hand it means that there exists some non-commercial feeling towards the paper, the kind of feeling consultants might have for their hospital or officers for their regiment. It means that men have been known to turn down better offers in order to continue *Punch* work, without any guarantee except that good work would be taken. I got two articles accepted out of hundreds in my first eleven years of trying. Part of the driving-force was simply narrowness, the great *Punch* vice. There were so many things I could never do and the only way I could exist was obviously by converting my inadequacies into something else. One of the things that first attracted me was that *Punch* seemed to be one of the few papers that let you do what you wanted. One felt its boundaries were not fixed but that if one invented something quite new they might be extended to include it.

I really got going in the summer of 1942, when I was pulling out of a bad nervous breakdown it is relevant to add. My various '*H.J.*' series [16] began as a fairly tight crazy world, a family with the father as narrator. Harmony Jenkins was a private scientist; his monologues were primarily a vehicle for separate jokes and his style gave me the maximum freedom by being, if not ungrammatical, some odd kind of dialect that enabled me to avoid the constrictions of grammar, about which, during years of teaching middle-school English, I had become vague. Later I kept on "H.J." because with anonymous work there is no better way of establishing a literary identity than by having a running character. Eventually I was writing poems, stories and articles and insisting on attributing them to "H.J.," until after seven years I was released by the concurrent grant of initials and a warning that "H.J." must be dropped. Essentially most of this work was separate jokes, comments, flashes, with a good deal of incidental burlesque, though very little parody, for which I lacked the ear. It appealed probably to a minority audience who enjoyed the inconsequential and the under- rather than the over-explained. It was, I suppose, upper-middlebrow humour, rather higher in density than much of *Punch*, and roughly in the tradition of Richard Mallett, of whom I regard myself as a follower, though not in quality or characteristics a very close one. Writing in solitude, desperately trying to escape, I had some of the amateur qualities of private frenzy. I now feel that the jokes could have been more efficiently presented—to-day I could probably handle the material more professionally but I doubt whether I could produce it with such fertility and freshness.

It is saddening to compare the status of *Punch* in the later Forties with its contents. The lack of advertising of individual contributors meant that the field of humour seemed to be left to the Americans, and a generation grew up to accept that the Americans were as much specialists in humour as the Swiss in neutrality or the Bushmen in use of the boomerang. The great Americans would have been great anywhere ; but they carried with them a number of other Americans who were pushed over here without being much better or worse than the native product. Only a few of the artists, largely through advertising work, and A.P.H., were "names." Mallett, Aude, Watt, Ellis and Boothroyd were a far more varied team than most periodicals could produce. All of them, in very different ways, were capable of building up and developing a solid reputation. But when they did succeed in getting a collection of *Punch* pieces reprinted it was never much advertised or made much stir. An interesting example of this is the success of Ellis's *Assistant Master* in America compared with its lack-lustre publication in England.

## IV

Verse under Evoe became less stilted than under Seaman. He reduced the amount of flat versifying of newspaper extracts, though he shared Seaman's pedagogic interest in strict form and, on the whole, the verse was noticeably less amusing than the prose. It gave the impression of not quite knowing where to go next. The dominant type of poetry in the Thirties and Forties was so completely different from the *Punch* tradition that no real rapprochement was possible. The right-wing satire of Wyndham Lewis and Roy Campbell was ignored. Left-wing satire was ruled out by the decision many years before not to make *Punch* a forum open to the whole of England. John Betjeman, most original of lucid poets between the wars, did not contribute to the paper until 1953. Much of the verse was rather sentimental country stuff, often tepidly old-fashioned. The verse of R. C. Scriven was superficially like that of the country poets and sometimes appeared with the same kind of illustration. Primarily descriptive of Yorkshire landscapes and wild life, it touched humorous verse based on dialect or local speech on one side and mystical verse on the other. Rhetorical, filled with wonderful metaphors and sometimes very beautiful, it was quite unlike other verse of the period. It was a little, though only a little, like the descriptive prose of H. E. Bates at his best. Scriven's plays written for the radio, one of which described an eye operation, have rather gained attention at the expense of his *Punch* work.

### HAYFIELD

The oil-filed teeth
chatter
with a criss-cross,
corncrake
cannibal clatter.

It was Spring
and you could cover
five daisies with your shoe :
O wonderful ! you said—
and a thousand miracles happened,
and each enchanted you :
the morning skies were grey,
the evenings red.

There came cowslips,
and buttercups,
bee-orchis,
milkmaids,
clover :
and the grass grew.

The grass, and the hundred different kinds of grass,
grew taller in sun and rain
a millionfold ;
flowered, and seeded,
lived in air and light,
drank dew,
and gripped the earth with roots untold . . .

The myriad insects that make the grass their home
spelled out their alphabets
of droning words :
the froghoppers spanned
their domes of Xanadu-glass,
alarms of fire disturbed the ladybirds.

The wind made love to the grass,
which laughed in the sun :
the butterflies played their masques
at midsummer ;
the crickets beat for it their thousand drums ;
hares brushed the thick dew
with their thicker fur :

and now the pageant's done,
the reaper comes.[17]

Of the younger light-verse writers in the classical tradition, Richard Usborne was one of the most reliable. He combined metrical control and accurate use of words with humour. Like Seaman, he was a clever man but his cleverness was kept sharp by honing on the granite of the real world. Justin Richardson was a neat manipulator of formal metres, but he made his name with irregular rhymed verse, *The Phoney Phleet,*[18] a series of naval tall stories. One of his most successful later series was *Backroom Joys.*[19] Here the attitude was, roughly speaking, that of the middle-class narrator of the domestic episode of Seaman's time given psychological observation, not unlike Ande's, and neatness with words.

The most successful comic verse of this period was the wildly imaginative. Patrick Barrington, who wrote *Songs of a Sub-Man* [20] and much else, combined fantastic invention with metrical clarity. He wrote with great accomplishment in many forms, but particularly liked Victorian and Elizabethan metres, the sentimental love-ditty, the greeting to spring, which he adapted to comic situations, or even just rendered incongruous by an occasional word. His limpid trills of pure humour contrasted oddly with the surviving verse of the Seaman tradition. R. P. Lister also used old tunes for new purposes and was to some extent a disciple of Chesterton. He produced fantasy as sharp-edged as a surrealist's ; he is a genuine minor poet :

THE FIELD OF DYNAMITE

We had a field of dynamite, and on that field we camped,
And we warned the wild asses to be careful where they stamped,
We warned the windy butterflies they must be careful too,
For if they stamp their little feet it's up with me and you.

It's up with you and me, my love, up in the morning sky,
A mile below my little toe, a mile above your eye,
And here a leg and here a hand, an acre in between,
Never a trace of either face that once before was seen.

They shall not say of us, my love, that we bewailed our plight,
Nor girded at the Fates upon our field of dynamite ;
We call it Sapper's Folly, and we never light the lamps,
And we ask the sober cart-horse to be careful how he stamps.

The kudu and the buffalo, the zebra and the pard,
We let them stamp a little but they must not stamp too hard ;
For this is all the life we have, and this is how we live,
When we are gone we may forget, but how shall we forgive ?

O night comes pouring down the west, a stream of liquid slate ;
Come, call to us, or crawl to us, but do not detonate ;
For this our field of dynamite is moistened by our tears,
But still it is not moist enough, though we may weep for years.

For still a little tiny spark may blow us from our beds
And fling us to the Pleiades, where we shall lose our heads.
Long is the night and chilly, and we have got the cramp,
But still we do not light a fire, and still we dare not stamp.[21]

## V

Evoe's first big find on the art side was "Pont" (Graham Laidler). *The British Character* [22] was a curiously transitional series. The drawing was free, descended from W. Bird rather than Townsend, with some distortion. The treatment of reality was impressionistic, though the style was far from impressionism. The subject—the English laughing at themselves—was the old subject and the national characteristics were chosen tactfully. It shows how dilute the satirical purpose of *Punch* had become that Pont's gentle jibes should have seemed sharper than anything for years. In fact, *The British Character* was not as imaginative as some of his work outside the series. Where Pont scored was where the *Punch* artists generally had been weak in this period, in comic drawing. Turn over the pages rapidly. Something hits your eye. In this period it is nearly always Pont. The caption and the idea that the caption describes may be no more penetrating than that the British write to *The Times*. The face of the particular British citizen in the picture will be cruelly accurate. Pont did a double-bluff. The kind of people he made fun of liked to see him making fun of their friends. They took him as the pictorial equivalent of all the writers who drew thin fun out of the tendency of neighbours to borrow lawn-mowers or to show snaps of their holidays. Instead, he satirised them by showing the way that life had drained out of their faces. The empty expression of the Pont characters, each with an individualised emptiness, the unhealthiness of them, taken with the pseudonym that Laidler adopted, presumably from Pont St., suggests he was consciously registering the physical and mental decline of a class.

*19th January, 1938* *Pont*

THE BRITISH CHARACTER

ABILITY TO BE RUTHLESS

Unlike later stylisers he causes no suspicion that he drew like that because that was the only way he could draw : some of his colour work in the 1941 Almanack was as delicately accomplished as *Punch* has ever printed. Pont's background detail was very varied and, something rare in *Punch* hitherto, satirically treated. His death at thirty-two was one of the worst blows *Punch* had ever received ;

he had been placed under contract and his work did not appear elsewhere, an almost unprecedented arrangement in this century.

Although Thomas Derrick contributed comparatively few drawings, he was an important link between the *Punch* of the early Thirties and the kind of smartish, fashion-like drawing to be found in the glossy weeklies and in advertising. His fluid, charcoal sketches were quite unlike any of the main *Punch* traditions of draughtsmanship. His faces were weak and his jokes, when they strayed outside a stimulus to the response " So they do " were uncertain. When, in fact, he was doing the same kind of thing as other men, he did it on the whole less well. What were important were his full-page compositions in which time and space became plastic, as in a Disney Silly Symphony. Reality was patterned and a social point that would be dull presented in a unitary setting gained enormously by being presented rhythmically and decoratively, for instance his *Country Cousins* of 19th January, 1938, or *News*, 4th May, 1938. This side of his work looked forward, perhaps to the 1960s.

When Kenneth Bird succeeded George Morrow in the Art Editorship in 1937, a little progress had already been made towards ending the long caption and speeding up jokes and improving the look of the paper by the removal of rules between columns and round pages and drawings. Headings were also modernised. Now for the first time there was detailed direction of the Art. One of the first difficulties was the lack of new men. It took time for it to become known that *Punch* wanted work submitted to it. Gradually new artists were found and encouraged. Systematic selection, arrangement and foresight made the Art editing arduous but worth it. The efficiency of the trained engineer was directed to improving the look of the pages, to varying the type of pictorial humour within each issue, to ensuring that there were not too many jokes on the same topic in the same period. Artists were encouraged to call at the office to discuss their problems and to receive criticism or encouragement. What was taken for granted as the minimum of editing in most magazines at last reached *Punch*. The new policy

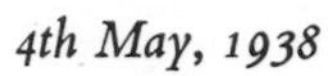

*4th May, 1938* *Thomas Derrick*

NEWS

was a return to the older *Punch*, the *Punch* of Leech. The object of the paper was redefined. It was a humorous paper and therefore the first point about a picture was whether it was funny. The one-line caption became the norm and the drawing that was able to make its point without words the final aim. What had been elegant and lifelike and detailed became distorted and grotesque and bare. The American influence was strong though late. The time was, in fact, ripe for a swing back the other way.

The limitations of subject-matter in pictorial humour were even more marked than in written humour. There was very little social comment ; but at least the jokes about the stupidity of the poor went. One began to feel each joke was the best of a good bunch. The reaction of the sillier readers to this belated introduction to the characteristic humour of the Twentieth Century was hysterical. There was something in their complaint that the shop-window for English black-and-white was now occupied by men some of whom were cheerfully aware that they could hardly draw at all. Yet the amount of incompetent drawing, in the sense of inability to realise an intention, was quite considerable before the change. Some of the tea-parties and dances were villainously ill-drawn.

The cartoon continued throughout this period unchanged in conception. In 1935, Raven Hill was succeeded as second cartoonist by Ernest Shepard, who was rather wasted on the work. Partridge had been anxious to retire but in response to urgent entreaties from the proprietors and the Editor he carried on until his death in 1945, when L. G. Illingworth took over. Illingworth was a superb draughtsman in a job that needed one. His joke drawings had always had a clarity and an authority of line that made them stand out ; they were both decorative and representational. His cartoons matched early Tenniel for drawing and some of Raven Hill for bite. A fiery, genial Welshman, he was often savage in the *Daily Mail* and has shown no embarrassment when given savage subjects in *Punch*.

The *Charivaria* page was greatly strengthened by Fougasse, whose illustrations managed to add a dimension to the items by endless invention within narrow limits. They may not have been noticed apart from the text by many readers but they had the expertise, the completely individual handling that *Punch* should have been able to command more often than it did. J. H. Dowd illustrated the film criticisms from the beginning, with great skill at getting a likeness. He was succeeded by R. S. Sherriffs, a remarkable caricaturist who, apart from the inevitable occasional failure, managed to get likenesses week after week. He says he regards himself as a disciple of Thomas Derrick ; this must be a psychological influence as nobody else can see it in his work, which is sculptural, the face built up in rocky planes on a base of firmly apprehended character. He has often been assumed to derive partially from early Picasso. A bitter fantastic with a whirling imagination, he stands apart from most of the other artists. His training was heraldic and some of his best work has been formalised decoration. His drawings of celebrities in the *Tatler* first brought him into notice.

With the gradual increase in the amount of space devoted to drawings, the number of *Punch* artists increased. The casualties among the fairly regular older contributors were heavy. The change had been so long delayed that it inevitably had to be violent when it came, if the paper were to survive. A good deal went, it seems now, that might have still had something to contribute. As, in fact, *Punch* art became considerably more varied than it had been under the previous Art Editors there was obviously no narrow orthodoxy. By the time he handed over the Art editorship, Kenneth Bird had made *Punch* the leading humorous art journal in the world, hampered only by limitations of subject that applied with far more deadening effect to the text. Professional humorous artists gave *Punch* the first refusal of their work. Youngsters were discovered, encouraged, criticised, looked after. The trouble began to be not, as it had been, that there was nothing to put in the paper but that there was too much. Contributions too good to be lost piled up and artists began to complain that they had to wait for publication, which in those days meant payment, for months and even years.

PEOPLE WHO LIVE IN GLASS HOUSES . . .

"Douglas" (Douglas England) had links with the world of the smart advertisement. Often his pictures burlesqued the glossy hats, the stylish prance of advertisement characters. He was fertile in jokes that depended on this kind of contrast between the smart and the tripped-up. In the Thirties he did a good deal of full-page work, including some gay and poster-like colour pages. Later he first shared the *Charivaria* illustrations with Fougasse and then took them over altogether. It made a decorative page, with his strong blacks, quite unlike any other *Punch* work, but he was trying to carry on a tradition created by another man and *Punch* lacked his own jokes

*22nd July, 1953* *Douglas*

until he moved to a strip, first at the end of *Charivaria* and later at the end of the paper.

In the transitional period between the complete realism of the Townsend school and the self-explanatory, detail-less, formalised drawing that was the full expression of the Kenneth Bird policy, there emerged a group of new artists whose strong individual capacities maintained them in independence of the fashionable trend. The setting was often a room in a house, the garden of a house or the road outside one. The drawing still contained a good deal of background detail. The human figure was distorted in varying degrees, but this distortion was a form of emphasis. The aim was to give an impression of real people in real homes. There was a common assumption that the speed of apprehension of the average reader had suddenly increased. William Scully, often regarded as a disciple of Peter Arno, filled his space with exuberant and decorative lines and often with objects which, while unnecessary to the joke, gave pleasure by their appearance. His humour, even when topical, had often something oblique and eerie about it ; he covered a wide range of comedy and never under-rated the reader's intelligence. Of this group, L. H. Siggs was the most naturalistic, the most careful delineator of the suburban background, and also the most poetic and fantastic in humour. W. A. Sillince was an ambitious and versatile draughtsman, always hankering after the genre drawings that later he was enabled to do in illustrating descriptive articles. Sillince probably had the best eye for country of the new arrivals.

Acanthus (F. Hoar) was an architect and, as a specialist, able to bring to *Punch* pages a high degree of specificity, one of the qualities most lacking in the modern period. He showed his training not merely in the jokes that made an architectural point, but in the composition. He could make a building funny in itself, and his precision made a point of rest in the paper when other drawings were less determinate in outline. With him may be considered Ionicus (J. C. Armitage). Although he concentrated less on architecture than Acanthus, the clarity of his method made it well adapted to drawing buildings. His people had normal skeletons, his furniture normal structure. There was space and solidity about his pictures that contrasted effectively with the odd, private suddenness of his humour. Although Norman Mansbridge used cartoonists' tricks of distortion and short-hand, he was at first essentially a realistic artist. If he drew a scene in a ship's cabin he always suggested that it was not an abstract cabin but one enclosed by a real hull, forced through the real seas. His period at sea in the war gave him a good deal of new material to add to his predominantly domestic backgrounds. From time to time he did editorial decorations and became a useful odd job artist ; but in the Thirties and Forties he was primarily an inventor and illustrator of jokes in which the joke was intended to be more important than the illustration.

David Langdon was the great master of the topical comic idea. His almost diagrammatic buses and houses and little shouting men gave immediacy to his perfectly phrased captions. He claimed to have introduced the open mouth into humorous art. His fertility has been astonishing. He has done a lot of advertising and contributes

*22nd June, 1938* *David Langdon*

"How many noughts in a million?"

regularly to several papers. His starting point was generally the newspaper or a walk in London. His jokes varied with the audience to which they were addressed in subtlety and assumptions of knowledge. Basically they were quick-witted comedian's jokes, some from the top of the bill at the music-hall, some from the top radio show, some from the political cabaret. They lacked the fantasy and the knowledge of Hollowood's, but they were more consistent in their appeal to the widest *Punch* audience. No other contributor united so many kinds of reader. The world was that of Bert Thomas after the changes of a generation. We laughed with, not at, the policemen, foremen, wardens, shopkeepers and *Daily Express* readers who peopled the pictures. David Langdon's sense of humour was extraordinarily constant. His recent *New Yorker* pictures have shown that translated to a different tradition he can draw on a reserve of humour of a kind hitherto untapped. After many years of very severe work each Langdon was still taut and, one felt, *ad hoc*. More individual styles, more elegant contributions to graphic art have palled more quickly. Turn back twenty years and often it is the Langdon in an issue that is still fresh and amusing.

An individual genius who probably influenced more artists than Pont was "Paul Crum" (Roger Pettiward, Peter Fleming's companion in *Brazilian Adventure*. He was killed early in the war.) He began contributing only in 1936, but in this short time he had established a new style of bleak, fantastic humour, in which drawing and joke formed a unity. He created a world of precise insanity.

*21st July, 1937* *Paul Crum*

"I KEEP THINKING IT'S TUESDAY"

Objects might be recognisable, but only as in dreams. He was not, in the strict sense, surrealist—there has been very little true surrealist art in *Punch*—but his humour, like that of many *Punch* artists after him, did cause a *frisson* not entirely explicable in logical terms. He led the way to a humorous art that could be responded to without complete cognition.

J. W. Taylor was one of the most consistent of the crazy artists. His sombre men in black hats, schoolchildren and sinisterly effusive dogs appeared in endless variety of combination. He was, perhaps, best when barest, nothing distracting attention from the purity of his nonsense. He belonged to that small, select class whose real

*26th March, 1952* *J. W. Taylor*

*"Never mind me—get cracking on the reviewers."*

individuality lies in their jokes being funnier than other people's. Even as a headmaster he has maintained his levity uncontaminated. " Anton," a brother and sister, H. Underwood Thompson and Mrs. Antonia Yeoman, in partnership, was one of the busiest of *Punch* artists. They had a very individual sense of humour. The jokes stayed good volume after volume. The drawing was decorative and the massed blacks showed up well on the page and made a change as one went through the paper. The world of tall men politely inclining forward, of spivs and forgers and waiters and duchesses

*"Well, if you've never seen a six-pound note before, how do you know that's not a genuine one?"*

and wonderful dining-room tables was calmly, courteously mad. Although the characters and settings and the topics were few the number of combinations seemed infinite. I have never understood why for some minds a deliberate limitation of field leads to fertility, while other minds it stunts and parches. Anton gained enormously from it.

L. H. Starke lived in a dreamland of monks and company directors. He was an extremely efficient, all-round comic artist of the less representational kind, but for some years editorial timidity meant that many of his best jokes, jokes that came from the deepest level, appeared elsewhere. With Anton and Taylor, he represented the first generation of crazy humorists at their best.

Now that with proper editing it was no longer possible for an artist to produce the same picture week after week, there was more experiment, more willingness to learn, more determination to meet competition by better work in your own line. As in the Victorian *Punch*, there were several types of comic humour appearing at once. During the war, there was a return to the pictorial investigation of reality and to fancy. Emett became the biggest new name after Pont. He marked the return of the decorative tradition and expressed some of the wartime nostalgia for fantasy and detail and the past. His derelict local railways, pleasure steamers in Cornish coves and gipsies by gnarled copses had a passion behind them that gave them a wide appeal. It was probably only gradually that his drawing and colour began to be appreciated in isolation from his comic ideas and his fantastic world. He soon found himself under the pressures that had tried to restrict Heath Robinson to inventions and Bateman to colonels and Rackham to twisted trees. At one time he did not draw a train in *Punch* for over a year. His design for the railway at the Battersea Festival Gardens in 1951 made him world-famous and he did some TV appearances and an increasing amount of work in America. His early drawings had simple, very strong comic ideas. Gradually he became more elaborate ; some of his full-page decorations were almost consumed by their detail. He showed in the illustrations to his children's books that he was becoming happier away from joke-illustration and the pictures of a tour in the U.S.A. that he did for *Life* transmuted things seen into comic fantasy.

Russell Brockbank had a different background from most of the artists. He was a Canadian who served in the Navy and had spent

*25th March, 1948* *Emett*

"*. . . some footlin' nonsense about a right-of-way or something . . .*"

periods in industry. Like many of the best humorists, he was a man with an obsession. He was absorbed in motoring and, secondarily, aeroplanes, thus being one of the few *Punch* artists, except the illustrators of sporting scenes, to share an interest with their readers. He made a number of visual jokes about the cars he drew, most of which were different, with minute variations enabling the expert to date them and notice obscure points of antiquarian lore, in addition

*" From a purely aesthetic point of view I do hope they take the right fork."*

to the main jokes which could be enjoyed by the non-motorist. The Brockbank world was positive, Twentieth Century, technologically abundant. He never got humour from recessive qualities. His favourite recreation was to work in the pits at International Motor Races. His humour developed steadily in range, penetration

*5th September, 1951* *ffolkes*

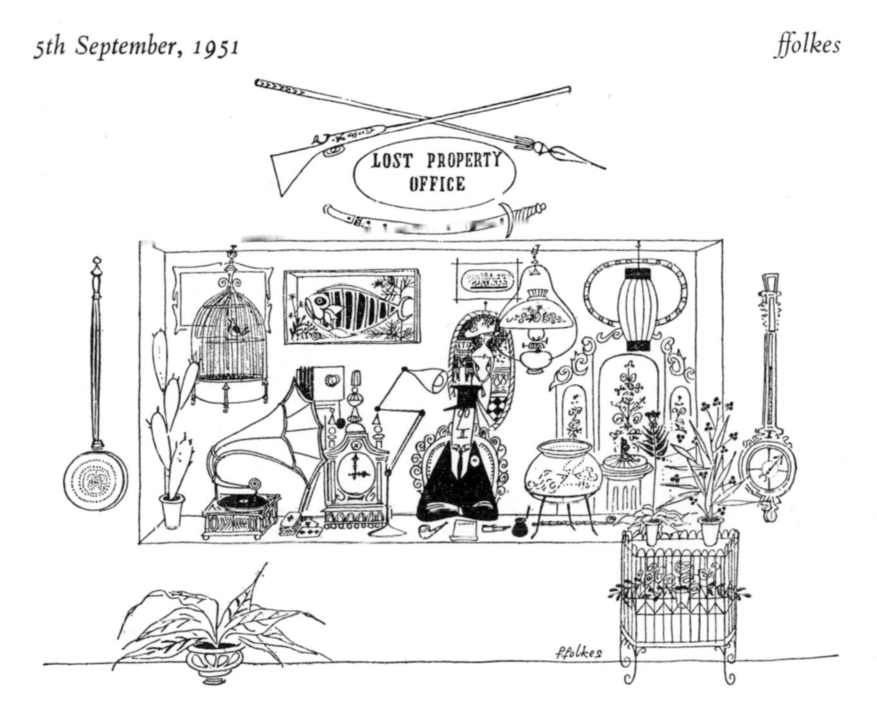


and subtlety. His drawing was better with things than with people, who tended to be rather repetitively horrified or eager or ferocious or terrified, though he could depart from this convention, which was probably based on the primacy of the machine, and the series of four pictures of a headmaster he drew in 1953 summed up the whole history of English education in tracing the deterioration of a character. As a colourist he was bold and decorative and did some striking covers.

Michael ffolkes was one of the decorators. He was influenced by the Rex Whistler–Oliver Messel world of masques and rococo interiors and periwigs and statues, though his range was very wide and he was in no way a specialised artist. His humour was light, fantastic, often very funny indeed. Like Emett, he could please

*11th April, 1951* *Sprod*

" *She's been immortalized by Mr. Wordsworth.*"

and amuse with his designs ; his comic invention was much more fertile. George Sprod, an Australian, was another decorator, less light and whimsical than ffolkes, often macabre. He liked caryatids, urns, madness and the frenzy behind the cairngorm. He has done most things including political pocket-cartoons. Not since Doyle and early Tenniel had there been so much poetry in *Punch* art as in the Emett, ffolkes, Sprod group. André François, a Rumanian domiciled in Paris, brought into *Punch* the great continental tradition of comic draughtsmanship. His line was quite unlike any English artist's and this alone made both a pleasant change to look at and a stumbling-block for the reader who had at last got used to Langdon.

*28th July, 1948* *André François*

*"Medals, medals, medals . . ."*

François seems to me to have been the next step in humorous art, almost pure humour, untranslatable into any other form. Often without caption, sometimes with a word or two that was only obliquely relevant, he juxtaposed ideas of different provenances, of different weights. Far more imaginative than the frequently rather mechanical surrealists, François made no concessions. Either you were amused or you were baffled and if you were baffled the joke generally could not be explained any more than you can explain a statue or a Persian carpet. One was conscious with François of following an exploration of new territory.

Although Kenneth Bird deserves the credit for the revitalisation of *Punch* art, it must be remembered that he had been appointed by Evoe, who was very much Editor in his own paper, had the final say in the selection of pictures and made the principal editorial decisions. The revitalisation took place in his reign.

CHAPTER NINE

# NEW LOOK

## *Kenneth Bird's Editorship, 1949–1952*

IN 1949 Evoe retired and was succeeded by Kenneth Bird, with H. F. Ellis as Literary Editor and Russell Brockbank as Art Editor. The problem before the new team was to try to recapture in the post-war world, now several years old, the public that *Punch*, in common with other periodicals, had found during the war, to revive interest in the paper and to direct attention to it. Unfortunately the very substantial improvements they made were not noticed by the public in sufficient quantities to free the situation from danger ; but some of the improvements to which Malcolm Muggeridge later succeeded in attracting attention were, as he has often pointed out, made by his predecessors. *Punch* is a tough little paper and its vitality has had periods of latency rather than extinction.

The first problem tackled was appearance. Fougasse had always been interested in the technicalities of magazine production, in lay-out and make-up and typography. *Punch* had grown to look old-fashioned, having once led the field. Evoe had been more interested in content than appearance and provided the pages were legible and accurately printed he considered that that was enough. The type was now redesigned and a wider range of types used for headings. There was far more space on the page and each page was planned as a whole. Long paragraphs were broken up and every chance was used of introducing dialogue or italics or other variations in the look of articles. Every page now had to have at least one drawing or decoration of some kind. There were gay headings, changed each week, to many sections.

*Punch* looked more attractive to the casual dipper. The chief weakness was that there was less in it than before. The article which needed to be long and solid was cut or broken up or not used. If the advantage of the new look was that it was visually enticing its weakness was that it made the paper bitty. The standard of accuracy in proof-reading had always been high and under Seaman the office never seemed to do anything else. Kenneth Bird was interested in accuracy and as time went on he directed more and more of the staff's attention to detailed revision and there was a slight drying of the first enthusiasm and inventiveness.

The second cartoon was dropped (to the surprise of the staff without a single complaint from the public), and Ernest Shepard was restored to decoration. Perhaps not many readers recognised the quality of his headings, but week by week they played variations on typical Shepard themes. By being not old-fashioned but deliberately out of fashion, to paraphrase *Horizon*'s defence of Piper's cover, they retained their freedom and freshness. Illingworth was increasingly restricted to statements of fact in the cartoon. Evoe had sometimes, in some moods, enjoyed the controversial and the infuriating. His successor was temperamentally in favour of agreement and hated to hurt feelings. This personal lack of the combative afforced the theory that *Punch* should not reduce circulation by alienating subscribers. Unfortunately this sometimes resulted in tameness and timidity. Once, as Burnand had discovered, you have begun to avoid offence to groups of readers, the number of possible causes of offence seems to increase. The paper's note became even more muffled.

There was a genuine difficulty here. Roughly half the population supported the Conservatives and half the Socialists. If *Punch* were to be a National Institution, should it take sides? It might have found it easier simply to satirise the weaknesses of both Parties, a plague o' both your houses attitude. Alternatively would it have been necessarily any less of an Institution if it had taken a point of view and stuck to it? After all, this is what it had done at its beginning. The decision was left suspended and *Punch* was, even more than it had been, a Conservative organ without the courage of Conservative convictions.

Various experiments were made with the *Charivaria* page, first by the Assistant Editor, B. A. Young, and then by J. B. Boothroyd, who left the literary side of banking for the *Punch* office. The items sent in by correspondents were more rigorously selected and rewritten and longer paragraphs dealing with current events, peculiar news stories and the like were tried, to get away from the formula of invented news items and endless jokes about jobbing-gardeners and motorists and policemen. The length was a difficult one to handle without either taking an item that would be complete in twenty words and spinning it out to a hundred and fifty or trying to compress a short article into a single paragraph. Direct reporting, as in *The New Yorker*, required more space and anyway the *Charivaria* page in its old form did appeal to very many readers. During this transitional period, while the tone and form were retained on the whole, items of a different kind were slipped in and eventually the feature painlessly became more varied in approach and subject matter and composition.

The Booking Office, which had been run by Hugh Kingsmill during the war, consisted of a couple of pages of reviews, each about 250 words long, and initialled. They were written by Kingsmill, by other men in the office and by a corps of outside reviewers, some of them dating back many years. The two ends of the paper published work by several long-service *Punch* writers, who tended to get overlooked simply because they had gone on so long: D. A. Gulliver, for example, the most consistent of *Charivaria* contributors, or Mrs. H. P. Eden, a very intelligent reviewer of considerable scholarship and width of mind, who normally dealt with the kind of books that many people did not realise *Punch* covered at all. The Book Reviews have always been a strong point with *Punch* and on looking back on them one sees how different they are from the outside picture of "a nice novel" or "a book for the country-lover " which to many people still seems to sum up *Punch*'s choice of books to review and praise. The chief criticism of the reviews in the Forties is, in fact, that they neglected to cover the field of light literature adequately, a field that *Punch* once usefully considered its province, and that they were so anxious to be good criticism that they sometimes failed to be light in the hand.

The new régime reorganised the Booking Office, and put it in charge of Richard Mallett, who made it into one of the best-balanced literary features in London. The selection and arrangement and, of course, impeccable editing, of the section gave it a unity of tone. It now began with a longer composite review of up to four books, though sometimes a single book might be used. Generally this was written by Eric Keown and myself alternately. There followed a varying number, about four or five, of shorter reviews. The instructions to be fair to the writer, fair to the possible reader of the book and fair to the reader of the paper who might not want to read the book were still the guiding principle, but the last received more attention than before. Much more trouble was taken over the actual writing of the Booking Office. The short reviews were followed by a number of short notes, written in a variety of telegraphic styles. This device variegated the page and enabled many more books to be referred to.

Russell Courtney (Guy Eden) continued to cover Parliament as he had been doing for some years. Impartiality having to be his watchword, he made much of small incidents and could not really let himself go on major issues. He carried out a difficult assignment with urbanity and style. Lucy had been able to use his store of political gossip and sometimes to be near-libellous. Tom Taylor had been fervently partisan, if not very entertaining. Shirley Brooks had been witty but generally witty *against* something. Guy Eden had to report without giving opinions of either events or men and he did it as well as it could be done.

One of the most important parts of the new policy was to be a rapprochement between *Punch* and reality, a return to the tradition of describing what the world was like. Each week there were two double-page spreads with two-thirds text to one-third illustration. These reported on various aspects of the world and attracted a completely new audience to the paper. One hard-bitten newspaperman gloomily remarked that *Punch* now contained the best descriptive reporting in the British Press. One of the articles was fairly serious. In alternate weeks Bernard Hollowood in *An Industrial Journey* [1] described factories, laboratories and exhibitions of industrial and commercial interest and Eric Keown described voluntary social services. Occasionally Keown was let loose on something less worthy but gayer ; but on the whole he took the reader's face and turned it pretty firmly to the misfortune that still existed and the efforts made by charities to deal with it. The expressed intention of balancing all the news in the papers about the Welfare State with an account of the work that was still being done by personal philanthropy sometimes seemed to make enormous efforts to ignore what the State actually did ; but it gave a sober and vivid picture of still existent conditions, and contained almost the first pity for the poor shown by *Punch* for about eighty years. Both Hollowood and Keown tried innumerable devices to maintain interest in their serious topics, but the best guarantee of interest was simply in the topics themselves, which on the whole were probably new to many readers. There was inevitably a feeling of repetition when another clinic or another factory turned up and it was a pity that the series were not varied more, giving both of the reporters some topographical work or overseas visits.

The other weekly Feature was intended to be primarily a comic article about visiting some place of interest or seasonal event. The distinction between the informative and the entertaining was not always clearly indicated and they tended increasingly to be fairly straight description. The topics selected included events that always had been covered, like the Royal Tournament, and places of interest, like The College of Arms. Many of the *Punch* writers collaborated on these and several contributors who had shown promise in articles were tried out on descriptive writing. Gradually a nucleus grew up headed by J. B. Boothroyd, who set the standard and the tone of the whole series. He had great industry and enterprise in getting into close contact with his material, a wonderful eye for the revealing or comic detail and a style that, as far as I know,

THE NEW HOUSE OF COMMONS

*22nd February, 1950* *D. L. Mays*

is unrepresented in anthologies of modern prose, simply because the kind of men who edit that kind of anthology were not, in those days, looking at *Punch*. Boothroyd was very sensitive to quality of light ; his writing had at times a Fabergé glitter. Everything was swift and neat and elegant. He was a deceptive writer because the works were hidden. The solid information on which the casual article on Ice Hockey or Fairs was based never appeared. The surface was both easy and taut ; it was loquitive prose that was never slack or chatty. Boothroyd never forgot that he was there to entertain and his method would vary from slapstick to analysis. In his ordinary articles he often started from derision or disgust ; but when he was unfavourably impressed and could not, because of the hospitality and assistance he had received, express his full feelings he often did one of his most deadly jobs. B. A. Young and P. M. Hubbard, with an occasional brilliant contribution from Ande, were the other leading Feature writers.

Most of the more regular artists were tried on illustrating the Features. Some proved unhappy, some showed that being able to draw something without having to think of a joke first was a liberation. For years D. L. Mays had been illustrating jokes about children or fashionable women in the tradition of du Maurier, though the jokes had far less satiric bite. Perhaps because he was an illustrator rather than a humorous artist, he was much the most successful. His new House of Commons [2] for example, was illustration of a quality that *Punch* had not seen for years. Quite apart from whatever effect the policy had on readers it was a very good thing for contributors, getting them out of ruts and forcing them to develop new skills and driving them into contact with the world. Norman Mansbridge developed considerably during a somewhat gruelling amount of Features-illustration.

## II

As Literary Editor, H. F. Ellis hurried to reverse Evoe's policy of doing as little editing as possible. The improvement in the " tail " of *Punch* was very marked. Lazy writers who expected to get in week after week with virtually the same article were downed. New writers who showed promise or even a serious desire to write for *Punch* were encouraged and trained. Ellis made the regular contributors work against a standard of what he considered their own best work. What mattered was to begin building up a corps of writers who were likely to be useful over a period and for this the important thing was the maintenance of the average standard of their work. Articles were rejected frequently. Articles were sent back and back for revision. The result of this was a sharp rise in quality, especially, of course, in the qualities that could respond to editing, like economy, lucidity and pace. The editing never bore down on the contributor like Seaman's and was, in any case, far less pedantic and detailed. The good work was, for the first time for many years, praised, and praise is the most powerful instrument the Editor of a humorous periodical possesses. An occasional sharp rap over the knuckles reminded the momentarily-complacent that *Punch* could not be taken for granted. Contributors were now invited to call at the office for interview, invited even to make an appointment for a general discussion when they felt depressed about their work—and this, which may seem small to the non-contributor, changed the whole of life. Under Evoe, to nearly all contributors *Punch* was a dread, chill building that a few of the boldest walked past every few years or so. Now the sun shone. Colleagues met others who suffered the same fits of depression, the same inability to get ideas, the same belief that the office had suddenly gone insane. There were binges for the contributors and if there was a lot of mutual backslapping it was cheering and, more important, inspiring. This policy had long been followed by Kenneth Bird on the Art side and Ellis adopted it enthusiastically. New men came along and were retained, not just allowed to drift away.

Ellis had a wonderful sense of the comic possibilities of an article. He could put his finger on the weak spot or suggest the change that made all the difference. His judgment of an article was almost infallible. He would probably have liked to make the paper not only contain more topical and immediate writing but sharper stuff. Here the editorial policy became increasingly inflexible. In a way

Evoe and Ellis were complementary. It is a pity that they were not, apparently, complementary at the same time. Ellis had far more idea of relating what the paper did to what it would do in the future, a far more positive aim in editing and far more expert skill in working on an article. On the other hand Evoe was broader in his tastes, he liked more different kinds of humour and he was, though with gaps, more aware of what was going on and what might be going to go on. Ellis was deeper and narrower in his tastes. He improved men's professional efficiency and raised the standard of actual writing in the paper but, on the whole, cultivated a smaller area. There was less of Evoe's random planting or sense of marginal growth, and he lacked Evoe's intermittent power of standing outside his own background, education and environment and meeting an article or poem on its own ground. It is probable that after the work of improving the day-to-day editing had been accomplished he might have relaxed and allowed himself a wider curiosity and developed a more versatile palate.

Of the new men who came in towards the end of Evoe's Editorship or during that of Kenneth Bird only a few can be mentioned. The fact that the pressure on space becomes overwhelming shows the rise in standard of the average article. Great stars are, to some extent, incalculable, can be seized on but not created. The existence of so many good supporting players is evidence of good editing.

Alex Atkinson is a good example of the man who got into the paper through tilling a small field and then, with encouragement, launched out. He was a Repertory actor who had contributed to many papers and written plays when he began writing in *Punch* about Repertory theatres, about the audiences and the plays and then about his landlady. It was his freshness rather than his humour that first attracted. This was new ground, even though he was approaching it in an old way. It is a common mistake for *Punch* beginners to play for safety by basing their approach on established writers and simply altering the *milieu.* Soon Atkinson began to reveal a personality. When at last he was granted initials and no longer had to establish his property in each article by dragging in the same characters he shot ahead, broadening out from the stage into subjects taken from the press and then into parody. With the added confidence that came from the successful reception of his novels he produced some brilliant work.

P. M. Hubbard, Newdigate Winner and ex-Indian Civil Servant, was a tremendous find. He began with poems of childhood, of the countryside and summer that managed to provide sentiment instead of sentimentality. He never fell off into the ordinary poem of affection or regret, partly because he was technically a far more accomplished verse-writer than most of the sentimentalists, partly because his attitude was always positive rather than negative—childhood is a valuable state, this threat to the country must be fought. His prose articles began from personal experience but as soon as he had found his own voice they became quite different from other articles of personal experience. He was strong where the old *Punch* article of misadventure or habit was weak, in seeing the detail. He would take a paragraph to describe a man putting his boots on and this would give solidity to everything that followed as well as being entertaining in itself. His style, hard, disciplined and very apt in comparison, could be gentle without mawkishness and savage without being muffled by fear. He turned out to be an admirable writer of Features, with a wonderful eye for the odd, amusing fact and the unexpected relationship. Gay, nostalgic, bitter and funny, Hubbard raised the problem of why anybody who wrote so well and showed such comic invention in conversation and letter-writing should not have found himself forced into print by his ability years before.

Marjorie Riddell, it has been remarked, may play a one-string fiddle but she produces a considerable number of tunes from it. Her laconic accounts of correspondence and telephone calls between a fussy, vague, associatively-minded Mother and her bachelor daughter [3] in the Big City had a double appeal, to the older type of *Punch* reader who could identify with the daughter, remembering just such another Mother in her own family, and to the reader who liked to see an anecdote stripped of irrelevances, embodying different kinds of observation and told with carefully-concealed experiment in the use of dialogue, variation of pace and all the rest of it. The great test of the *Punch* domestic article is what it looks like in a volume of reprints. Marjorie Riddell's pieces improved by reproduction. Side by side they reflected light from surface to surface. The " How " attracted attention as well as the " What." The family was shown to be not just a sketched-in background but a firm invention. The social background, the problems of living alone, the sadness of the incompatibility of protection and freedom, the incompleteness of freedom as a way of life, were delicately handled but not avoided. One step in either direction might have resulted in disaster. As it was, the articles about *My Mother* came off perfectly, another evidence of what craftsmanship can do with unpromising material.

*Punch* had often used monologue and dialect duologue but gradually it died out except for an occasional Scot or Irishman. A.P.H.'s *Topsy* had been one of the few attempts to try to draw a character through speech habits. In a series about a child, in which each article began ' Mummy, mummy ', [4] Marjorie Redman did succeed in conveying the urgency of infantile demand for attention by syntax. There was a real child there, desperately trying to communicate. Mrs. D. J. Saint wrote about conditions in a Junior School with an implied protest about the overwhelmingness of the *Forty* [5] that came into every title. This was monologue by the teacher with the voices of the children echoing through it, as it were. Both these series unfortunately found it a little difficult to know what to do after making their point. Alan Hackney brought the flavour of speech fully back into *Punch*. *Snax at Jax* [6] was built round casual arguments in a snack-bar, reproduced with extraordinary phonetic fidelity. You might like it or dislike it, but here was living speech. The incidents were few, tangential, often merely decorations of eccentricity. The characters emerged murkily, as in life.

One important departure was the regular publication of serious or semi-serious poems on the two centre pages, with illustrations, generally by Ernest Shepard. These included some of the older writers who had been writing on equine and pastoral subjects for some years, one or two of the newer recruits who learned how to do what was wanted, R. C. Scriven, who gave the feature a distinction it otherwise lacked and a few poets who gave the impression of whooping for joy to find that the kind of verse they had written for many years before was not, as they had feared, unsaleable. This editorial change aroused considerable controversy. It was defended on the ground that, judging by the letters, many readers liked this unexacting branch of literature, having given up reading poetry in despair before 1914, and that it increased the non-humorous, general magazine appeal of *Punch* and gave an opportunity to the illustrators to keep alive the tradition that *Punch* meant black-and white as well as humour. It was criticised on the ground that to print dilute pre-1914 verse after the Second World War was to throw away the advantages gained by the other improvements. The trouble was that some of the verse was good, though not in a contemporary style. What made the younger reader feel he was back in the *Punch* he had slowly seen renew its vitality was the amount of tepid country verse without any character, the amount of metrical drooling. Scriven's precision, the freshness of his memory as his sight faded, showed this up badly.

The centenary of *Punch* in 1941 could not be celebrated, as had been hoped, with a *History* and a Memorial Number because of the war. The opportunity of the Festival of Britain was taken to use some of this material to produce a Special Number, the largest Special Number ever produced by *Punch*. This Festival Number had a central section consisting of extracts from the prose, verse and pictures of the past hundred years. The rest of the issue was loosely organised round an imaginary Exhibition in Bouverie St. and formed a kind of Almanack or Summer Number with rather more colour than usual, special colours being tried and the production of the issue being of some importance in the history of colour-printing.

## III

The policy in the Art during the Fougasse Editorship did not alter except in the direction of having rather more of it and of having some of it serious illustration. As Art Editor, Russell Brockbank maintained the Fougasse tradition of encouragement, accessibility and technical expertise. He probably appreciated more varieties of humorous drawing than Fougasse and his sensibility continued to develop. G. L. Stampa retired from illustrating the dramatic criticisms and was succeeded by Ronald Searle, who had contributed a few little joke drawings since the end of the war. He had made a big reputation outside *Punch* for his fiendish schoolgirls and shark-like managing directors. As a theatrical caricaturist he was the first *Punch* contributor for many years to produce real caricatures. His magnified, pointed jaws and spindly extremities, though sometimes they masked a likeness, introduced rhythms of some elegance into a part of *Punch* that had not aimed at being more than competently photographic since the Nineties.

One marked change since the First War had been the decline in the pictorial humour of

character and *milieu*. There was no special reason why the jokes should be rooted in any part of the world. Porters carried goods on their heads through jungles, but it was never any particular jungle. There was no registration of differences between parts of London or parts of the country. The regional joke completely died out. Cars, aeroplanes and modern furniture were almost the only appearances recorded. Only Mays was really interested in costume. Since Belcher, hardly anyone had drawn people. There was no graphic equivalent of Alan Hackney. Lloyd, Sherriffs and Searle drew *ad hoc* caricatures but celebrities generally were left alone and temperaments and types were ignored.

Of the new artists, Kenneth Mahood was in the Crum tradition. The danger is that this is so hit-or-miss. Unless the joke is different in quality from other jokes placed near it in the paper, it loses its effect. When Crum pushed unity of joke and drawing further than before, he sacrificed visual delight *per se*. In his followers, there is only one kind of pleasure to be gained from each contribution, though that pleasure may be of the most intense kind. Mahood, at his best, could invent wonderful situations, but in the drawing he did not aim at more than stating what the situation was. Here he may be compared with Eric Burgin, an even more fertile inventor of the fantastic. But Burgin scored in that the shapes in his drawings were themselves often funny, like some of the Miro shapes. With the blazing imaginations of Mahood and Burgin, perhaps this particular tradition has developed as far as it can.

*22nd April, 1953* *Giovannetti*

There was an enormous welcome waiting for anybody who could devise a new formula. Roy Davis made a very pleasant change, with his little, doll-like guardsmen, which had some of the appeal of Leech's Brook-Green Militia-Man. Because the style of drawing was different they gave variety to the page, quite apart

*21st May, 1952* *W. Hewison*

from the merits of the humour. His jokes were always agreeable and often funny, but their narrow range involved a self-denying ordinance not to compete all along the line, rather like that of some of the earlier specialists, the drawers of humanised animals, for example.

A very popular new star was Giovanetti, an Italian-Swiss, whose hamster, Max, was the most endearing arrival in *Punch* since Emett's train. The eager, undaunted gaiety of Max (the last panel in the strip usually showed him puzzled after disaster) has been absurdly considered to throw light on human courage, and to perform all kinds of philosophical feats. This is nonsense. What was enjoyable in Max was that, with him, some of the humours of animal and child returned to *Punch* purged of sentimentality. The parents of the Twenties and Thirties having fought and won the battle against whimsy, the children of the Fifties could relax guiltlessly with Giovanetti.

*12th May, 1954* *Thelwell*

François has had little direct influence, partly because his madness was encapsulated in a continental tradition to which few English artists had access. One new *Punch* artist who found his inspiration obviously valuable was Smilby (F. W. Smith), who to some extent married the tradition of Crum with the new tradition of François and produced something, not only individual, but showing signs of potentiality for development, both in idea and in the expression of it.

The principal recruit in the decorative tradition was William Hewison, who started from a mixture of Pre-Raphaelitism and historical illustration. His humour might be wild but his drawing was realistic, or rather, of reality with its comic aspects heightened. Like ffolkes, he was an accomplished drawer of decorative initials and headings. The last new artist of Kenneth Bird's editorship for whom space must be made is Norman Thelwell. His drawing was purely realistic and he excelled in studies of animals, especially horses and birds, but his humour was, on the whole, purely crazy. His space was crowded with minutely-rendered detail. His jokes belonged to the tradition, not of Townsend, but of the poetic, fantastic humorists who usually had expressed their vision with completely unnaturalistic drawing. For example, a picture of a man lying in bed with birds perched neatly on every available inch of bedrail was drawn as the scene would look if it had actually happened. Though even this was not strict surrealism (there was rarely any horror in Thelwell), it was at least nearer to it than a lot of the humour that, fifteen years ago, was inaccurately labelled with the name.

CHAPTER TEN

# BACK IN THE MAIN STREAM

## *Malcolm Muggeridge's Editorship, 1953–*

SALES AND advertising were declining and, though circulation was not as low as it had been at one time, the sharp drop from wartime sales was worrying, and even more worrying was that the decline was proceeding at an accelerating rate. Kenneth Bird had taken the post only to make changes in make-up and organisation and had not expected to remain away from his drawing-board for very long. The Proprietors decided to break with tradition and call in an outside opinion. They appointed Malcolm Muggeridge, the Deputy Editor of *The Daily Telegraph.*

At the time the breach with tradition seemed far greater than it seems in retrospect and considering the history of *Punch* as a whole. Small things loomed big and what had become again a rather inbred society shuddered to think of the iconoclasm to which the paper, the National Institution, was being subjected. Malcolm Muggeridge was the son of a Labour Alderman, M.P. and early Fabian ; he married a niece of Beatrice Webb's. After leaving Cambridge he taught in India and Egypt and entered journalism through taking an interest in nationalist politics. He became a leader-writer on the *Manchester Guardian*, which later sent him to Russia as its Moscow Correspondent. At that time he was a professed Communist ; his Russian experiences threw him violently the other way. He had always hated the liberal mind from the left ; now he hated it from the right. In a period when journalism was full of clever young men reacting against a Tory childhood, perhaps he reacted against a Fabian childhood. He wrote a novel satirising the English fellow-travellers in Moscow. After a period in India on *The Statesman* he joined the *Evening Standard* and later *The Daily Telegraph*. At different times he was its Washington correspondent, leader-writer, literary editor, principal literary critic and Deputy Editor.

His experience in journalism has included most kinds of work but has been predominantly on features work. He has written articles about foreign affairs, about politics, about new books, rather than reported or sub-edited or administered. In the war he worked in Military Intelligence in England and Occupied France. He has always got through a good deal of outside writing. His books include a study of Samuel Butler, which is really an attack on the generation of " progressives " before his own, and some sportive collaborations with Hugh Kingsmill, by whom he was greatly influenced.

As few *Punch* men knew him personally, at first he was judged by his work, which was often derisive and spiteful. He jeered at politicians and especially at Socialist politicians. He criticised the Conservative Party from what seemed to be the right of it. On the radio his voice aroused hostility and his remarks were often rather negatively destructive. When interlocutors tried to get him to state his positive beliefs, he either passed the question by or denied having any or airily committed himself to any belief that occurred to him at the moment. He did not sound the kind of man who would consider himself a new boy amid the panelled walls, the memories of Thackeray and Tenniel, the collegiate atmosphere of *Punch*, nor did he sound the kind of man who would realise that in trying to raise the circulation too violently he might lose the paper the very many loyal readers it still had.

The first thing that struck many people about Muggeridge was his approachability and his kindness. It became an absurd situation when infuriated traditionalists wanting to find a sympathetic ear for complaints about the new Editor thought first of " Malcolm," who was quite ready to discuss himself in the most detached way. He realised fairly quickly that *Punch* could not be, as he had hoped, a kind of overflow from general journalism, written mainly by the leading professional journalists, and in time he came to think that it needed a hard core of writers on whom both Editor and readers could rely. He had never read *Punch* much and disliked what he knew of it, feeling it was stuffy, weakly collaborationist in politics, muffled in comment, handicapped by its fear of causing offence. He bounced in, determined to make changes fast while the revolution was in progress and to change too much rather than not enough, arguing that this was the only way in which changes could be made. He poured out ideas enthusiastically and sometimes sulked when his Staff turned them down. Half-unconsciously he relied on the balance between his own impulsiveness and the critical abilities of the men he found there and the men he brought with him. As he read more of the old volumes, listened to what the Staff had to say, argued with H. F. Ellis, watched and learned, he began to try to combine something of the best of the old with the new. *Punch* after three years of Muggeridge was much more like the old *Punch* than *Punch* after three months of him.

In a broadcast to America, Muggeridge said he had hardly any beliefs except that life on earth was part of a pilgrimage of unknown destination but beneficent purpose. Either everything was worth while or nothing was. Progress was impossible because man is unchanging, a creature born to exist in time while envisaging eternity. The pursuit of Golden Ages, like the pursuit of happiness, was likely to end in disaster. He has said in another broadcast that he does not believe in the existence of quality. This odd creed, a kind of Tory anarchism, leaves the individual irresponsible, with no rights or duties. There is no need to love the highest when we see it because there is no highest. Man must endure and enjoy without self-pity or wishful thinking. Following Hugh Kingsmill, Muggeridge, rather uncertainly, took the side of imagination against will, imagination being rather the mystic's gleam than the artist's vision.

Muggeridge believes in directness of response, frankness of speech—sometimes using words not even in Partridge—fun, high-spirited gossip, hitting at what you hate, satire, parody, which he regards as a form of invective rather than of criticism, the present as against the past or the future, cynicism rather than credulity, Eighteenth Century common sense rather than the " romanticising of the unattainable ideal," Johnson and Blake as against Rousseau and Shelley. He has read considerably, if lop-sidedly, and surprises sometimes by the speed of his apprehension, which he attributes to many years in journalism ; but it has some links with the academic world. After all, he has taught in Universities. It is impossible to describe him closely because he has a protean quality. He is quite unlike other people ; his qualities and defects cannot be inferred from one another. With all his excitement about the press and tendency to see contemporary history as a series of newspaper headlines he has serious literary interests. He is as likely to be found writing on D. H. Lawrence in *The New Statesman* as on a politician's memoirs in *The Daily Telegraph.*

All this made him come into *Punch* as something more than an experienced journalist, case-hardened by C. P. Scott, Beaverbrook and the Berry brothers. He had a theory of satire and a point of view that was sufficiently extreme to give his arm freedom. Puckish, unpredictable, irresponsible, he probably thought it would be fun to wield the national bladder and turn it into a flail, to take on a fight, and it was likely to be a hard fight, and to cleanse something he very much disliked.

On the whole, Muggeridge is strongest where his actions go against his theory. There can be no justification in his bleak, solipsist creed for kindness, generosity and charity. There is, unfortunately, every justification for living only in the moment. Divisions of time between the minute and eternity do not exist for him. This makes him a good judge of what news to put in an afternoon edition and with an effort he has slowly made himself a fair judge of what will be topical by the time *Punch* has been made up, gone to press and been published. Believing that the paper must be ultra-topical to live he has weakened its long-term appeal. A copy gets stale now whereas at one time it bumbled on for ever. To-day is too apt to be to-day's newspapers and he has a childlike love and wonder for the Press. His heroes are often journalists, however cynically he talks about journalism. He feels the existence of the bound volumes of *Punch* as a threat to the week's issue, which is all that matters and which ceases to exist for him on publication.

As the moment is all-important, consistency is a vice rather than a virtue, a denial of life. He revels in being inconsistent, yet through all the shifts of his policy he has driven a pretty consistent course. He may make life difficult by frequent changes of opinion about what is to go in an issue ; he may buy stuff he decides not to use, ask men to take on an assignment and then not want it, be swayed by the last man he has talked to into a complete change of opinion about a contributor ; but a pattern is clear all the same. Possibly if he had not had a strong-minded Staff some of the wild swoops of editorial policy might have wrecked the paper, but more probably the wild swoops would not have taken place. Muggeridge wants his men to write rapidly, with immediacy, to get about and get on and know people and enjoy life. He was puzzled when he came into the office that some of the contributors were not better known, were not trying to migrate to bigger papers, regarded *Punch* as the summit to which they aspired. He insisted that every article should be signed and the long battle for recognition of the writers equally with the artists was over. A slight change had been made under Kenneth Bird, when full names instead of initials or pseudonyms were allowed to those who had been given their " colours."

He began by trying to make use of writers he already knew, some of whom were born *Punch* men but some, while no doubt admirable Foreign Correspondents or good hands with a budget forecast, seemed lost when expected to entertain. He also introduced celebrities. One *Punch* disease he diagnosed was that nobody had heard of the people who wrote it and drew in it. *Punch* had never believed in building up its contributors. Hardly anyone with an outside name was to be found in the pages and Muggeridge introduced a policy of getting in " names." Some of the celebrities simply tried to remember the *Punch* of their childhood and write the kind of article that had appeared in it. There were little essays about going away for the week-end or being a novelist or interviewing one's bank manager. Some of them, deciding sensibly enough that they would do better to stick to the line that had made them celebrated, sent stuff that was good of its kind but might or might not suit *Punch*.

This question of suitability is fundamental. Muggeridge decided that as the shape of *Punch* had often varied in the past it might well vary in the future. To begin with he seemed to think of *Punch* as a kind of weekly feature-page extended to periodical length. Then he began to recognise that he was Telegraphing his *Punches* and tried to bulge the frontier out, as it were, in different places. He printed extracts from the forthcoming set of *Boswell Papers*.[1] This was a very good idea. It established the fact that anything entertaining could be published in *Punch* if it were good of its kind and that the existing categories could be added to. Boswell was one of the great British comic characters. Owing to the difference in texture and pace from other articles the mental adjustment demanded from the reader was considerable. It was a clever move because it put the traditionalists on the defensive. The extracts were intelligent amusement. Was the fact that nothing similar had been published within living memory to exclude them ?

The turnover of contributors was rapid. *Punch* had always had a number of men who wrote only when the spirit moved them and a number who made one hit to a succession of misses. Both these groups often produced work that was fresh, had new backgrounds and a good basic idea. Probably many of these contributors might have liked to try something sharper and more topical and closer to actuality, but they would have had to be trained slowly and systematically. In his early months, Muggeridge dispersed the collection of outside contributors that had been built up and deprived himself of a possible asset. When later he swung towards a mixture of leading professional writers and experienced *Punch* men, there was some shortage of usable material. All these experiments asserted the principle that *Punch* was neither a closed shop nor the haunt of the amateur. It would pay competitive prices for celebrity material.

The public began to wonder what they were missing by not looking at *Punch* regularly, not only in the way of quality but in the way of news. There were scoops, indiscretions. Almost everybody you had ever heard of turned up in the pages. The first year produced a substantial number of new contributors of the greatest value, and some old contributors, like P. G. Wodehouse, were coaxed back.

Muggeridge felt that *Punch* was evading the real world and that the shock of the first war had made the middle-class frightened and escapist, hence the concentration on rural life in an urban civilisation, childhood in a period in which the expectation of life was growing fast and on domestic trivialities when most waking-hours were spent in work. He also disliked the anti-intellectualism, the slightly snivelling philistinism. Therefore he sharply put an end to the sketch, the little anecdote, the article which started from invention, from the private rather than the public. It was probably time that brisk changes were made; but to cut out the humours of marriage and children and leisure was to limit the range of human activities covered. In fact, having, like previous Editors, extended *Punch* in one direction he contracted it in another. Perhaps this is the way organisms progress. Later he relaxed as far as allowing articles sited in the home or car or cinema-seat, but liked them linked with something in the news.

Muggeridge claimed to have no sense of humour, in the ordinary, or perhaps the dying, sense of the term. This turned out not to be the insuperable obstacle that it sounded at first. (In any case, a man who was humour-blind as men are colour-blind would be infinitely better than a man who had a cheap sense of humour, who was amused only by bathing-belles having their bottoms pinched and chaps at the local froth-blowing and discussing the little woman and income-tax.) He had a sense of fun, something more ebullient than the rather subdued tone of the *Punch* office since the days of Burnand. He was gay. He enjoyed the oddities of human behaviour and the gossip that has a psychological point. He knew a lot of people and lots about a lot of people and in his dashing way he restored to the *Punch milieu* that sense of amused participation in the world where decisions are made that it had lost since Shirley Brooks. He had a taste for satire, believing it to be the articulate man's duty to hit what seems wrong to him and to hit it laughingly. He never really distinguished between satire and invective and, being a "What," where Evoe and Ellis had been "Hows," he was apt to judge an article by whether it were about a subject he felt strongly on and then by whether it were hostile. He liked the madly logical development of an initial absurdity provided, and this he maintained consistently and toughly, that the development was not in itself fantastic. He liked burlesque and parody, though he did not distinguish between them. Partly this was due to his belief that, like quality, style was an illusion. If nothing matters but the moment then spontaneity and speed of writing are the chief literary virtues. Hence parody and satire that can delight by subtlety and perfection do not exist for him, or at least did not in the first, formative months. He is apt to under-rate the satisfactions of the craftsman and only slowly came to realise the connection between applause and creation in the entertainment world.

He was temperamentally opposed to the deadpan joke, the ironical, the humour between the lines, the delicate inflection, feeling in the typical *Punch* quietness nothing but lack of vitality. He wanted humour to be ruder, earthier. What he uprooted was a tradition still capable of development and, in fact, it has slowly and warily re-emerged, purged of its spinsterishness and encouraged, now so many bans are removed, to try new fields. He complained that *Punch* was too well written. There was a little in this, in the sense that adventurousness of subject had been replaced by concern with smoothness of style ; but now that articles are no longer sent back for revision, the standard of *Punch* prose has fallen.

## II

The cover had changed several times in the early years. Then it remained the same, apart from the removal of advertising and the addition of a bit more colour, except for the Special Numbers, which were gay and bright and beloved of book-stall managers. Muggeridge did not, as he might have been expected to, throw away the advantages of visual continuity and have a different cover every week. Nor did he stick always to the cover as it has been so long known and loved. Within the general pattern drawn by Dicky Doyle he allowed redrawing for specific numbers—some figures would be replaced by skiers or dogs or caricatures of celebrities concerned with the particular activity to which the number was devoted. Soon the reader had been trained to take even bigger alterations without losing his sense of continuity.

B. A. Young, now Assistant Editor, took over the *Essence of Parliament* and with the new encouragement of out-spokenness was cheerfully partisan, vivid and witty, so that two pages of the paper regained the vitality they had had in Lucy's time. J. B. Boothroyd was allowed a sharper style in *Charivaria* with full use of names, and wrote most of it himself. The illustrated poems were dropped.

The critical sections, which had been placed at intervals through the paper, were now collected together at the end with a fanciful heading. The Music and Ballet, previously covered by Miss D. C. Barker, was divided. The Ballet was placed in the hands of Canon C. B. Mortlock, Ecclesiastical Correspondent of the *Daily Telegraph*. Serious art criticism began at last with Adrian Daintrey. Music, predominantly operatic, was covered by Charles Reid, a find. Writing with a sardonic eye for detail and in a very neatly witty style, he solved the difficult problem of how to write about music for a possibly non-musical public by dealing very largely with production, but never failing to acknowledge that it was the music that mattered. A regular Radio and Television page by Bernard Hollowood was started. This was incisive, straight journalism, sensibly and fairly done. It was received with some respect by its victims. Later, a Country Feature by Ronald Duncan and a City Report, a mixture of economic causerie and straight tipstering signed "Mammon," were introduced.

In the cartoon, Illingworth continued to execute the designs hammered out in argument by the Table, now reinforced by John Betjeman, Anthony Powell and Christopher Hollis. However, it became much more sharp and striking and the basic ideas were nearer to the great Nineteenth Century cartoons.

On the whole Muggeridge is not particularly interested in verse and is content if it expresses some strong-minded sentiment. P. M. Hubbard contributed a weekly poem of varying savagery but unvarying verbal and metrical accomplishment. He had always hated compromise, the smooth insincerity, the tactful half-truth. No-one else was temperamentally so fitted to the new policy of outspoken satirical writing. He is very varied in pattern and phrasing ; he can be funny in several ways and uses humorous techniques quite different from those of any other contributor.

### TOP-LEVEL CONTACT[2]

I wonder what he's really like, this wonder of the one-half earth ?
Of course, one has seen the photos, but one knows how little they're
worth.
A shave can make such a difference, and the voice leaves plenty of
scope,
And that curious smell of foreigners one always hopes is the soap.
I must say, he does things nicely—that clock with the platinum face
And this splendid silver cigar-box with the tape-recorder in the
base—
Real good solid stuff, not just turned out for the trade.
I'd like one of those myself. I wonder where he gets them made ?
Can't just ask him, unfortunately. The worst of this kind of show—
Never can ask the things one is really yammering to know.
Wouldn't make a good impression, which is what I'm being paid
to make.
Better get my right hand aired against the preliminary shake.
Formidable, some of these foreigners, doing it the way they do :
Have to get a good grip early, in case he's been practising too.
Voice ? Yes, comes out nicely. Must concentrate on carriage of
the head,

Especially when I move to meet him. And what was it that Madame
 said
About keeping my weak eye open despite the dazzle of the lights ?
Can't quite remember the method : should have brought her along
 by rights.
Bound to be pretty impressive, for all they say he's a swine,
With a hundred-and-twenty-odd million against my seventy-nine.
Still, it's the culture that counts, not the size of places on the map,
And the figures are always phoney, and—Gosh, what a funny
 little chap.
Pigeon-toed, or I'm a Dutchman ; but tough, no doubt, in his way.
Ah well, on with the motley. Now—what was it I had to say ?

Muggeridge believes that the young do not like the humour of the amused contemplation of domestic predicament nor the crazy humour of association and illogicality that followed it, though his attitude on this varies. He insists that they like the humour of fact. One of his most successful moves has been the introduction of more articles that report on the world and supply entertaining details about it. These fall roughly into three classes. There is the report of first-hand experience in the great world. Claud Cockburn, one of the most improbable and most successful of the new-comers, has wonderful material, for example leaving the staff of *The Times* to join *The Daily Worker*.[3] All his life he has lived, as someone has remarked, as though he wanted to be in a book. His Irish articles, his accounts of his life as a Communist, his odd comments on news items are exuberant and quite fresh in outlook. He experiments with language ; it is healthy to find somebody trying out methods of writing in *Punch* and the Editor's support for this shows his odd flair. His response to individual writers is often superior to his theory.

Anthony Carson, who writes both in *Punch* and *The New Statesman* and is one of the signs of a rapprochement in personnel that is long overdue and has been characteristically carried out by *The New Statesman*'s most fanatical opponent, writes generally the shaped and worked-up reminiscence, often of his experience in the tourist business or in Australian farming. This may sound superficially like the kind of thing that *Punch* has always published and that has often been very well done indeed. The difference is partly in greater freedom. Carson has walked the world in liberty and, short of a prosecution for blasphemy, sedition, obscenity or libel, he can write about what he has met. The attitude is that of the modern upper-class intellectual, spivish, fugitive from trammels. The writing is laconic, selective, tart, vivid. It is much nearer to ordinary contemporary prose, looser, rougher, more varied in source of metaphor than the prose of the best of Evoe's disciples. It has gained a dimension and lost a dimension, perhaps characteristic of the whole of the new *Punch* in this.

Then comes the specific investigation. This is the basis of the normal newspaper-article, and in particular of the normal feature. Muggeridge objected to the feature-articles of the Kenneth Bird régime, partly because they did nothing but praise and be tactful, partly because they were too carefully well-written, perhaps also because he felt they avoided obvious material and stuck to safe subjects, though one would have thought that factories and slums were as much part of the British scene as the more revolting aspects of the Ideal Home Exhibition. Patrick Balfour, Lord Kinross, is far the best of the new investigators of reality. He has a wonderful eye for the unpleasant detail. His articles are full of fact, represent a great deal of hard work and are grimly funny simply by the piling up of horrifying information without comment. They have a drive and efficiency that tend to kill the quieter tones of sometimes subtler work near them. His chief weakness is that the implied criticism of the modern world conveyed by his quotations from promotional literature is not based upon any discernible positive attitude about what is preferable. In article after article he drags in references to The Century of the Common Man or the Common Peer without committing himself to open justification of the Century of the Rich Man or the Century of the Nobleman or the Century of the Poverty of the Poor. His briskness of style, power of selecting targets and aristocratic disdain of good taste enable him to make his sneers at the names chosen for their houses by Labour Peers or the spreading of the joys of gastronomy to Tom, Dick and Harry both amusing and apparently a defence of civilisation against vulgarity, of style against cheapness, of standards against desires ; but essentially he is doing what George Mikes in his book *Eight Humorists* accused the pre-Muggeridge *Punch* humorists of doing, fighting not for a better present but a better past.

The third class of new articles that report on actuality is the careful composition, the word-painting, the verbal transcription of reality from a new angle, the face that is new but recognisable. G. W. Stonier, the *New Statesman* critic, went about London and produced completely individual descriptions.[4] His style is fantasticated, impressionist, full of acute observation, broken lights, touches of poetic comedy, pieces of curious information, and what have so well been described as curlicues ; it is quite different from anything else that appears or has appeared in *Punch* and is now one of its literary glories. Muggeridge's shy remark that one must sometimes put things in just because one likes them shows another facet of him. He, in fact, responds to Stonier's quality ; but then there is no such thing. Stonier obviously cannot be defended as the firm base of a go-getting circulation campaign, as a blow in the cold war or as the literary expression of a revulsion from the post-Fabian world. Nor can he be defended as one of the necessary hangovers from the old *Punch*. He is there simply because he is good ; but he makes hell of the theory.

John Betjeman, who should have been in *Punch* years before, was an important new recruit. His verses and some of his topographical articles were something new for *Punch* yet obviously right. It was another clever appointment. His dazzling performances as a metrist, the precision of his evocations of buildings, places and moods, the fruitful ambivalence of his attitude to the past and, above all, his complete separation from all other traditions of light verse and *belles lettres* meant that he not only brought with him a ready-made readership but that he brought to existing *Punch* readers a quality undreamt of in a genre they liked. In his more elegiac moods he makes a link between the older *Punch* tradition of loving the past at the expense of the present and the more positive likes and dislikes of the attitude that has succeeded it. His verse about places, with its wonderful detail and breath-taking command of rhythm, makes an odd comparison with the vagueness of early-Twentieth Century nostalgia and the uninventiveness of early-Twentieth Century light verse.

Anthony Powell came from *The Times Literary Supplement* to take charge of the Booking Office. It is difficult to think of any new man, at least since Phil May, who has arrived with so considerable an outside reputation, with his wide acquaintanceship in literary London, considerable scholarship, experience on the *Daily Telegraph*, in publishing and in the more recherché branches of the Army and his works of Seventeenth Century research, in addition to the novels. Like the Editor, he enjoys the comedy of the fight for power and the humour of personal idiosyncrasy. He shares his Toryism, though he is less interested in day-to-day politics. His distaste for the old philistinism of *Punch* and his interest in the Arts indicate, together with the cast of mind revealed in his novels, what he probably brings to the making of *Punch* policy in editorial discussions.

Powell retained the services of some of the old *Punch* reviewers and brought in new ones, usually better-known. He abolished the short notes on the grounds that if you noticed a book at all it should be done at reasonable length : the short condemnation was unfair to the author and a string of plaudits would be valueless and unreadable. He did most of the long book articles—the rest were written by Malcolm Muggeridge, J. Maclaren-Ross, R. G. G. Price and others—and with gentle persistence accustomed readers to the scholarly discussion of books that could support scholarship. It was the first time that *Punch* readers had been addressed in that tone. His writing is much quieter than the rest of the paper and until one is used to it the jokes, often complex, may be invisible. His articles in other parts of the paper are private, amused and sometimes, like his *Steerforth on Copperfield*,[5] brilliant. Where he shows his quality is on the borderland of literary and social observation, as in the article he wrote about the gainful occupations of writers.[5a]

Christopher Hollis, then Conservative M.P. for Devizes, was appointed to the Table to strengthen its political knowledge. A Roman Catholic, a publisher, a busy journalist and an active, extravert public figure, like Anthony Powell he is an Etonian : of all members of the Table he is probably nearest to the Editor in outlook. He has a flow of good farcical ideas, fluently deployed in prose and verse. What he does best is taking a subject much enshrouded in platitudes, like N.A.T.O., and worrying away at it logically. The strength of his work is vivacity, knowledge of current affairs and satirical ideas ; its weakness is sometimes an appearance of haste and amateurishness in presentation. In the early days nobody else showed so clearly the sharp decline in literary standards ; latterly he has tightened up his writing and shown more signs of taking trouble to plan, to revise and to cut, and a genuine talent for political journalism has been given a chance to emerge. He did not stand again for election in 1955 and took over the *Essence of Parliament* from B. A. Young.

Gwyn Thomas, the Welsh novelist, has been a strong reinforcement. His dense prose, with its profusion of comic metaphor, needs to be read at a different rate and with a different eye from other *Punch* prose and it has probably taken time for readers who did not know his novels to get used to it. He writes stories of depressed, embittered but not sombre mining villages, filled with the poetry of peasant speech and the fun of local folk-lore. Richard Gordon writes on medical subjects funnily and well. Geoffrey Lincoln does much the same kind of thing with the Law, lacking Gordon's power of phrase but having an even larger supply of amusing information. J. Maclaren-Ross does a good deal of varied work. He is an experienced reviewer and was brought in to strengthen the Booking Office. He writes most kinds of article. He obviously found the reminiscent article, his own established line, difficult to cut to the over-short *Punch* length. Muggeridge has tried to get lengths varied more but it is very difficult. There is simply not enough room in *Punch*. Some people argue that if there were more to read in it readers would be put off, others that it would be an attraction that would outweigh the extra cost. Perhaps one reason why there was in the past so little interchange between *Punch* and general journalism was the highly specialised nature of this length. It demands quite different density, tension and pacing from the usual article or story. This may be why some of the genuinely distinguished new-comers seemed to be so thin. They were writing extensively in a necessarily intensive medium. (It may be admitted that sometimes earlier in the century experienced *Punch* men seemed to be writing in the same way.)

Geoffrey Gorer, the social anthropologist and journalist, did get the length. He wrote a series called *Modern Types* [6] which were illustrated by Nicolas Bentley, and lucidly described typical examples of various people to be found in a country town, the doggy woman, the discontented left-winger and the like. They were intended to satirise all kinds of opinion and character but were far shriller dealing with the left than with the right. Although efficiently written they lacked the originality and bite of Gorer's anthropological investigations and rather oddly emerged as dilute E. M. Delafield. They seemed to belong, both in matter and manner, to the *Punch* of an earlier day.

The few survivors of the existing *Punch* writers adapted themselves with the hope of gradually getting back to normal ; but, as probably Muggeridge intended, normality seemed different after the adaptation had been made. H. F. Ellis had always used reality as a jumping-off point, whether the reality of an experience—one of the great virtues of the *Assistant Master* was its diabolical accuracy—the reality of domestic life or the reality of the world as reported in the papers, especially *The Daily Telegraph*. The new régime has cut off his domestic end, as it were, but he has remained, as he has always been, one of the *Punch* men most interested in the topical, though his attitude to the topical is not quite what Muggeridge in his pursuit of it means. Under considerable difficulties, Ellis has remained funny, stylistically inventive and above all individual. By flatly refusing to compromise, except in loyalty to the policy that allows only part of his original material to be used, he has remained safely within the compression chamber where his genius best flourishes.

The most striking example of the continuity of *Punch* tradition, the power of *Punch* as an institution to work through men who have grown up in devotion to it and to treat any change of régime as a natural and healthy swing of the pendulum, is J. B. Boothroyd. The master of the predicament article, the infuriated account of the anfractuosity of things and people, the complaint of domestic life or morning train life or office life, he had always kept alive a taste for burlesque, especially of the Press. Now he showed a range of power hitherto unsuspected. Always one of the best *writers* on *Punch*, Boothroyd established himself in new territory. He burlesqued. As *Charivaria* Editor he watched the Press closely and he based a good deal of his work on picking out incongruous items, noticing shifts of policy and treatment.

## III

One of the emphases of the new policy was on mockery of the Press, the corner of the collectivity that Muggeridge knew best and one traditionally covered by *Punch*. *The New Yorker* parody [7] was, perhaps, the biggest success, but several of the series, which varied in elaboration upwards from a single page, were nearly as brilliant. Mansbridge and Brockbank, who developed into outstanding parodists, and Boothroyd burlesqueing the text were the stand-bys, though in *The New Yorker* Richard Mallett's Perelman was perhaps the high-water mark. (In a way, this was a return match as many years before *The New Yorker* had parodied *Punch*, under the title *Paunch*. *Punch* was also parodied at various times by student magazines at Yale, Harvard and Annapolis. Except occasionally in the pictures, the alumni found obvious difficulty in producing a likeness.)

Of all Muggeridge's devices for increasing interest in *Punch* two stood out, the Press parodies, with their typographical gaiety and literary quality, and his calculated exhibitions of what die-hard readers considered bad taste and potential readers considered a sign that *Punch* was not dead after all. The cartoon urging retirement on a corpse-like Churchill [8] said openly what people were saying privately ; but no other Editor since Taylor would have printed it, still less inspired it. It lost a number of regular, inherited readers, solid subscriptions of habit that it would take years to replace. On the other hand it showed that *Punch* had returned to being a claimant for power. Disliking Socialists as well as many Conservatives, Muggeridge was in an admirable position to annoy without being labelled traitor. He hated Eden, perhaps because of his League of Nations affiliations and his approach to Moscow in the Thirties. The cartoon showing Eden returning from Geneva [9] looking like Chamberlain returning from Munich annoyed many people but again it attracted attention and, as every publicity man will tell you, abuse is better than silence.

Muggeridge's outside activities, which suddenly shot him into headline fame, were an important factor in getting *Punch* back into the news : for the first time for years it began to be mentioned in the editorial columns of other papers. He did a lot of miscellaneous journalism and in America became a name in the cold war. He broadcast frequently and would often fly to another continent and talk on the radio. One of his strong points is his flow of comment. He has always something to say. It was Television that really put him on the map. As a performer in programmes like *Press Conference* and *In the News*, as previously on radio in *The Critics*, he amused or irritated or interested, his line of being against any kind of political action, including voting, enabling him to dodge any awkward questions. With a regular " spot " in *Panorama* as an interviewer he aroused comment in nearly every national paper. His strong individuality, his refusal to be simply a machine asking questions, his mannerisms, his gnome-like, Puckish quality, his sudden swoops between sense and nonsense meant that he was there, whether

*Norman Mansbridge*

## COUNTRY WEDDING FOR A 1949 DEBUTANTE

*WAITING to receive their guests after the wedding in the Church of St. Anne, Bury, were Mr. and Mrs. Christopher Gulby. The reception was held at Coney Castle, the home of the bride's father, Mr. Percy J. Hobb. Behind them is a bust of Lord North, in his day famous for his hospitality and sporting interests and also a popular Prime Minister* you approved of him or not, and *Punch* reaped the benefit.

In the Art he made very little difference, saying he knew nothing about it and then oscillating between saying he thought it all dreadful and not a bit funny and claiming that he had inherited from Fougasse the finest collection of humorous artists in the world. His removal of the old bans has widened the field of humour open to artists. In one of his many interviews he has said he finds sex funny but that it would have to be introduced gradually. Painlessly it has arrived, not dragged in as a selling point but simply and naturally ; if a joke is funny it goes in and if the subject is sexual within the limits of obscenity, and these are rather strictly interpreted, this does not bar it. There is a clear, though previously ignored, distinction between what has sex as its theme and what is directly anatomical. A reference to a prostitute is quite different from the kind of joke on seaside post-cards, which nearly always gets down to detail.

Michael Cummings of the *Daily Express* replaced A. W. Lloyd on the *Essence of Parliament* and was given space to do illustrations that sometimes approached Sambourne's in elaboration. " Emmwood " (M. Wood), *Tatler* and Beaverbrook Press cartoonist, and for a short time Editor of the *Junior Express*, came in to illustrate, very efficiently, Hollowood's Television and Radio column. Fougasse came back on the *Charivaria* illustrations that he did incomparably. Occasional page cartoons were used in addition to the existing main cartoon drawn usually by Illingworth. There was encouragement of topical pocket-cartoons, in which Langdon and Hollowood were joined by Sprod. Ronald Searle did an occasional cartoon and a very successful series of six-panel pages called *The Rake's Progress*,[10] following typical careers in the contemporary world. The wicked selection of detail was a model. This was the approach that Muggeridge wanted, carried out with independent invention.

Ardizonne (signing Diz) was brought in to strengthen realistic illustration, and provided a mannered and characteristic series of London scenes to accompany G. W. Stonier's perambulatory essays.[11] Completely outside any of the *Punch* traditions, Ardizonne helped to show the readers that the isolation of *Punch* from serious or semi-serious art was not complete, a point made rather differently by employing the bright young fashion artist, Marc Boxer, on decorative headings and work like the little illustrations in the

*12th January, 1955* *Ronald Searle*

middle of the main Booking Office article, in which many of the *Punch* artists shared. There was no marked trend among the joke drawings. Ronald Searle was encouraged to be as decorative, fantastic and disquieting in *Punch* as he had hitherto been outside it.

The balance-sheet of the latest régime cannot be struck yet. In many ways Muggeridge belongs to the tradition of Jerrold and A. P. Herbert. He has swung *Punch* back towards the early years, even in little points like having himself begun as a dramatist and in persuading a theatrical management to put on a *Punch Revue* in 1955. Characteristically he rushed into it and the Revue when it finally appeared had very few items by *Punch* contributors, although those there were got the best notices. It is significant, however, that the adverse newspaper criticisms nearly all took the line that the material was not good enough for the revived *Punch* to which Muggeridge had restored vitality and bite. He has made the previous period seem like a deviation. *Punch* has changed sides, of course, but is back on the attack. The attack, however, is not very consistent. In a way Muggeridge is too kindly to be the type of Editor he would like to be. Sometimes he seems to prefer the bludgeon to the rapier as less lethal. His strength is in his readiness to consider new things, his removal of the scabbard from *Punch*'s flourished sword, his realisation that humour can spring from actuality and his essential toughness. His weakness is his dislike of detail, his love of sudden decisions, an occasional lack of awareness of the second-rate, his obsession with politics and his lack of appreciation of fancy. He has arrested the decline and reversed the trend ; he has made people look at *Punch* and has made writers of repute wish to contribute to it ; he has withered the poetry of farce. *Punch* is, at least, still well within one of its three main traditions and little by little the oblique, the incongruous, the accomplished are creeping back.

*Punch* is a National Institution in a way that no purely commercial magazine can be. Look at *Punch* as the early Editors saw it and you see a miracle of survival. Look at it as it seemed in its middle period and you see something as majestically unchanging as cliffs, and as liable to erosion. To-day, whether *Punch* lives or dies it will obviously do it with a bang, which means it will live, and if it lives it will grow. *Punch*'s future is more interesting than its past.

APPENDIX ONE

# SOURCES OF QUOTATIONS, *PUNCH* REFERENCES, AND END-PIECES

References are to *Punch* unless otherwise stated.
V = Volume ; P = Page ; 1 = line.

For convenience of reference, dates are substituted for volume and page numbers as soon as the change was made in the heading of the paper.

References to *Spielmann* are to his *History of Punch* unless otherwised stated.

## *CHAPTER ONE*

[1] " Never mind." V. I, p. 2.

[2] *Candidates.* V. I, p. 7.

[3] *Synopsis.* V. I, p. 3.

[4] Conversation between cab horses. V. I, p. 5.

[5] Dialogue between *Punch* and stage-manager. V. I, p. 6.

[6] *Ode.* V. I, p. 11.

[7] " Young Kean." V. I, p. 12.

[8] *The Westminster Review,* July–October, 1842.

[9] A later proprietor—F. M. Evans : Henry Silver's Diary, 23rd July, 1862, in *Punch* Office.

[10] Description of Coyne : *A Mid-Victorian Pepys : Letters and Memoirs of Sir William Hardman,* Ed. S. M. Ellis (1923).

[11] " Lemon's likes stronger than dislikes " : *With a Show in the North* (1871), Joseph Hatton.

[12] " I was made for *Punch* " : *ditto.*

[13] Hans Andersen quotation : *Edmund Yates : His Recollections and Experiences* (1885).

[14] " Editorship became centralised " : Letter from F. C. Burnand to Spielmann, 9th January, 1895, in *Punch* Office.

[15] " Free of grossness " : *Sunday Times* quoted by *Spielmann.*

[16] *Somerset County Gazette :* quoted by *Spielmann.*

[17] Leech's *The Great Social Evil :* 12th September, 1857.

[18] G. M. Young : *Victorian England* (1937).

[19] Evans : Henry Silver's Diary, 1st November, 1865, in *Punch* Office.

[20] " Shilling fly " : *Mr. Punch : His Origin and Career* (1882?)

[21] Lucy's letter : *Nearing Jordan* (1916), H. W. Lucy.

[22] " ikon of Montgolfier " : *The*

*Adventures of George Augustus Sala* (1895).

[23] Coyne—" filthy lucre" : *Spielmann.*

[24] " Mile and milestone" : *Douglas Jerrold* (1918), Walter Jerrold.

[25] " Wounds of the dead . . ." : quoted by Blanchard Jerrold from *The Monthly Magazine* in *The Life and Remains of Douglas Jerrold* (1859).

[26] " Earth is so kindly in Australia . . ." : quoted in *ditto* from *Douglas Jerrold's Weekly Newspaper.*

[27] Masson : quoted in *Douglas Jerrold and Punch* (1910), Walter Jerrold.

[28] Lord John Manners. V. VI, p. 241.

[29] Thackeray letter : *The Uses of Adversity : 1811–45* (1955), Gordon N. Ray.

[30] *Comic Blackstone* : began Vol. V, p. 165.

[31] Jerrold and Albert Smith : *Douglas Jerrold and Punch* (1910), Walter Jerrold.

[32] Rule and Albert Smith : *Glances Back Through Seventy Years* (1893), Henry Vizetelly.

[33] Kenny Meadows and Nature : *The Brothers Dalziel* (1901).

[34] Kenny Meadows at dinner : *ditto.*

[35] Letter from Francis Eason to Spielmann, 4th August, 1895, in *Punch* Office.

End-piece : V. I, p. iv.

## *CHAPTER TWO*

[1] " Your weakness, not my strength": *Douglas Jerrold and Punch* (1910), Walter Jerrold.

[2] *The Second Tree from the Corner* : E. B. White (1954).

[3] Jerrold letter : *The Life and Remains of Douglas Jerrold* (1859), Blanchard Jerrold.

[4] Hard-hitting : *Thackeray* (1932), Malcolm Elwin.

[5] Half-monstrous Cornish giant : *Spielmann.*

[6] Letter about resignation : *Thackeray* (1932), Malcolm Elwin.

[7] Louis Napoleon cartoon. V. XXI, p. 275.

[8] Thackeray letter : Bradbury Album. 10th May, 1852. In *Punch* Office.

[9] Queen's Speech set to music : V. IV, p. 56.

[10] *Lions of London* : V. II, p. 175.

[11] *The New Timon and the Poets* : V. X, p. 103.

[12] Watering-places : V. III, p. 41.

[13] Thackeray's *Snobs* : began V. X, p. 101.

[14] Dickens on Thackeray's *Novelists* : *The Showman of Vanity Fair* (1947), Lionel Stevenson.

[15] " I am quite pleased with myself . . ." : *Thackeray* (1932), Malcolm Elwin.

[16] Leech's Special Constable : V. XIV, p. 172.

[17] Taylor's father : Press-cutting, origin unknown. In grangerised *An Evening with Punch* in *Punch* Office.

[18] " Must not attack man . . ." : *Recollections of a Humorist* (1907), Arthur à Beckett.

[18a] *The Brothers Dalziel* (1901).

[18b] *The Drawings of John Leech* : (1950) June Rose.

[19] Ruskin : *The Art of England* (1883).

[20] *Manners and Customs* : began V. XVI, p. 114.

[21] Often quoted. Unpublished book by Lewis Lusk on Doyle in possession of Adrian Conan Doyle says authority a Mr. Everitt.

[22] Description of Brooks: Anonymous writer quoted in *A Great Punch Editor: Shirley Brooks* (1907), George Somes Layard.

[23] "That generation were boozers": *ditto.*

[24] "We don't want Rubens on *Punch*": *Spielmann.*

[25] Tenniel drawing: Sir John Tenniel (English Masters of Black and White, 1948), Frances Sarzano.

[26] *British Lion's Vengence*: 22nd August, 1857.

[27] *Dropping the Pilot*: 29th March, 1890.

[28] *Bang went saxpence*: 5th December, 1868.

[29] Keene letter: *The Life and Letters of Charles Samuel Keene* (1892), George Somes Layard.

[30] "Bakewell tart": *Sixty Years in the Wilderness* (1909), Sir Henry W. Lucy.

[31] British Museum and Exhibition Catalogues: V. XX, p. 34.

[32] *Brook-Green Militia-Man*: e.g. V. X, p. 55.

[33] *General Février*: V. XXVIII, p. 95.

[34] Wellington Memorial: 13th June, 1857.

## *CHAPTER THREE*

[1] Lines on Lincoln's assassination: 6th May, 1865. (Erroneously attributed by Spielmann to Brooks.)

[2] Lemon's Falstaff: *With a Show in the North* (1871), Joseph Hatton.

[3] Burnand and Gilbert: *The Two Pins Club* (1925) Harry Furniss.

[4] Lemon on Brooks: *With a Show in the North* (1871), Joseph Hatton.

[5] "He seized the place": Carlyle on Cromwell, quoted by Winston Churchill in Commons on death of Lloyd George.

[6] *Naggletons*: began 6th September, 1862.

[7] *Table Talk*: began 28th October, 1865.

[8] *Mokeanna*: began 21st February, 1863.

[9] *Happy Thoughts*: began 23rd June, 1866.

[10] "Clever old cockalorums": *A Long Retrospect* (1936), Anstey Guthrie.

[11] Cockhorse Nightmare: 30th September, 1865.

[12] Tom Tit marries giantess: Almanack and January, 1866.

[13] Lemon to du Maurier: *George du Maurier* (English Masters of Black and White, 1948), Derek Pepys Whiteley. (Slightly different version in *Spielmann.*)

[14] du Maurier letter to Lucy: *Sixty Years in the Wilderness* (1909), Sir Henry W. Lucy.

[15] Keene joke: 19th May, 1866.

[16] Frith's story: *My Autobiography and Reminiscences* (1887), W. P. Frith.

[17] Wilberforce-Westbury Obituary poem: 2nd August, 1873.

[18] Gladstone conundrum: 24th June, 1871.

[19] Brooks on *Punch* writers: Letter to William Bradbury, 26th September, 1871. In Bradbury Album at *Punch* Office.

End-piece, Charles Keene: V. LII, Index, 1867.

## *CHAPTER FOUR*

[1] Victoria and Czar: V. VI, p. 255.

[2] Tenniel quotation: Letter to Philip Agnew, 1900. *Punch* Office.

[3] Sambourne's malapropisms: *A Long Retrospect* (1936), Anstey Guthrie.

[4] *'Arry*: began 13th October, 1877.

[5] Gladstone Pun: 10th April, 1880.

## *CHAPTER FIVE*

[1] Lucy quotation: *Diary of a Journalist* (1920), Sir Henry Lucy.

[1a] *Nearing Jordan* (1916), Sir Henry Lucy.

[2] Bryce quotation: *Sixty Years in the Wilderness* (1909), Sir Henry W. Lucy.

[3] *Nottingham Express* quotation: C. L. Graves Manuscript History of *Punch*, Folder VI. In *Punch* Office.

[4] Agnew—salads: *Reading, Writing and Remembering* (1932), E. V. Lucas.

[5] Lady Edmond Fitzmaurice quotation: *Nearing Jordan* (1916), H. W. Lucy.

[6] *Dropping the Pilot*: 29th March, 1890.

[7] Ear-trumpet: *Spielmann.*

[8] *Thames Weather*: 1st June, 1904.

[9] Lehmann on Light Verse: 28th December, 1910.

[10] *The Idyllic*: 25th May, 1889.

[11] *'Arry at the Seaside*: 10th September, 1887.

[12] *Another Little Holiday Cruise*: 1st September, 1883.

[13] *Conversational Hints for Young Shooters*: began 8th October, 1892.

[14] *Mr. Punch's Prize Novels*: began 4th October, 1890.

[15] *Voces Populi*: began 29th October, 1887.

[16] Anstey letter: June 1895, in *Punch* Office.

[17] *A Bayard from Bengal*: began 12th September, 1900.

[18] *Vi-Kings Essence*: began 29th April, 1903.

[19] *Diary of a Nobody*: began 26th May, 1888.

[20] *Mrs. Medwin*: 28th August, 1901.

[21] Townsend's remark: Oral tradition.

[22] *Sometimes I sits*: 24th October, 1906.

[23] Partridge's complaints: Letter to Spielmann (1897 ?) in *Punch* Office.

[23a] Partridge broadcasting on *Punch* Centenary, 1941.

[24] Partridge letter: to Canon A. Rhodes, 1939. Copy in the *Punch* Office.

[25] Furniss tramp: 26th April, 1884.

[26] *Prehistoric Peeps*: began Christmas Number, 1893.

[27] Reed's *Contrasts*: 31st August, 1889.

[28] Burnand on *Trilby*: *Sixty Years in the Wilderness* (1909), Sir Henry W. Lucy.

[29] May on Keene: *Phil May* (English Masters of Black and White, 1948), James Thorpe.

[30] May on Sambourne: *ditto.*

[31] May technique: *ditto.*

[32] May quotation: *ditto.*

End-piece, E. J. Wheeler: 11th May, 1889.

## *CHAPTER SIX*

[1] Seaman quotation: C. L. Graves's Introduction to *Owen Seaman: A Selection* (1937).

[2] Burnand on veto: Letter to Furniss in *Punch* Office.

[3] *It's Too Late Now* (1939), A. A. Milne.

[4] A letter of 1894: Charles Geake to Spielmann, in *Punch* Office.

[5] Quotation: *It's Too Late Now* (1939), A. A. Milne.

[6] Apollinaire par: 20th September, 1911.

[7] Quotation: *It's Too Late Now* (1939), A. A. Milne.

[8] Quotation: *ditto.*

[9] *Nonsense Novels* review: 19th July, 1911.

[10] *The White Prophet* review: 25th August, 1909.

[11] *The Woman Thou Gavest Me* review: 20th August, 1913.

[12] *Dew and Mildew* review: 12th February, 1913.

[13] *Glossary*: 29th April, 1908.

[14] *Androcles and the Lion* review: 17th September, 1913.

[15] *Magic* review: 19th November, 1913.

[16] Menagerie: 4th September, 1907.

[17] *Answers to Correspondents*: 3rd June, 1914.

[18] *Stanzas on Tea Shortage*: 24th October, 1917.

[19] *Protest from Parnassus*: 31st March, 1909.

[20] *Inspiration*: 27th May, 1914.

[21] *Coal*: 4th June, 1919.

[22] *Tempestuous Petticoat*: 14th July, 1909.

[23] *Bevis Marks*: 6th December, 1916.

[24] *Newington Butts*: 3rd January, 1917.

[25] *There are Fairies at the Bottom of our Garden*: 23rd May, 1917.

[26] Valentine: 20th February, 1924.

[27] *Potted Films*: e.g. 2nd February, 1916.

[28] *Entertainments*: e.g. 19th October 1932.

[28a] *Royal Academy Depressions*: e.g. May 11, 1910.

[28b] Morrow's oat: 23rd November, 1921. Oral tradition.

[29] Lucas on Raven Hill: *Reading, Writing and Remembering* (1932), E. V. Lucas.

[30] Evoe interview with *Manchester Guardian*: 1st July, 1935.

[31] *In Flanders Fields*: 8th December, 1915.

[32] Langley's bombed town: 21st June, 1916.

[33] Margarine par: 9th May, 1917.

[34] America and Ireland par: 2nd May, 1917.

[35] Bulgaria par: 9th October, 1918.

[36] *The Anniversary*: 7th May, 1919.

End-piece, A. W. Lloyd: 13th May, 1914.

## *CHAPTER SEVEN*

[1] Rima: June–July, 1925.

[2] Seaman and octopus: Oral tradition.

[3] *Mr. Maximus Beerbohm*: 29th April, 1925.

[4] Seaman quotation: *Friends and Adventures* (1931) by "T" (of *Punch*).

[5] *When We Were Very Young*: began 9th January, 1924.

[6] *Misleading Cases*: began 9th July, 1924.

[7] *Ballads for Broadbrows*: 11th July, 1928.

[8] Seaman letter: In *Punch* Office.

[9] *Simple Stories*: began 18th August, 1926.

[10] A few late *Kai Lung* stories appeared in *Punch*, starting 20th November, 1940.

[11] *1066* began 10th September, 1930.

[12] Reynolds Obituary: 29th April, 1953.

End-piece, Fish: 8th June, 1932.

*CHAPTER EIGHT*

[1] Emett illustrations to de la Mare poems: began 26th March, 1941.

[2] *Assistant Masters*: began 30th November, 1938.

[3] *For Men in Aprons*: II: 13th February, 1946.

[4] *Translations from the Ish*: began 1st January, 1936.

[5] *The Flames*: 18th November, 1931.

[6] *Yet Another Way of Love*: 21st October, 1903.

[7] *The Rencontre*: 26th July, 1922.

[8] E.g. *Café Rezzonico* (*after Mr. Aldous Huxley*): 9th December, 1925.

[9] *The Warden*: 26th January, 1944.

[10] *Smith Minor*: began 10th July, 1940.

[10a] *Molesworth*: began 9th August, 1939.

[11] *Lady Addle's Domestic Front*: began 8th March, 1944.

[12] *Home Guard Goings On*: began 3rd July, 1940 (varying titles at first).

[13] *Letters to a Conscript Father*: began 28th January, 1942.

[14] *My Lifetime in Basic Industry*: began 31st October, 1945.

[15] *Port-fed Stilton*: 12th November, 1952.

[16] *H. J. Talking*: began 1st July, 1942.

[17] *Hayfield*: 4th August, 1948.

[18] *The Phoney Phleet*: began 23rd December, 1942.

[19] *Backroom Joys*: began 1st March, 1950.

[20] *Songs of a Sub-Man*: began 17th May, 1933.

[21] *The Field of Dynamite*: 24th December, 1947.

[22] *The British Character*: began 4th April, 1934.

*CHAPTER NINE*

[1] *An Industrial Journey*: began 1st March, 1950.

[2] New House of Commons, 22nd February, 1950.

[3] "My Mother" series: began 12th January, 1949.

[4] "Mummy, Mummy" series: began 25th August, 1948.

[5] *Forty* series: began 9th February, 1949.

[6] *Snax at Jax*: began 20th June, 1951.

End-piece, D. L. Mays: 27th December, 1950.

*CHAPTER TEN*

[1] *Boswell on the Grand Tour*: began 26th August, 1953.

[2] *Top-Level Contact*: 17th November, 1954.

[3] *The Willing Worker*: 2nd June, 1954.

[4] London articles began: 18th February, 1953.

[5] *Steerforth on Copperfield*: 29th July, 1953.

[5a] *Profession or Occupation*: 27th April, 1955.

[6] *Modern Types*: began 5th August, 1953.

[7] *New Yorker* parody: 7th April, 1954.

[8] Churchill cartoon: 3rd February, 1954.

[9] Eden cartoon: 19th May, 1954.

[10] *The Rake's Progress*: began 3rd February, 1954.

[11] Diz illustrations to Stonier's London articles: began 14th October, 1953.

## *APPENDIX SIX*

End-piece, Linley Sambourne.

APPENDIX TWO

# NOTE ON SOURCES

*[Dates refer to edition used]*

THE MAIN source is, of course, *Punch* itself. Convenient reprint of first fifty years—two years to a volume—published by *The Times*, 1900, with introductions and notes, some of them apparently taken over from an earlier reprint edited by Lemon. Complete set of *Punch* with original advertisements and covers in Managing Director's room at *Punch* office. Full indexes begin in 1902, at first showing some lack of practice. Useful anthology of pictorial humour, *A Century of Punch*, R. E. Williams.

*The History of Punch* (1895), M. H. Spielmann : invaluable, especially for identification of contributions and collection of testimony of survivors of early period. Facts not invariably reliable and some half-concealed gaps in information ; but as a whole an indispensable piece of industrious research. (According to Arthur à Beckett a few of the references to deceased contributors were corrected in proof by spirit-writing.) Spielmann had a good deal of co-operation from *Punch* men, including a man who offered to provide an Appendix on contributors with Romany blood, these apparently being himself and Andrew Lang.

Spielmann intended to produce a second edition but did not do so and passed his material over to C. L. Graves, who prepared a Centenary History that was not published but exists in manuscript in the *Punch* office. It is a record of *Punch*'s response to public affairs rather than a domestic history ; but it contains a certain amount of useful information and some valuable corrections by Alan Agnew, Kenneth Bird and the General Manager, Herbert Heather. It was written by a very old man and is not really very much help. Perhaps its chief value is the light it throws on the attitude of the Seaman circle. (Rather charmingly it judges all dramatic critics by their opinion of Ruth Draper. Incidental outbursts include a sharp attack on the decadence in the nursery shown in the supersession of dolls by golliwogs.)

Owing to the destruction of records in the early 1930s and again in the salvage drive, documentary evidence is sparse. The ledgers listing the authorship of contributions week by week begin in 1843. There are several box-files of letters deliberately preserved from destruction in the Managing Director's room, including some of Spielmann's correspondence on historical points. There is also an album of letters and other documents once owned by Miss Mabel Bradbury. Much of this material is concerned not with *Punch*, but with the mid-Victorian publishing business of Bradbury & Evans. The same bookcase contains several grangerised volumes—Spielmann, Bunn's *A Word with Punch*, etc. The material includes a letter from Landells to Bunn attacking Bradbury & Evans and some useful press-cuttings; it also includes some wildly diverse items, a letter from Tennyson—"Dear Sir, It will suit me to receive the mortgage money from Lord Thurlow on September 29th",—a portrait of Lady Blessington and a letter from Melbourne about a Scottish Poor Law appointment. *Punchiana* is a commonplace book kept by R. F. Sketchley between 1877 and 1891. He was a member of the Table for a time and a librarian at the Victoria and Albert Museum. It contains extracts from books, newspapers and magazines relating to *Punch* and is of some anecdotal value. The Editorial Department has some folders of miscellaneous material, some kept in the basement. There are a few letters and a number of odd facts, many of these, particularly dates of artists' contributions, being inaccurate. Some letters and copies of letters sent originally to Mr. Keown in response to a request, and now in my possession, will be returned to the *Punch* office on completion of this book. The manuscript *Diary of Henry Silver* records the conversation at the *Punch* Table 1857–70. Extracts have been printed by E. V. Lucas in an article on Thackeray's table-talk in *The Outlook* and by Professor Gordon N. Ray in his *Life of Thackeray*.

The *Encyclopædia Britannica* is useful, especially on the Art side: Spielmann was at one time Art Editor. *Chambers's Encyclopædia* has an article on *Punch* by E. V. Knox. The *Dictionary of National Biography* generally summarises information to be found elsewhere but some of the Twentieth Century entries of *Punch* men are by friends and contain personal details: E. V. Knox's *Owen Seaman* is flintily fair: Lionel Cust's *Ebenezer Landells* includes some information from his daughter. Grove's *Dictionary of Music and Musicians* (1878–9) for Mendelssohn's amusement at *Punch*'s *Antigone* review. (I owe this reference to Mr. R. S. Lazarus.)

For the earlier historical background the last two volumes of the Oxford History of England, *The Age of Reform 1815–1870:* (1938),

E. L. Woodward and *England 1870–1914* (1936), R. C. K. Ensor, with *Victorian England* (1937), G. M. Young. *Mr. Punch's History of Modern England* (1921), C. L. Graves. The *Cambridge History of English Literature* (1915, 1916), mainly useful bibliographically.

*The Development of English Humour* (1930), L. Cazamian. Erudite rather than enlightening. *The Field of Nonsense* (1952), Elizabeth Sewell. Brilliant study of nonsense in relation to logic, psychology, etc., starting from Carroll and Lear. *English Newspapers* (1887), H. R. Fox Bourne, for the early Press background. *The March of Journalism* (1952), Harold Herd, is a useful sketch. *The Street of Ink* (1917), H. Simonis, gives some gossipy background and one or two *Punch* references. *Roaring Century: 1846–1946* (1946), R. J. Cruikshank, for the *Daily News*.

For Art, *The Pre-Raphaelite Tragedy* (1942), William Gaunt, *The Aesthetic Adventure* (1945), William Gaunt and *Victorian Olympus* (1952), William Gaunt give a gossipy account of the art circles with which *Punch* was chiefly concerned. *The Art of England* (1883), John Ruskin, on the *Punch* artists. *The Illustrators of the Sixties* (1928), Forrest Reid, is mainly bibliographical and intended for collectors but it is important for the relation of book-illustration to periodical-drawing and for the work outside *Punch* of *Punch* artists. *English Illustration : The Nineties* (1935), James Thorpe, is much inferior. It contains a list of the names of draughtsmen roughly arranged under periodicals and differentiated by rather slap-dash praise and blame. *From Hogarth to Keene* (1938), Henry Reitlinger, for " high " comic art. *The Brothers Dalziel : A Record of Fifty Years Work* (1901) is important for engraving and illustration. The Dalziel artists overlap with the *Punch* artists. *English Book Illustration 1800–1900* (King Penguin, 1947), Philip James, gives very clear short descriptions of the various processes of reproduction.

Other miscellaneous background material : *The Victorians and Their Books* (1935), Amy Cruse. *Lyra Elegantiarum* (1867), Ed. Frederick Locker, the first anthology of Light Verse. Locker's Introduction is the classical statement of the field of Light Verse. Cf. R. C. Lehmann's article on R. M. Leonard's *A Book of Light Verse* in *Punch*, 28th December, 1910, and W. H. Auden's Introduction to the *Oxford Book of Light Verse* (1939). *Satire and Satirists* (1854), James Hannay, gives an early-Victorian view of satire by a very intelligent and vigorous writer. *Poems from Punch : 1841–84* (1908), Introduction by F. C. Burnand. *Later Poems from Punch : 1887–1908* (1909), Introduction by Arthur Waugh. *Poems from Punch : 1909–1920* (1922), Introduction by W. B. Drayton Henderson.

*The True Story of Punch* in *London Society* (1875–6) by Joseph Hatton ;

summarised in his *Journalistic London* (1882). *Mr. Punch: His Origin and Career* (n.d.—Spielmann says 1882, but written as memorial to Lemon, who died 1870.) F. C. Burnand in *Pall Mall Magazine* (1903), articles on *Punch* forerunners and rivals. *A Jorum of Punch* (1895), Athol Mayhew. *Westminster Review* (July–Oct. 1842), article on comic press. *Notes & Queries* (25th May, 1889), R. B. Postans on origins (9th Mar., 13th Apr. and 11th May, 1889), information on *Punch* publications. *British Museum Catalogue*, misleading on *Punch Pocket-Books*. The information in the text is based on a check of the Museum copies, the copies in the *Punch* office and the collection left by Linley Sambourne. *Punch in the Sixties*, by C. L. Graves in *The Eighteen Sixties* (1932), Ed. Drinkwater. *The Women Poets of the Seventies*, by V. Sackville-West in *The Eighteen Seventies* (1929), Ed. Granville-Barker. *At Home and Abroad*—Second Series (1862), Bayard Taylor. *Mr. Punch's Pageant 1841–1905* (1909), Leicester Galleries, Introduction to catalogue by E. V. Lucas. *The Church in the Pages of Punch* (1912), The Rev. D. Wallace Duthie (author of *A Bishop in the Rough*).

*Grand Man* (1954), Nancy Cunard—for Germans' burning *Punch* volumes. *John Gibson Lockhart* (1954), Marion Lockhead, for Murray's story that Doyle was forced into resignation by the Church. *Times Literary Supplement* (1st July, 1955), letter from M. E. Grenander saying Ambrose Bierce on *Fun*. *Six Tennyson Essays* (1954), Sir Charles Tennyson, for Forster's sending Tennyson's *New Timon and the Poets* to *Punch*. For *Peccavi* see *Notes & Queries* (Nov. 1853, Dec. 1907, Nov. 1913, Mar. 1917, Sept. 1917). See also *Punch* (6th Dec. 1950). *Eight Humorists* (1954), George Mikes. *Ross and The New Yorker* (1952), Dale Kramer. *Night and Day* (1937). *The Second Tree from the Corner* (1954), E. B. White. *Paunch* (*New Yorker*) (1934). *Harvard Lampoon* (17th Dec., 1950). *Paunch* (*Yale Record*) (4th Dec., 1952). *Log* (Annapolis) (27th Mar., 1953).

Biographies and Autobiographies of the *Punch* circle include: *With a Show in the North* (1871), Joseph Hatton—an account of Lemon's Falstaff tours with a good deal of miscellaneous Lemon material by an admirer. *Thomas Hardy* (1954), Evelyn Hardy—for Lemon's discouragement of Hardy's dramatic ambitions. *A Great Punch Editor* (*Shirley Brooks*) (1907), George Somes Layard. *Wit and Humour* (1875), Shirley Brooks, short Introduction by Reginald Brooks. *Records and Reminiscences* (2 vols., 1903. Abridged edition by E. V. Lucas, 1917), F. C. Burnand; very little on his Editorship. *Happy Thoughts* (with introduction by E. V. Knox, 1954), F. C. Burnand. *Owen Seaman: A Selection* (1937), Introduction by C. L. Graves; very short memoir. *This I*

*Believe* (1953), Ed. Edward P. Morgan. Broadcasts that include Malcolm Muggeridge's *credo*.

*The à Becketts of Punch* (1903), Arthur William à Beckett. *Recollections of a Humorist* (1907), Arthur William à Beckett. *Green-Room Recollections* (1896), Arthur William à Beckett. *The Life and Remains of Douglas Jerrold* (1859), Blanchard Jerrold ; vigorous work by Jerrold's son, a busy journalist, Napoleon III's apologist and Editor of *The Epicure*. He was always trying to get the cost of heavy feeding out of the paper's owners on the grounds it was a reasonable expense for the Editor of a journal devoted to good living. *Douglas Jerrold* (2 vols., 1918, but Preface 1914), Walter Jerrold. *Douglas Jerrold and Punch* (1910), Walter Jerrold : account of Jerrold's connection with *Punch*, a list of his contributions and a reprint of some of his series. *Thackeray* (1932), Malcolm Elwin. *The Showman of Vanity Fair* (1947), Lionel Stevenson : much better than it sounds. *Thackeray : The Uses of Adversity, 1811–46* (1955), Gordon N. Ray : the authorised biography, based on *The Letters and Private Papers of William Makepeace Thackeray* (4 vols., 1945–6), Ed. Gordon N. Ray. *Letters of Anne Thackeray Ritchie* (1924). *Chapters from Some Memoirs* (1894), Anne Thackeray Ritchie. *Hitherto Unidentified Contributions of Thackeray to " Punch "* (1899), M. H. Spielmann : *Corrected and Amplified for the Period 1848–1855*, by Gordon N. Ray in *The Times Literary Supplement* (1st Jan., 1949). *Quarterly Review* (Dec. 1854) : Thackeray's article on Leech that annoyed his colleagues.

*John Leech* (2 vols., 1891), W. P. Frith : more Frith than Leech, but a little useful material. *John Leech* (1883), F. G. Kitton. *The Drawings of John Leech* (English Masters of Black and White, 1950), June Rose. *Horæ Subsecivæ : No. 3* (1882), John Brown. *The Noble Science : John Leech in the Hunting Field* (1948), Thomas Bodkin, with Introduction by Sir Alfred Munnings. *Notes & Queries* (5th Nov. 1864). *Charles Keene* (1947), Derek Hudson. *The Life and Letters of Samuel Charles Keene* (1892), George Somes Layard. *The Works of Charles Keene* (1897), Joseph Pennell. *Richard Doyle* (English Masters of Black and White, 1948), Daria Hambourg. *Sir John Tenniel* (English Masters of Black and White, 1948), Frances Sarzano.

*George du Maurier : The Satirist of the Victorians* (1913), T. Martin Wood : this brilliant book ought to be better-known *as* a book. *The du Mauriers* (1937), Daphne du Maurier : gives the background and atmosphere down to du Maurier's youth. *The Young George du Maurier : A Selection of Letters 1860–67* (1951), Ed. Daphne du Maurier. *George du Maurier and Others* (1937), C. Hoyer Millar. *George du Maurier* (English Masters of Black and White, 1948), Derek Pepys Whiteley. *In Bohemia with du Maurier* (1896), Felix Moscheles. *Century Magazine* (May 1883), Henry James on du Maurier and London Society. *Harper's Magazine* (Sept. 1897), Henry James on du Maurier. *Social Pictorial Satire* (1898), George du Maurier. *Phil May* (English Masters of Black and White, 1948), James Thorpe. *The Confessions of a Caricaturist* (2 vols., 1901), Harry Furniss. *My Bohemian Days* (1919), Harry Furniss. *The Two Pins Club* (1925), Harry Furniss. *My Lady Cinema* (1914), Harry Furniss. For Furniss's film work see *The History of the British Film : 1906–1914* (1949) and *1914–1918* (1950), both by Rachel Low. *Bernard Partridge and Punch* in *Image* (Autumn 1952), Derek Pepys Whiteley. *Daily Mail* (10th Jan., 1901), for interview with Linley Sambourne on his succeeding Tenniel as principal cartoonist. *Country Life* (4th Apr., 1952), Christopher Hussey on Sambourne's house.

*Sixty Years in the Wilderness* (1909), *Sixty Years in the Wilderness : Second Series* (1912), *Nearing Jordan* (1916), *Diary of a Journalist* (1920) and *Diary of a Journalist : Later Entries* (1922), all by Sir Henry Lucy, are repetitive but full of important political gossip and should be better known. *A Long Retrospect* (1936), Anstey Guthrie. *Selected Verse* (Introduction by Alfred Noyes, 1929), R. C. Lehmann. *The Whispering Gallery* (1955), John Lehmann. *Out and About* (1933), Archibald Marshall. *Reading, Writing and Remembering* (1932), E. V. Lucas. *It's Too Late Now* (1939), A. A. Milne. *Friends and Adventures by "T" (of "Punch")* (1931), J. Thorp. *They Make Us Smile* (1942), Percy V. Bradshaw. *Independent Member* (1950), A. P. Herbert. *About Kingsmill* (1951), Hesketh Pearson and Malcolm Muggeridge.

Autobiographies and biographies that give glimpses of *Punch* men have become rarer as *Punch* men have ceased to mingle in the busy social world. Finding this kind of material is, of course, a matter of chance. *Memories of My Times* (1870), George Hodder. *Glances Back Through Seventy Years* (1893), Henry Vizetelly. *Edmund Yates : His Recollections and Experiences* (1885), *The Life and Adventures of George Augustus Sala* (1892) and *The Memories of Dean Hole* (1892) are important. Of some minor *Punch* interest are : *My Autobiography and Reminiscences* (3 vols., 1887), W. P. Frith. *A Mid-Victorian Pepys* (Sir William Hardman) and *The Hardman Papers* (1923–30), Ed. S. M. Ellis. *Early Days Recalled* (1891), Janet Ross. *The Fourth Generation* (1912), Janet Ross. *Memories of Ninety Years* (n.d., probably early 1920s), Mrs. E. M. Ward. *Victorian Sidelights* (1954), A. W. M. Stirling from the papers of Mrs. Adams-Acton. *The Light of Other Days* (2 vols., 1890), Willert Beale. *A Barrister's Life* (1882), Serjeant Ballantine. *Paxton and the Bachelor Duke* (1935), Violet M. Markham. *Reminiscences of Sir Henry Hawkins* (1904).

*Georgian Adventure* (1937), Douglas Jerrold. *Gerald* (1934), Daphne du Maurier. *Those Days* (1940), E. C. Bentley. *A Book of Recollections* (2 vols.) (1894). John Cordy Jeaffreson. *Personal Recollections* (1900), H. Sutherland Edwards.

APPENDIX THREE

# THE EARLY HISTORY OF PUNCH

SOMETIME IN the late Thirties, Henry Mayhew began discussing a possible paper called *Cupid* and even assembling staff. He took a " dummy " to Mr. Johnson of the National Steam Press, who refused to take it on. Late in 1840 or early in 1841, Joseph Last, who had been the printer of *Figaro in London*, and the engraver Ebenezer Landells were starting a periodical called *The Cosmorama*. Last introduced Landells to Henry Mayhew, son of his solicitor. When there were difficulties over *The Cosmorama*, Mayhew brought out his dummy of *Cupid*, disliked it, and refashioned it with the help of some copies of Philipon's paper he got from his sister in Paris. According to Mayhew's story reported by his son, he persuaded Last and Landells to switch their energies from *The Cosmorama* to this new paper. According to the tradition in the Landells family, which is accepted by Spielmann, Landells made the first suggestion but did not see the full possibilities : Mayhew took up the idea and developed it. Last's family claimed that the idea started with him, that he called on Mayhew, they talked about staff and only then did Last think of Landells as the engraver. à Beckett's son said it all started with a suggestion to revive *Figaro in London* . The Jerrold family claim that the obvious progenitor was Douglas Jerrold's *Punch in London*, the tone of which is that of an individual addressing his readers, much more the tone of the final *Punch* than that of *Figaro in London*.

At the inn kept by Mark Lemon's mother, the Shakespeare's Head in Wych Street, at which Lemon, then a young brewery clerk, tried to create a literary atmosphere, there was an attempt to start a weekly paper called *Pen and Palette*. Contributions were put in a box under pseudonyms and then read aloud and discussed once a week by Mark Lemon and the habitués. In some way that is not clear, Mayhew brought fellow-members of this circle into the enterprise with Last and Landells. There were several meetings at pubs, probably one in Last's offices and one at the house of the artist Joseph Allen.

At one or more of these meetings, two things happened. The name *Punch* grew out of a casual conversation about the ingredients of the beverage and was applied, probably by Mayhew, to the new paper, though there was a slight delay while it was discovered whether Jerrold felt he had an exclusive claim to it. The other was that two documents were produced : an Agreement, which was finally made at a solicitor's but had been discussed in outline convivially—it settled that the Proprietors were to be Last the printer with one-third share, Landells the engraver with one-third share and three Editors, Henry Mayhew, Mark Lemon and Stirling Coyne with the remaining share—and a Prospectus. The draft of this is in Lemon's writing, but it seems probable that most of the wording was Mayhew's. It announced that at the price of 3d. " A new work of wit and whim, embellished with cuts and caricatures, to be called *Punch* or *The London Charivari* " would be published. It rather depressingly continued : " This Guffawgraph is intended to form a refuge for destitute wit—an asylum for the thousands of orphan jokes." It ended with a drawing of a row of " Funny Dogs with Comic Tales."

In the course of several meetings, mainly at inns like the Edinburgh Castle in the Strand and later the Crown Inn in Vinegar Yard, Drury Lane, the contributors were gathered. Mayhew was the link with Jerrold, then abroad, the star contributor on whom the venture depended. Some of those approached were cautious. Percival Leigh and " Phiz " wanted to see a copy of the publication before they would commit themselves.

*Punch* was printed at Last's works in Crane Court, and published by Bryant at 13 Wellington Street, Strand. Sales were insufficient to cover costs. Last refused to go on ; his rival printers, Bradbury & Evans, declined to buy his share and eventually Landells acquired it, though Last's son claimed that he did sell it direct to Bradbury & Evans. Difficulties increased. The printing was executed successively by Mr. Mitchell and by Mills, Jowett & Mills. The first Almanack gave the paper a tremendous boost, but sales were still insufficient. Bradbury & Evans became the printers. Lemon and Jerrold called on them and persuaded them to buy " The Editors' share for £200 which they advanced on the security of the whole." Spielmann's phrase is obscure. He strongly supports Landells throughout, and may be intending to suggest that the Editors somehow committed the engraver's share without his approval. Landells began protracted negotiations to try and win back control of the enterprise. These dragged on, with all the time the printing bill mounting. Finally, he sold his share for £350 on the understanding that he should continue to do the engraving, though Bradbury & Evans said this was not part of the agreement and dropped him after a fortnight. By

Christmas, 1842, Bradbury & Evans were not only printers, but Proprietors.

Under Bradbury & Evans, Lemon was sole Editor, with Mayhew in a vague advisory capacity, which he resigned before long. Gilbert à Beckett was dropped but came back fairly soon. Bradbury & Evans had no general publishing experience and used W. S. Orr & Co., the London agents of Chambers, who got the paper out to the booksellers on sale or return. This firm had been helped out of financial difficulties by Bradbury & Evans, according to Spielmann. According to a bitter letter from Landells to Alfred Bunn, now in the Bradbury & Agnew records, there was a respectable book-seller used as a catspaw " to get a third share more out of the original proprietor. . . . They managed to get rid of him altogether as soon as they found the thing likely to be a good property." I cannot discover what this intervening phase was.

This reconstruction is based on an attempt to extract a coherent story from the following :

Spielmann's *History of Punch* (1895) gives much credit to Mayhew, but the honour of the first suggestion to Landells, and is rather vague about Bradbury & Evans, though it gives a useful list of the legal documents and the text of the Agreement constituting *Punch*. *Mr. Punch : His Origin and Career*, said to be by Sidney Blanchard, but Spielmann says mainly by Last's son. Athol Mayhew called it " facts by Last and fiction by Blanchard." *A Jorum of Punch* (1895) by Athol Mayhew—everything claimed for Mayhew. This book was much resented by the Jerrold and Landells families. *Memories of My Time* (1870), by George Hodder—companion and hanger-on of Mayhew, whose claim he supports. *The True Story of Punch* in *London Society* (1875–6), by Joseph Hatton, summarised in *Journalistic London* (1882), Joseph Hatton—Useful and gossipy, very pro-Lemon. *Notes & Queries* (May, 1889)—account by R. B. Postans of early meetings, pro-Mayhew. *Dictionary of National Biography*, sub. Landells, by Lionel Cust—information from Landells's daughter. Manuscript *Diary of Henry Silver:* in *Punch* office, includes stories about early years told by Lemon, Evans, etc. *The à Becketts of Punch* (1903), Arthur à Beckett. *Glances Back Through Seventy Years* (1893), Henry Vizetelly. Details of Cambridge periodicals in Cambridge University Library, *per* letters from Robert Swartwout to Eric Keown. *English Newspapers* (1887), H. R. Fox-Bourne. Articles by F. C. Burnand in *Pall Mall Magazine* (1903) give information on forerunners. Letters in Bradbury & Agnew archives from Alice Chaplin (née Landells) say Mayhew was quite out of it when *Punch* passed into Bradbury & Evans's hands. Letter from Henry Vizetelly—repeats very malicious gossip.

APPENDIX FOUR

# DRAWING AND REPRODUCTION

*by Kenneth Bird*

NO ONE can look through old volumes of *Punch* without being struck by the changes that successive periods have brought to the pictures—not merely in their subjects, costumes and background details (which naturally move with the times), but even in their fundamental character. These changes are too great to be accepted as entirely due to changing conditions and changing habits ; in fact, their explanation lies just as much in the changes that have come about in the methods used for reproducing them upon the printed page.

And so a short untechnical description of these methods, and changes, may be of interest :

In 1841, when *Punch* was born, photography was not available, and therefore it was not possible to obtain a true facsimile reproduction of any drawing : the " block " used to carry the design which was to be inked and transferred on to the paper had to be made by hand—and by a hand other than the artist's.

This block was made of boxwood (a wood hard enough to stand up to the wear and tear of printing a large edition) and the design to be reproduced was drawn by the artist on its face, with either pen, brush or pencil.

The wood-engraver then took over, and cut away the surface of the block, leaving in relief the lines that the artist had drawn. When this cutting was finished, the block was fixed in its place on the flat bed of the printing press, the type in its forme was fitted round to make up the complete page, and printing ink was rolled over the whole surface—the surface of the type letters and of the lines in the drawing left in relief—to give an impression on a sheet of paper then laid upon it.

It is obvious that the process of cutting away from the surface of the wood block all the white areas in the drawing must have been a long and laborious one : only line drawings could be reproduced (since a wood block could only give solid black where the surface of the wood remained

**A PATHETIC APPEAL.**

" *Mamma, shall you let me go to the Wilkinson's Ball, if they give one, this Winter?*"
" *No, Darling !*" (*A pause*)
" *You've been to a great many Balls, haven't you, Mamma ?*"
" *Yes, Darling,—and I've seen the* folly *of them all.* (*Another pause*)
" *Mightn't I just see the folly of* one, *Mamma ?*" (*A very long pause*)

(*Wood-engraving after George du Maurier*)

standing, and white where it was cut away) and no shade of grey was possible. And so, if an artist wished to draw a scene in fairly elaborate tone (as they usually did in Victorian times) he had to resort to cross-hatching, which (being merely two sets of shading-lines at an angle to one another) was very easily and quickly done by the artist (*see illustration A*), but very troublesome to the block-maker, who had to cut out laboriously by hand each and every little white island left between the lines (*see*

*B*

(*Enlarged detail of preceding, showing the work of the wood-engraver*)

*illustration B*). It is not surprising, therefore, that the cutting of a full-page block took twenty-four hours, whereas a modern process block can be produced in as many minutes.

Twenty years after the birth of *Punch*, a slight relief in time was obtained with a method by which a large block could, when the drawing had been made on it, be cut up into smaller blocks, each of these being given to a different engraver and finally collected and clamped up together with the others to make a complete whole, the time required being thus reduced to a quarter or less. (In large blocks of the Sixties and after, it is often possible to see the white lines which indicated the joins ; one of them is visible in *illustration A*, running vertically through the back of the dog and the shadows of the trees above.) A slight relief was also given to the artist, in that he was allowed to make his drawing on a piece of paper, which was pasted down on to the block and cut away with it.

But no considerable relief arrived until the 1880s, when photography suddenly made it possible to carry out the drawing on a normal piece of drawing-paper or board, the drawing being then photographed on to the surface of the boxwood block. By this development, the artist was released from the necessity of making his drawing the exact size of its intended reproduction and was made free to choose the size, or scale, that suited best his particular style ; furthermore, with this method, only the photograph was destroyed with the cutting of the block, the drawing itself remaining untouched and intact for posterity. (It is a sad thought that of all the drawings that appeared during the first forty years of *Punch*, before this photographic method was introduced, not a single one is left ; every one of them was destroyed in the cutting of the block, and all that remain to us are a few preparatory studies.)

The final development, which did more than anything that had gone before to change style and character, was the introduction of the "process" block ; this was a metal block, on to which the drawing was photographed. Then, instead of a laborious cutting-out of all the whites in the drawing, acid was used to eat them away, leaving the black lines, photographed on to the block and protected by an acid-resisting solution, standing up in relief.

The importance of this change lay in the fact that it provided a true facsimile of the artist's line, instead of a translation of it by an engraver—and so for the first time the artist could indulge his own particular style in his own particular way, unhampered by thoughts of the difficulties that his drawing was putting in the way of the engraver, or fears of what the engraver might think of it (*see illustration C*).

In common fairness to all concerned, perhaps it should be added here that some of the greatest of *Punch* artists of the earlier days were not in the least hampered by thoughts of the difficulties that their drawings put in the way of the engraver, nor, apparently, by any fears whatever as to what the engraver might make of them. Charles Keene, although he must have been perfectly well aware that a wood block could only give a black line on a white surface, very frequently watered his ink for the background, giving pale grey lines for the far distance, as a contrast to the heavy brown ones used for the foreground and figures. And du Maurier, intent on getting the fullest possible range of tones from pure white to velvety black, used masses of cross-hatching, with entire disregard of the fact that every minute piece of white left between the lines must be cut out with so much care that none of the care so taken showed on the surface.

*C* *14th September, 1895. Phil May*

**MUCH ADO.**

" *Mamma-a-a ! Boo-hoo ! We's crying ! Tum up 'tairs an' see what's de matter wiv us !* "

(*Drawing by Phil May reproduced by process*)

Week after week the wood-engravers produced magnificent blocks, in spite of all the difficulties inherent in a method that had to try to convey the freshness and feeling of a free-hand line drawing by cutting up the unresponsive surface of a block of wood, and when an artist complained that his work was spoilt by the engraver's lack of skill, the engraver might usually with greater justice retort that *his* work was spoilt by the artist's lack of consideration.

The first process block appeared in the issue of 3rd December, 1892

*D* *December 3rd, 1892*

(*First drawing to be reproduced in* Punch *by process block* [*line*])

(*see illustration D*), and since then only one major refinement has been added to the method—a development which gives shades of tone in addition to full black, and thus makes it possible to reproduce drawings carried out in wash or pencil.

This development is known as " half-tone," and roughly consists in putting a glass screen, ruled with closely-spaced vertical and horizontal lines, between the drawing and the camera, so that the drawing, as seen by the camera, is split up into a large number of little squares. The lightest parts of the drawing come through the screen as minute dots in the middle of the squares, and the darkest parts come through as solid black, entirely filling them. The first example of half-tone appeared in *Punch* on 25th January, 1896 (*See illustration E*).

One special application of half-tone allows full colour to be introduced. In this case, three half-tone blocks are made, the drawing being photographed through three colour filters, each of which allows one only of the three primary colours to pass through it. Each of the blocks is then printed in its appropriate colour, and, if the impressions so made are exactly superimposed on the paper, the result gives a full colour reproduction of the coloured drawing.

Frequently a fourth block (black) is now added, to give depth and body—and also to allow the letterpress belonging to the drawing to be printed in black instead of blue, a minor refinement which makes a considerable difference to the look of the page.

The first full-colour drawings to appear in *Punch* are to be found in the Summer Number of 1920: these were in three colours only. The fourth block was added in the Summer Number of 1938, and has continued to be used ever since.

In the sixty-odd years since the adoption of the process block, many improvements have naturally been made in it, but all of them improvements of quality rather than changes of method, and to-day the *Punch* pictures are still reproduced by substantially the same process, line drawings by line blocks, wash drawings by single half-tone and coloured drawings by four-colour half-tone. (The traditional weekly cover is reproduced by a black line block, with a red line block added.)

The modern process reproduction, in the hands of a skilled blockmaker, gives a truly remarkably accurate copy of a line drawing—so accurate, in fact, that if a reproduction is made exactly the same size (and printed on the same paper), as the original drawing, even the artist himself can hardly tell which is which. And, considering the number of different stages that make up the method, from the photographing of the drawing on to a sensitized film on the metal plate, through the developing, fixing, washing and eating away with acid, the squeezing of papier mâché pulp into the surface of the block, the drying out and bending of this papier mâché, the pouring of molten metal into the papier mâché mould thus formed, the cooling, the fixing of the resultant curved metal plate on to a cylinder, and its rotation so that it alternately picks up ink from a roller and transfers it to a band of paper running past it, on to the folding,

THE LAST DAY OF THE MISTLETOE.

*Adolphus and Dolly confide to each other their opinion as to " The Age of Love "*
*(First drawing to be reproduced in* Punch *by process block [half-tone])*

cutting and pinning together of this band of paper into a complete copy of *Punch*, it really is a fairly remarkable performance.

As to the changes in the style and character of the drawings that these changes in the methods of reproduction have brought about, the position of affairs when *Punch* was born in 1841 was that Victoria had only recently come to the throne, and humorous art was still very definitely Georgian : that is to say, it derived at its best from Rowlandson and Gillray and, at its worst, from the crude wood-cut illustrated pamphlets, ballads, tracts and broadsheets of popular tradition. The first drawings in *Punch* followed these influences : there were attempts at the fierce caricature of Gillray and the more urbane "social" of Rowlandson, and there were also child-like productions fairly closely related to the broadsheet.

*F* *Vol. I. 1841. P. 275*

(*Wood-engraving of 1841, showing influences of etching*)

Now, Rowlandson and Gillray "drew for the copper" ; that is, their work was in general reproduced by etched or engraved lines on a copper-plate, these being usually drawn quite freely with a needle on a black acid-resisting varnish on the surface of the plate, and then eaten into the plate with an acid which attacked the plate wherever the varnish had been scratched off by the needle.

Thus their style was entirely different to that imposed by the slow cutting of a wood block—and much of the early *Punch* work shows in consequence a considerable freedom of draughtsmanship that came down from the etching, (*see illustration F*) although it was often combined with a crudity of drawing that came up from the broadsheet (*see illustration G*).

But very soon the pattern altered : Georgian freedom disappeared under Victorian disapproval, and, in order to be accepted as respectable enough for polite society, the drawing was forced to approach in style as nearly as possible to its more solemn relations.

John Leech was early enough to be comparatively free (*see illustration*

*H*), and his line still showed many traces of the etching : Charles Keene, who followed, was very largely wood-bound, although his own genius and the wood-engraver's skill combined to make a wonderful job of it, (*see illustration K*), while du Maurier, the next great regular contributor drew for the paper in a style that was truly academic and, beyond a certain exaggeration in the expressions where considered necessary, almost indistinguishable from his more serious illustrations to his own novels.

G *Vol. I. 1841. P. 58*

(*Wood-engraving of 1841, showing influences of broadsheet wood-cut*)

By the time Keene and du Maurier between them were filling most of the paper every week, the static wood-engraving period was at its peak : it was a period of great draughtsmanship and great wood-engraving, but to those brought up on the freedom of modern work, it seems a period that left too little to chance or imagination, that insisted that every coal in the grate must be given its full value, and that the drawing must continue right out into each of the four corners of the rectangle reserved for it in the type.

(It would not be fair to put all the blame for this on the wood-engraving : in part the style of drawing was, as already mentioned, imposed by the Victorian revulsion from Georgian licence, and in great part it was imposed by a public taste which associated black-and-white either with steel engravings after oil paintings, endeavouring to give in monotone the originals' fullness of tone and of detail, or with serious illustrations of serialised novels in popular weekly periodicals.)

At all events, this static style, with a few individual risings and rebellions here and there, persisted right up to the arrival of process, in the early Nineties, and by then the Victorian revulsion from Georgian humour was nearly forgotten, and the next revulsion was due.

**A STREET FIGHT.**

*Wife of his Bussum (to Vanquished Hero) : " Terence, ye great Ummadawn, what do yer git into this Thrubble for ? "*
*Vanquished Hero (to Wife of his Bussum) : " D'ye call it Thrubble, now ? why, it's Engyement ! "*

*(Wood-engraving after John Leech)*

When process arrived, artists were for the first time, as we have said, able to draw in whatever style they liked (provided that the editor liked it too) and with as much freedom as they wished, confident that the new photographic method would give them a genuine facsimile of their original—and it is interesting that the first major artist to take advantage of this freedom was Phil May, the master of the graphic epigram, whose

*K* *28th September, 1867*

ARTFUL—VERY!

*Mary :* " *Don't keep a Screougin' o' me, John !* "
*John :* " *Wh'oi bean't a Screougin' on yer !* "
*Mary (ingenuously) :* " *Well, y' can i' y' like, John !* "
(*Wood-engraving after Charles Keene*)

dynamic lines would inevitably have lost a great deal if they had been dependent on the wood.

It is, incidentally, equally interesting that, when he arrived, public taste was still so firmly fixed to the tradition of the solid static meticulously detailed wood-engraving that, before his new virile shorthand could be accepted as art, it had to be established to general satisfaction that Phil May was really quite as academic as the rest, that he, like them, did in fact put in every line in the folds of the coat, the only difference being that, unlike them, he then rubbed out again all the lines that were not absolutely necessary.

It is truly remarkable that this explanation was so widely accepted as satisfactory, for such an operation is, of course, just about as impossible as the production of a sonnet out of a full-length novel by removing all the unnecessary words. The style line that indicates, in artistic shorthand, all the creases in a sleeve has got to be a true shorthand : it has got to be an epitome, a précis of a hundred separate lines, and cannot really correspond with any single one of them.

In course of time, Phil May was accepted on his merits, without need of explanation or apology, and the way was open for all the free and lively work which followed him, and which eventually developed into the vast range of styles that make modern black-and-white drawing so interesting (and serve to demonstrate that contemporary humorous art in this country is at least as virile, as varied and as technically accomplished as any other branch of art).

Only one other happening remains to be recorded as having had a considerable effect of the development of pictorial humour—the arrival of radio and the talking-films.

Here the revolution was not a technical one, but took place in the mind of the reader (and also, of course, of the artist—and editor) : up to the time of this arrival, about thirty years ago, amusement and instruction were almost entirely provided by the printed word, the visit to the theatre or the lecture being to most people a very rare occurrence. Then suddenly, as it were, a cinema with continuous performances sprang up at the corner of the street, and a wireless set came right into the house, giving out, if required, a continual stream of speech and music from 8 a.m. to midnight. The effect on the average individual and, through him, on the printed page, was remarkable—and also remarkably swift in comparison with, say, the effect of the arrival of process, the twentieth anniversary of which still found many artists working with traces of the old wood-cut technique and the old wood-cut attitude that went with it.

The reader found that with radio and talking films he could no longer refer back or " recap " ; he had to " listen the first time." But, as soon as he had learnt to do so, he became increasingly fond of the hare, and increasingly critical of the tortoise. In other words, the first impact of a drawing, or a subject, became of increasing importance and its contemplative content of correspondingly diminishing value—and the changes in the styles and methods of presentation of pictorial humour directly due to the arrival of these two innovations are undoubtedly far greater than those ascribable to any other cause within the period we are considering.

No doubt television will in time bring another change, but not, probably, such a great one, since the psychological effect of TV is more or less the same as that of radio and the talking-film, and that has already taken place.

The change due to TV is, in fact, more likely to be of a more or less technical nature ; and it will not probably have its full effect on humorous art until a technical method has been produced by which pictorial humour may be presented and drawn (and possibly animated as well) by the artist himself in front of the viewer. When such a method has been perfected, as presumably it must be fairly soon, it will undoubtedly have a considerable effect on the humorous art of the printed page—all the same, it can hardly be an effect comparable to that of those two great entertainer-instructors who got in their impacts first, the talking-film and the radio ; and for the next really important development, we have probably got to wait for something more revolutionary still.

APPENDIX FIVE

# MISCELLANEA

## *Proprietorship*

BRADBURY & EVANS finally acquired control of *Punch* in December, 1842. In 1865, the firm became a company as Bradbury, Evans & Co. and the House of Agnew, the Art dealers, became associated with it. In 1872, F. M. Evans, the son of " Pater " Evans, left the firm, which then became Bradbury, Agnew & Co. W. H. Bradbury, the son of William Bradbury, married a daughter of Thomas Agnew. In 1893, Lawrence Bradbury succeeded his father, W. H. Bradbury, as Joint Managing Director. He retired in 1920. The Agnew Managing Director until 1910 was Sir William Agnew, Bart. (He was a Liberal M.P. from 1880 until he lost his seat as a " Home Ruler " in 1886.) He was succeeded by his son, Philip Agnew. In 1938, Philip's nephew, Alan Agnew, became Managing Director and Lawrence Bradbury came back as Chairman until his death in 1953. Alan Agnew succeeded him as Chairman and was himself succeeded as Managing Director by his son Peter Agnew in January, 1956.

## *Offices*

*Punch* was first printed at Last's, 3 Crane Court, Fleet Street, and published by R. Bryant at 13 Wellington Street, Strand. Bradbury & Evans were at 11 Bouverie Street, just by the second turning on the right-hand side going down, later used by the post office. Swain the engraver was at 6 Bouverie Street. Bradbury & Evans moved up the street to number 10 in 1867. The banqueting room here was rebuilt in 1898. The *Punch* office was a one-story building, 85 Fleet Street : there used to be a party to watch the Lord Mayor's Show from the leads. It moved to 10 Bouverie Street in 1900, the building being demolished and replaced with the present building in 1930. The printing works are at Mount Pleasant.

## APPENDIX FIVE

*Famous Jokes*

Peccavi—I've Scinde : *11th May: 1844*. Advice to Persons About to Marry : *Almanack: 1845*. Bang Went Saxpence : *5th December: 1868*. The Curate's Egg : *9th November: 1895*. Lunatic and fisherman, " Come inside " : *21st August: 1897*. Tramp's soap testimonial—" Since then I have used no other " : *26th April: 1884*. " Sometimes I sits and thinks " : *24th October: 1906*. Old lady who wanted the Bank of England : *30th November, 1895*. " Feed the Brute " : *31st October, 1883*.

Two ancestors of *ITMA* jokes :

HOSTESS : Come and hear a whistling solo by my husband.
SMITH (*whose hearing is a trifle indistinct*) : A whiskey and soda with your husband ? Well, thanks, I don't mind if I do have just one! *31st October, 1900*.

" Wot a life. No rest, no beer, no nuffin. It's only us keeping so cheerful as pulls us through." *27th September, 1916*.

*Forecasts*

Underground : *26th September, 1846*. Cooking by electricity : *14th November, 1857*. Long-range guns : *17th May, 1862*. Telephonoscope : *Almanack, 1879*. Sky-writing : *Almanack, 1888*. Hunting by Aeroplane : *12th December, 1906*. Aerial refuelling : *20th October, 1909*.

APPENDIX SIX

# NEWSPAPER CUTTINGS

[*A Selection of newspaper cuttings sent in by readers that in primmer days were not considered printable*]

The day's play had a result highly gratifying to Victorian golfers, for it placed on top of the list the girl champion of a year or two back. She appeared in something like her true colours, although her long shorts were not coming off with the desired regularity.

No definite cures were announced, but several of the sick fainted when Pastor Jefferys laid his hands on them and prayed.

Two war-time organisations sandwiched the individual items. They were the string orchestra of 14 players, all local amateurs, born as a result of fire-watching.

MISTAKEN FOR RABBIT

Barking Girl Accidentally Shot.

LUMPY BEDS

Mrs. Winston Churchill told members of Y.W.C.A. committees in Liverpool recently : "Ninety per cent. of the mistresses on Y.W.C.A. hostel beds are not fit to sleep on. They are lumpy and uncomfortable."

Ancient Office of Lord Warden of the Cinque Ports was assumed by Lord Willingdon, ex-Viceroy of India, at Dover Castle yesterday—new Lord Warden acknowledging cheers during procession to Town Hall. With him is Lady Willingdon.

HOO-RAY AND UP SHE RISES !

Two attractive young ladies would like to meet two tall gentlemen with cars and things. Sincere. *Box K 277.*

*Body Found in River*

The police are trying to establish the identity of the woman whose body has been recovered from the Thames above Chertsey, he told the Committee, amid laughter.

## HANDS OFF DISTRICT NURSES

*Straws in the Wind are Causing Anxiety*

## OBITUARY

The usual *Ije* or the Seventh Day was observed in connection with the death of Madam Adefowoke the Alagbo of Ita-Marun, Imusin on the 9th instant. The Olugbo-yega Band Set was in attendance ; there was a heavy downpour of rain throughout the day which marred the jollity of the occasion to a certain extent.

## SHARK EATS FINANCIER

## " DISGUSTED "

Mr. Bottomley said he was so disgusted with the tone of the conversation that after 20 minutes he put down the receiver.

A verdict of " Death from natural causes " was returned at an inquest at Coventry yesterday on ——, who died in the Market Square on Sunday while listening to the Salvation Army band.

After the two bloodhounds had been given a scent of a sleeping-suit belonging to Miss —— they leapt forward in two directions.

# INDEX

*[Figures in italics refer to illustrations]*

# INDEX